1/06

NATURE'S KEEPERS

NATURE'S KEEPERS

The Remarkable Story
of How the Nature Conservancy Became
the Largest Environmental Organization
in the World

BILL BIRCHARD

JOSSEY-BASS
A Wiley Imprint
www.josseybass.com

Published by Jossey-Bass
A Wiley Imprint
989 Market Street, San Francisco, CA 94103-1741   www.josseybass.com

The many references to and excerpts from Nature Conservancy documents and
speeches throughout the book are used with the permission of the Nature Conservancy.

Jossey-Bass books and products are available through most bookstores. To contact
Jossey-Bass directly, call our Customer Care Department within the U.S. at
800-956-7739, outside the U.S. at 317-572-3986, or fax 317-572-4002.

Jossey-Bass also publishes its books in a variety of electronic formats. Some content
that appears in print may not be available in electronic books.

Credits are on page 252.

Library of Congress Cataloging-in-Publication Data

Birchard, Bill, date.
   Nature's keepers : the remarkable story of how the nature conservancy became the
largest environmental organization in the world / Bill Birchard.
       p. cm.
   Includes index.
   ISBN 0-7879-7158-8 (alk. paper)
   1. Nature Conservancy (U.S.)—History. I. Title.
   QH76.B57 2005
   333.72'06—dc22

                                                              2005000723

Printed in the United States of America
FIRST EDITION
HB Printing   10 9 8 7 6 5 4 3 2 1

CONTENTS

PREFACE

E VERY BOOK HOLDS ITS SURPRISES—even, as I've found out, those you write yourself. There were two big surprises for me in writing *Nature's Keepers,* and they make the story of the Nature Conservancy worth telling.

The first surprise was where my research would lead me. When I began thinking about the Conservancy, I imagined spending days with impassioned activists out on the land. My story would start, I thought, by capturing the lives of people like Terry Blunt, a young conservationist who worked for the Conservancy. Blunt got wind of plans to develop a pristine Atlantic island in the late 1960s. The developers were buying parcels by paying delinquent taxes—and throwing people off their property.

Snooping around a bit, Blunt went to one rattled landowner, a Maryland oysterman, and offered to pay his back taxes. He said the Conservancy would give the man and his wife lifetime tenancy—in return for selling their land. He even wrote a $75 personal check on the spot to buy the Conservancy an option on the land. With savvy and speed, Blunt snatched an ace property from the developers' hand of real-estate cards.

That kind of story had a lot of appeal as the bread and butter of my research. Here was a swift and clever fox, a man who ranged across a twenty-three-state territory, outmaneuvering a muscle-bound economic monster. That the Conservancy was a shoestring outfit in those days added to the panache of the story. The Conservancy's office was on a corner along K Street in Washington, D.C., modest digs above a prosthetics shop.

Blunt would often hear the thumping of a handicapped person mistak-
enly struggling up the stairs. He'd rush down to stop the poor soul and
save him or her a futile trip in search of the artificial-limbs office. If curi-
ous people did make it up the stairs, Jo Johnson, a stalwart of administration and membership, would often field the same question: How are
the Nature Conservancy and the artificial-limbs business related?

Alas, I found that however fun this land-saving story was on the
ground, the more important story of the Conservancy often took place
in offices and around conference tables—whether a stairway up from a
prosthetics shop in 1965 or, as today, in a handsome edifice a block
away from the National Science Foundation. To tell the tale of the making of a great organization calls for much more legwork on carpets in
corridors than across acres of ground under an open sky. Like most stories about organizations, this one takes place in the daily lives of managers. It is a story about people working with people, not about people
out on the land.

The second surprise had to do with the growing clout and competence of the people who manage nonprofit organizations. I've been writing about management for many years, and like so many people, I've
looked to corporations as models of excellence. Indeed, most professional
people do. At business schools, many aspiring managers figure they will
work most of their lives at corporations, and if they do well, devote a few
years later to public service.

But just as I started on the book, out came a most interesting survey.
Environics International asked people in fifteen countries which kind of
leader they trusted. Roughly two-thirds said they trusted nonprofit (or
nongovernmental organization) leaders; only one-third said they trusted
corporate and government leaders. This followed a joint Gallup and Environics survey that showed nongovernmental institutions to be the most
trusted (second to the Armed Forces) and corporations the least.

The answer to the question, What's the most trusted name in leadership? Not Corporate America.

Of course, even nonprofit leaders have plenty of work to do in raising
their stature. A two-thirds "trust" rating is something you could only brag
about to your mother. Still, the survey confirmed a turn of sentiment: the

zeitgeist that had zigged in the corporate direction in the 1990s had zagged the other way in the last few years. On the global scene, French Prime Minister Lionel Jospin's slogan helped capture this notion: "Yes to a market economy, no to a market society."

The message of the survey was timely: A look at leading nonprofits promises deep insights about high performance delivered by the most trusted leaders on earth. In a world hungry to measure value in more colors than green, the bare-bones shareholder value formula of the traditional corporation is losing its hold on people's imaginations. The citizens of the world are looking for leaders with a broader vision of how to create value. Maybe that's one reason that the number of nonprofits has soared. In just the United States, the tally of registered nonprofit organizations has grown from 633,391 to 800,972 in the last five years, according to IRS figures compiled by the Urban Institute.

To be sure, the management of a nongovernmental organization can be a lot different from that of a corporation or government agency. But there's a great deal of overlap, and the leaders of nonprofit organizations are far out ahead in meeting one challenge: injecting meaning into work. Today's jobholders want to make a difference. Nonprofits invariably help them do so. Many corporate chiefs have come to the conclusion in the last decade that, to excel, they have to do the same, if they want to retain motivated employees.

So the surprise—and delight—of this book is that the story reveals how talented leaders in a nonprofit have made this happen. Even if they once started out in drab offices above a prosthetics shop, they could—and would—build a team of administrators, dealmakers, fundraisers, scientists, and others to make a difference. On the frontier of better management today, whether in profit-making, nonprofit, government, or other organizations, the big challenge for leaders is both as simple as it is hard—figuring out how to give people something to work on passionately.

That's what Terry Blunt and Jo Johnson were given, even if the task at hand on many days was a humble one. If someone from the bus stop out front came to ask Johnson about the Nature Conservancy's artificial limb business, she didn't just point them down the stairs. She told them about the Conservancy and enamored them of the idea of saving land. And she sold them memberships, five dollars at a time. It's motivated people like Blunt and Johnson who make the story of the Conservancy worth reading.

Amherst, New Hampshire   Bill Birchard
January 2005

NATURE'S
KEEPERS

1

NO CRISIS UNANSWERED: How the Nature Conservancy Masters Challenges and Change

THE PEOPLE OF THE NATURE CONSERVANCY had plenty of warning that the *Washington Post* was going to sully their image. More than a year before a series of articles began on Sunday, May 4, 2003, reporters showed a taste for the Conservancy's knottiest transactions. Eight months before, they dug into the Conservancy's darkest deal—rustling natural gas from a neighbor's deposit in Texas. A few days before, they called to say the stories would run on the front page for three days in a row.

The *Post* reporters had done their homework on Conservancy foul-ups, and they were going to run an exposé that, in the eyes of Conservancy faithful, wasn't pretty. That much everyone knew.

But when the *Post* series broke, Conservancy insiders recoiled in outrage. They felt abused and violated. The Conservancy, said the *Post*'s first story, was the "the world's richest environmental group" and a "corporate juggernaut." It logged forests and drilled for natural gas. It sold its name and logo for profit and bought land to resell to insiders. The Conservancy's list of errors and indiscretions ran for eight inches down the newspaper column.

Many people wondered why the *Post* didn't look more at the Conservancy's success. After all, measured by revenues, it is the largest environmental group in the world, bringing in over $800 million each year. It employs 3,450 people operating from four hundred offices in fifty states and twenty-eight countries. No other organization surpasses the Conservancy's record of on-the-ground results. It protects more than a million acres of land a year, for a total of 120 million acres to date. As for foulups, well, they happen at any big organization.

The story of the Nature Conservancy's success actually starts fifty years ago. It is a story about men and women building a top-tier institution, one of the preeminent in the nonprofit world. This is a conventional success story. But this book is also a story about men and women overcoming crises and challenges—only the latest of which emerged as a result of coverage in the *Post*. This is the more complex story of people repeatedly taking steps to transform and improve the way they work—and continue to log achievements that count, and count big.

The story of any organization's success pivots on crises and challenges—crises and challenges experienced by the individual, the team, and the institution. The ability of people to weather and profit from these events, sometimes the most daunting or nerve-racking of their careers, separates organizations that thrive from those that do not. Still, these events are crucibles of learning that force people to rethink behavior, rewrite rules, reconfigure processes, and reinvent the way they work.

Among the crises and challenges that yield lessons about success at the Conservancy:

- Weak or inappropriate leadership, a crisis striking at the heart of almost every organization, challenged the Conservancy several times in its early years. The board had to face up to leaders poorly matched to the organization's evolving needs.

- Mission drift and confusion, a crisis in focus that creeps up slowly but nonetheless cripples organizational effectiveness, revisited the Conservancy more than once. At times, opportunism and indiscipline prevailed.

- Confused and weak organizational culture, a challenge that blocks an organization from achieving high-performance, faced the Conservancy in its adolescence. Conservancy leadership had not yet inculcated a mature organizational personality.

- A dead-end business model, a crisis that emerges as an organization tackles bigger societal needs, faced the Conservancy as it sought to break from a tradition of almost exclusively small-scale nature-preserve conservation. People stumbled as they learned the new capabilities required to operate at a broader scale and bigger scope.

- A disempowered board, the sleeper crisis in performance at so many nonprofit groups, perennially hampered the Conservancy, particularly on its state-chapter boards. Conservancy leaders struggled to go beyond asking their boards to give money and arrange connections with the rich and powerful.

- Ad hoc management, the make-management-up-as-you-go habit of small organizations, hobbled the Conservancy as it expanded to fifty state offices. The pluses of decentralized management became minuses for the performance of the whole.

- Homegrown international expansion, or using an ad hoc approach to expanding globally, created a promising but diffuse strategy for overseas conservation. Conservancy leaders eventually had to rethink their approach to meeting the needs of conservation internationally.

- A crisis in public accountability, triggered by the scrutiny of investigative reporters, took the halo from the Conservancy. Weaknesses in oversight combined with more demanding public expectations damaged the Conservancy's reputation, especially in the court of public opinion.

The Conservancy was an unglamorous start-up half a century ago, hardly influential enough to attract much attention from the likes of the *Washington Post*. At the December 4, 1954, meeting of the Conservancy board of governors, in the Portrait Room of the American Museum of Natural History in New York, executive director George Fell made it clear that the start-up phase of the organization was a crisis of its own. Noting that nearly five years had passed since they opened a full-time office, Fell, a thirty-eight-year-old Illinois native with degrees in botany and wildlife management, asked the eight governors and seventeen guests, "What have our five years of work produced?"

"The answer," he responded, "in comparison with the need, is so obvious I won't bother to give it."

So obvious because the answer was just about nothing—except for lots of "seemingly fruitless labor," he said, "confusion as to purposes," and "one after another golden opportunity slipping from [our] grasp."

Fell, who stood at the vanguard of a cast of star characters in Conservancy history, acknowledged that every worthy organization had begun this way. But the beginning for the Conservancy, a novel new force for saving natural lands, was lasting too long. Fell, along with other founders dating to the organization's start in 1950, aspired to build a national organization. The Conservancy, he said, should "have the size and strength to take its rightful place in a country that does things on a gigantic scale."

On this Saturday in New York in 1954, away from his home office in Washington, D.C., Fell was not feeling like the master of any world-changing cause. The Conservancy had promised an extensive program to preserve samples of all biotic communities in every natural region. Fell foresaw the use of legal instruments to protect land—direct ownership, lease, contract, trusteeship agreement, restrictive covenant. He envisioned the Conservancy establishing a nationwide system of wild preserves.

And yet he was not seeing the progress he hoped for. "Surely in five years we should be farther along than we are," he said.

The Conservancy had not yet preserved even one piece of property.

Fell represented the drive, commitment, and spirit needed to turn the vision of the noble cause into action. He was a man determined to have an impact and to participate in a movement that had an impact. But he faced a huge challenge in getting the Conservancy off the starting line. Initially the only full-time employee of the Conservancy, Fell had left Rockford, Illinois, with his wife, Barbara, in 1950 to open an office in Washington. He believed the movement to protect land in the United States was gathering steam, and it needed a national organization to train people, organize them, and raise funds to support their efforts. Remarkably, Fell moved to Washington with no salary. His wife, a medical technician, supported them both.

Fell designed a template for the national organization. He foresaw that the Conservancy would supply state chapters and local groups with criteria and standards for preserves, technical and legal advice, financial (seed) assistance, and a national fund available for emergency land-protection spending. Although in the early 1950s the organization had only six hundred members, mainly scientists, Fell's *Manual of Territorial and Project Operations* outlined the details for setting up state and local chapters.

Fell placed the Conservancy at the center of the natural-lands movement in the United States. Nature preservation until that time had centered on the large, spectacular, and scenic. The Conservancy would instead rescue from destruction typical examples of *all kinds* of wild nature—prairie, swamp, desert. "We need these samples of each sort of natural feature for their great scientific, educational, and esthetic values," he wrote. "They will be monuments; our heritage to be held in trust by each generation. They will be living museums of the primitive world of nature."

Fell spent money frugally to get the organization on its feet. By buying at government surplus sales, he boasted in 1954 that the average price of his office machines—three electric typewriters, a Vari-Typer, a Robotyper, two offset printing presses, a mimeograph machine, two folding machines, two Dictaphones—was 20 percent or less of list price. A man who had never run a printing press before, Fell figured out how to print all Conservancy materials himself, in 1954 producing 106,030 pieces of letterhead, form letters, *Nature Conservation News,* and reprints of popular Conservancy brochures. By 1956, he forecast in a 1952 white paper, the group would be at full operations, with a budget of $17,500.

Yet despite his sacrifice and devotion, and despite the tremendous work of scores of volunteers on a handful of projects, the organization was failing to meet his expectations. On that day in New York, with eight board members in attendance, the Conservancy board didn't even have a quorum. Fell told the board, "We have neglected the need for a strong organization to back up these projects and initiate others that are needed. . . . More money from more sources, more volunteers, will come when we have built an organization that commands respect."

And so Fell highlighted the crisis of the time, which in a sense is the challenge all nonprofit organizations face if they aspire to make a substantive difference in the world: how to build the organization with the management skills to deliver the benefits hoped for and promised—and then how to raise the organization's stature, skills, and sights to deliver more and more, year after year, decade after decade.

In the following pages, the answer to that question appears in the story of nine people from the Conservancy. These are nine men and women who faced crises and challenges, addressed them, learned from their mistakes, and changed their ways to achieve and maintain success. The account of these people's experience is not a history of the Conservancy. Although the book covers a lot of historical ground, it leaves out many turns in a history of more than fifty years. It scarcely draws on the annals of most of the fifty state operations or the personal archives of many former employees, donors, and partners.

Instead, the account reveals the work of these nine people who exemplify what made the Conservancy excel—and rise to such a position that it attracted the attention of a newspaper like the *Post:*

- Richard Goodwin, a Connecticut College botany professor, twice replaced the chief executive and guided two organizational restructurings. With quiet grit, he showed how to revamp leadership to bring an organization to a higher level of performance.

- Robert Jenkins, a Harvard-educated ecologist, redefined the science-based mission of the Conservancy. Brilliant and bullheaded, he created a culture and processes for making decisions systematically instead of opportunistically.

- Patrick Noonan, a real estate operator and master negotiator, gave the organization its heart and raised the money to launch it into the big leagues. With legendary chutzpah, he showed how to cement in place an enduring culture of action.

- Gregory Low, a polite North Carolinian of uncanny analytical talent, pressed the organization to develop new capabilities. He showed how to build an entirely new business to deliver the more powerful product of a growing organization.

- Kent Wommack, an earnest Yale forestry graduate, fired up the energies of his staff, board, and the citizens of Maine. He showed how to engage every possible constituency to deliver results far beyond the capacity of one organization alone.

- John Sawhill, the compleat corporate manager, installed professional management and modern systems reflecting his earlier tenure at McKinsey & Co. He taught the organization to work as one, to balance and multiply the efforts of headquarters and the field.

- Katherine Skinner, an inimitable lobbyist-cum-manager, as comfortable in a canoe as in the state house, led her team on a journey to shared leadership. She demonstrated how to develop herself and her people to practice the art of sophisticated team management.

- Kelvin Taketa, the cowboy lawyer in flip-flops, led the organization in expanding to the Asia Pacific region. Taketa, ever the strategist, showed how to launch and adapt global operations to survive and thrive from Indonesia to China.

- Steven McCormick, veteran manager of the Conservancy's biggest operation, in California, was named president in time to handle the crisis in accountability triggered by the *Post*. Ever focused on the silver lining, he showed that the public and lawmakers today demand a thorough revamping of board governance.

The stories of each of these people show off some of the best of the Conservancy. Through them there emerges a picture of the kind of individuals and the brand of management that makes the Conservancy so strong. To readers interested in what it takes to build a top-tier institution, the stories answer basic questions: What has made the Conservancy so effective? What can we learn from the men and women who made it that way?

To be sure, the Conservancy and its people have erred. The road to effective management does not follow a freeway and the icons of management do not perform without flaws. Some of the most valuable lessons people learn emerge from painful experiences, from time, money, and effort wasted, and from misadventures and missteps that look shabby or boneheaded in hindsight.

But in the end, these stories, stitched together from years of personal experiences, show that the organization that retains the ability to renew itself—whether forced to do so from a sudden crisis or spurred to do so by the challenge of constantly working smarter and faster—can survive to fulfill the growing needs of its constituencies, decade after decade. The stories here convey a sense of authenticity because they reflect the actual working lives of nine real people. The story lines are based on interviews with these people and other firsthand observers who agreed to speak on the record. They are fleshed out by board minutes, internal reports, letters, articles, books written at the time, and so on. Owing to the stories' personal nature, they not only inform and educate: they inspire.

As for the story of Fell, as so often happens with founders, he soon slipped out of the picture. Although he defined the managerial crisis the Conservancy would struggle with for its first decades, he was not to remain to guide its passage to the national organization he envisioned. Though he oversaw the organization from its birth through the earliest acquisitions of nature reserves, he eventually lost a battle for control of the organization to one of the visitors in attendance that very morning in December 1954 in New York: Richard Goodwin.

2

THE COURAGE TO LEAD: Revamping Leadership to Renew Performance

WHEN CONNECTICUT COLLEGE BOTANY PROFESSOR Richard H. Goodwin was elected president of the Nature Conservancy in August 1956, the organization was still tiny. It had 2,500 members. It had a full-time staff of one, the executive director, George Fell. It had a budget of $15,000. It was working on just a dozen projects. Its most recent purchase was the 21-acre Hellen Creek Hemlock Preserve in Maryland. The purchase price: $700.

Tiny as the organization was, Goodwin faced a giant divide. The people working on projects, volunteers in New York, Maryland, Florida, and elsewhere, were at odds with the man in headquarters. The volunteers groused about Fell's control of bank accounts, Conservancy bookkeeping, preserve access rules, and other details. They were piqued by Fell's insistence on building an administratively rigorous national organization.

Morale had nosedived. In June 1956 one board member who disliked the dutiful Fell demanded an investigation of his practices and books.

Several others told Goodwin they were ready to resign. The board was having trouble getting a quorum at meetings. Goodwin, the Conservancy's representative in Connecticut, was distressed by the split and discord. As he accepted the nomination for the post in August 1956—recruited by Fell—he knew he had trouble on his hands.

Goodwin, a brown-haired, blue-eyed stalwart for the cause, faced the challenge that often arises as organizations grow: the need to revamp leadership to move the organization to a higher level of performance. Goodwin didn't know just what the change entailed as he started in late 1956. But he did know he had to rearrange the people or structure at the top. Without his intervention, Conservancy growth would stall. Goodwin's work would ultimately reveal the difficulty, yet necessity, of leadership change and adaptation in a growing organization.

Goodwin was by no means an imposing organizational troubleshooter. At forty-five years of age, however, he had built a track record in the nascent but fervent natural-areas movement. While herbarium curator at the University of Rochester in the 1940s, he conserved his first property, a sliver of land in the Bergen Swamp, twenty miles west of town. The 2,000-acre wetland, filled with white marl (calcium) beds, offered habitat for the endangered massasauga rattlesnake, the white ladies' slipper, and Houghton's goldenrod.

Enamored with the biological treasures in the swamp, Goodwin talked to the fledgling Bergen Swamp Preservation Society and learned the group was making no headway in saving land. So he got a free Soil Conservation Service aerial photo, overlaid a county atlas, and created a picture of wooded swamp, field, and pasture with land-ownership marked. He visited farmers who owned pieces of the swamp and found one willing to sell a piece for $125. He talked Society trustees into parting with some cash, and became the man who kicked off the preservation of a national natural landmark.

Goodwin, who traveled to the West as a teenager at a time when roads beyond the Mississippi were still unpaved, loved the idea of saving land. When he moved to Connecticut College in New London in 1944, he assumed directorship of the Connecticut Arboretum and oversaw its expansion by acquisition of twenty parcels totaling three hundred acres. One of his triumphs was acquiring Mamacoke Island, a peninsula in the Thames

River next to the college. The wooded knoll, crowned by granite rimrock and hitched to shore by pristine salt marsh, was a gem. Goodwin raised the $15,000 purchase price from 257 individual donors in eight months.

Bitten by the land-saving bug, Goodwin took on the job as the Nature Conservancy's promoter in Connecticut in 1952. In 1956, he published "Six Points of Especial Botanical Interest," a menu of Connecticut preservation prospects. Research botanist and land savior, Goodwin drew notice from Fell and others as a man who knew how to take swift action.

Goodwin took over the Conservancy presidency, the volunteer head of the board, from another man of action, Richard Pough, a conservationist at the American Museum of Natural History. Pough, Conservancy president since 1952, was an extraordinary rainmaker. He courted and won donations from the Conservancy's first two major benefactors. Old Dominion Foundation of New York had given $10,000 each year to the Conservancy since 1954, and Theodore Edison (the inventive and business-minded son of Thomas Edison) gave nearly $8,000 in 1954. In later years, both would give much more.

Pough, as president, wanted to sideline Fell, but he didn't have the heart to do so. That's because he and Fell were both friends and foes. George and Barbara Fell had breathed life into the Conservancy, an organization that had been mostly a hobby for academics in the Ecological Society of America. Fell had worked full time for four years, 1950 to 1953, with no pay whatsoever and for another year and a half with a modest $2,500 honorarium. There would be no Conservancy bylaws, no accounting system, no membership solicitations, no structure—indeed, no Conservancy at all—without the Fells. They were, for all intents and purposes, the founding staff. The Conservancy was their baby.

But the style of the Fells and Pough clashed. Pough would court people and deals and ignore legal and financial details. He wanted to whip up enthusiasm, befriend people of wealth, put what he called an "arresting" land-saving project on the books. Fell and his wife, in contrast, wanted to install efficient machinery for conservation—the documentation, accounting, and control systems befitting a strong national organization. The Fells and Pough were the yin and yang of an organizational start-up. Neither would have worked without at least some of the talents of the other.

But the two points of view didn't sit comfortably as partners in the same organization. In the Conservancy, they actually reflected a divide that plagued the organization as a whole. Board members bent on creating a national organization worked to build a strong center, standardized systems, and an expansion plan. Local groups, trying to preserve pieces of precious nature, preferred transactional expediency. They wanted to save the gorge or marsh or woodland in their own backyard and cared little about the national bureaucracy. Pough, playing to the excitement of local committees, urged people to run their own shows, without "bossing" from headquarters. He scoffed at the "petty bookkeeping" in Washington.

Friction between the two points of view arose constantly, as it would in any start-up organization. In one instance, in the early 1950s, Pough arranged for the Conservancy to act as financial intermediary to receive funds for buying a property on Fire Island, New York. He agreed to solicit funds in the Conservancy's name, pass them to a local group called Wildlife Preserves, and give control of the property to a newly minted group, Sunken Forest Preserve.

Fell disliked the setup and argued that transferring the land didn't safeguard natural conditions in perpetuity, nor did a clause that gave Sunken Forest a say in handling proceeds should a government entity condemn the land. Neither he—nor some board members—liked how the cavalier Pough promised local people so much autonomy. Pough's laxity angered Fell, and Fell tried to intercede in this and other deals.

But Fell's actions peeved local preservationists. Labeling Fell "uncompromising," Pough called a special board meeting in June 1955 to talk through the dispute. "I want to make absolutely sure that you are in agreement with my understanding," wrote Pough to the board, "that in the absence of a specific policy formally adopted by the Board at a regular meeting . . . I, as [board] president, have the authority to use my best judgment as to what the Nature Conservancy's policy shall be."

Pough the rainmaker, Fell the organization man—they staked out irreconcilable positions. "Mr. Fell's actions must conform to my decision and my instructions to him," Pough added in his letter to the board. "I cannot continue to operate effectively as president of the Nature Conservancy unless my right to make the final decision where there is disagreement is recognized and my authority over Mr. Fell in such matters is unquestioned."

Such head-butting between the two went on and on. Over time, the board tired of the differences between the two men, and as Goodwin emerged as a candidate for president, many on the board—including Pough and Fell—urged Goodwin to accept. Thus it was that Goodwin inherited the dilemma over how to lead the Conservancy. Goodwin had to somehow reconstitute leadership at the top—at a time when the founding executive director was the heart and soul of the Conservancy's work.

Goodwin visited nearly every board member for advice, and smoothed the ruffled feathers of volunteers working on all fifteen Conservancy projects. He found that nearly all projects had bogged down over Fell's exacting approach—in spite of Fell's vision, passion, commitment, frugality, and integrity in handling Conservancy affairs. Thus Goodwin was faced with the greatest challenge of his volunteer life. He would have to overcome a preference to remain the nice guy so he could make the tough moves to rejuvenate the leadership of the organization.

DIPLOMACY FIRST

In late 1956, Goodwin cast about for solutions. For some time, he avoided meeting the problem head on. At first, he suggested hiring a paid president, someone to go over Fell. In that way, Fell could keep his title as executive director. Goodwin wrote Ernest Brooks, a board member and the vice president who held the purse strings at the Old Dominion Foundation: "If we should be able to find the right man for the job of Executive President, might the Foundation look with favor on financing his salary for a trial period?"

"If I can give the Conservancy the boost it needs and get the leadership into competent hands within the next two years," Goodwin added, "I shall feel a deep sense of accomplishment."

Goodwin didn't want to just cut Fell out. He even asked Fell for advice on management. "The Nature Conservancy cannot afford to have the President and the Executive Director at loggerheads," Goodwin wrote Fell. In return, Fell gave the board a Conservancy expansion plan in which eleven staff would man five departments managed by directors of organization management, business management, development, research, and lands. Reasoned and foresightful, the plan stimulated board discussion.

But Goodwin found that Fell mixed helpful suggestions with unwelcome recommendations. Expansion space at the office (in the Fells' home at 4200 22nd Street) was exhausted. Fell suggested a new location, preferably in a small city. Owing to a death in his wife's family, a large house in his hometown, Rockford, Illinois, was available. The central location, said Fell, was a good spot for the headquarters of a growing national organization.

The governors agreed that moving was urgent. But many worried that leaving Washington might hurt the organization's prestige. Goodwin, aware the decision couldn't wait long, sent a memo to the board listing the criteria for a new site—prestige, proximity to other conservation groups, postal service, accessibility to officers, central to people, wealth, and services, cost, and so on. In response, Fell continued to argue for the Midwest.

"What sort of office location fits in best with our conception of a well ordered society?" Fell wrote in a memorandum. "To me, there is something basically wrong about cities and congestion. . . . In the case of the Nature Conservancy headquarters, we have the opportunity now of deciding whether to locate where we will add our bit to perpetuation and extending urban congestion or find our place in a smaller community or a rural environment." Locating in Washington or New York for the sake of prestige was "the antithesis of conservation philosophy," he said, appending a two-page appeal for Rockford, Illinois.

Fell's argument had the reverse effect of what he intended. Goodwin, irritated, voted along with most of the board on September 21, 1957, to stay in Washington. The incident undercut Fell's standing with Goodwin and other governors, and they seemed less inclined to delay the handling of the leadership question any further.

Goodwin once again raised his idea for hiring a full-time paid president. This time, the governors took up the proposal formally. They directed the nominating committee to seek candidates who had a name in conservation, who would lend prestige to the Conservancy, and who had "proven talent as leaders." The board in effect voted for a two-tier leadership structure.

Fell wanted to stay in charge. In October, he presented graphs depicting the growth of the Conservancy under his tenure. Graphed in logarithmic scale, the results looked impressive. Income rose from $550 to $51,600. Membership grew from 130 to 2,900. Chapters grew from zero to nine. And areas owned went from zero to ten.

"The only real test of management is in results," he argued in his accompanying memo. "If I am to continue in this job in an effective manner, I must have the wholehearted support of every Governor. . . . We have suffered from a sort of organizational hypochondria."

And yet Fell seemed to vacillate. "I can continue on year by year as in the past," he added, "but it will be without enthusiasm. . . . I mention this so that you may take it into account in considering whether or not to support my tenure in office. There is little to be gained from a half-hearted effort and therefore if the Board feels it is essential to maintain the office in Washington it might wish to seek a manager who could carry out that policy with enthusiasm."

At the December 1957 governors meeting, the board summoned Fell after an executive session. Goodwin announced the results, and then the board secretary read several resolutions: Fell's position as executive director, and that of his wife as membership secretary, would be terminated on April 1, 1958. The Fells would be offered new jobs as executive secretary and assistant executive secretary at a 33 percent increase in combined salary (to $10,500).

So the board demoted Fell. The executive director job would be filled with a new candidate. Despite Goodwin's original intentions, the board couldn't hire a paid president because the bylaws wouldn't allow it. After Fell listened to the resolutions, he said he wished time to consider them. He might find the proposal of a new job unacceptable. He left Goodwin and the other governors hanging.

BRAWL OF THE DECADE

For Goodwin, the December meeting was a painful resolution to a year-long struggle to reconfigure the Conservancy's leadership. He hated demoting a man who put the Conservancy's welfare before all else. But he had determined that dislodging a founding leader was the only way to set the stage for renewed growth.

To students of management, this was not an ideal solution. The Conservancy would now get a new leader who would have the former boss as an employee. Two hard-headed bosses rarely work well together, especially when one comes from the outside. Yet this is the solution the board chose.

By February 1958, two months later, Goodwin had drawn up a list of ten new candidates, and in March, the board blessed a new executive director. Fell inquired whether the new man might not be named "conservation director." He explained that, in any case, if he stayed on, he did not expect to report to the new man. Since the governors hired him, it was the governors who would be responsible for reconciling disputes between him and the new executive.

But the board did not budge, and on March 21 Fell accepted the new post of executive secretary. "We have devoted 8¼ years to the Nature Conservancy," he wrote, "of which 4 years were without compensation, 1½ years with an honorarium for myself, 2 years with a salary for myself, and ¾ year with salaries for both myself and Mrs. Fell." He added, "We wish to state most emphatically that after devoting this much effort to the organization we have no intention of precipitately deserting it."

Not that Fell had the intention of submitting to the will of the new man. The board hired Edward Munns, a retired U.S. Forest Service executive and recent chairman of the Conservancy's advisory board in the West. Munns, sixty-nine, had years of experience in forest research and natural-areas protection. The board, adopting a specific resolution that the Fells would report to Munns, hoped Fell would defer to the seasoned manager, who started June 1.

The start was bumpy—Fell insisted that neither his name nor Munns's title as executive director appear on the press release announcing Munns's new position. But Goodwin felt the dust had settled by July 1958, when Fell and Munns seemed to be working together smoothly. At the July board meeting, Goodwin even announced that Fell had won the American Motors Conservation Award for 1958. Fell was one of ten professional conservationists to get the honor.

Goodwin felt he had the leadership problem in hand. A seasoned veteran in management, one with the prestige to talk with the rich and pow-

erful, paired with a founding organizer of the natural-areas movement—
this was a solid solution. The Conservancy could finally get back to its
core job of conservation.

But the apparent calm was prelude to a nasty bureaucratic brawl. In
July 1958, the board's nominating committee submitted a slate for the
August election of governors in Bloomington, Indiana. Goodwin, stepping down from the presidency, was nominated to continue as a governor. James Ross, a publishing executive, was nominated to succeed him.
Just three days later, however, the board received a bombshell: Board
member Alvin Whitney wrote to say he was nominating George Fell as
president and head of the board—and he offered a slate of opposition
board candidates to go along with him.

"I thought you would be interested to know that I have consented to be
nominated for the office of the president of the Nature Conservancy," Fell
wrote to the board four days later. "In the event I am elected, I shall serve
as a full-time volunteer and I hope the board of Governors will see fit to
grant leaves of absence from our staff positions to Barbara Fell and myself."

Fell was bypassing the board in his drive to regain the top post, taking his case directly to the Conservancy membership. He had gone into
league with Whitney to launch a board takeover. Thus began a battle for
the hearts and minds of Conservancy members—and the future of the
Conservancy's leadership.

Caught off guard by Fell's challenge, Goodwin realized he faced a
proxy fight, and he met with board members in New York and Washington to discuss what he should do. Some governors were angry. In a
handwritten note, one snapped: "Dear Dick, I favor dismissing George
Fell *now*. Isn't that within Ed Munns' power?"

But two governors, Whitney and Paul Herbert, stood behind Fell.
Herbert felt Fell was a well-qualified manager. "It would take many thousand words to fairly present the problems facing the Nature Conservancy
and the misdirected actions (as I have seen them) of the Board of Governors to solve them," he wrote to the membership. "Are Mr. Whitney
and I the only members of the Board of Governors who would like to see
an introduction of new thinking on the Board?"

The challenge by the dissident board members gave Goodwin no
choice. He would have to fight with Fell in public, in writing, in a form

far less dignified than using behind-the-scenes diplomacy. Goodwin learned that Fell planned to solicit proxies to win a majority vote in the fall meeting on August 28 in Bloomington. Goodwin would have to vie for that majority. He would have to engage in a full-blown campaign to win the support of members.

Goodwin, his reputation on the line, first sought to explain his own side of the story. Most members were unaware of the months of earlier wrangling. Goodwin wrote a letter saying it was the board's "conviction that the Nature Conservancy movement now requires the services of a man with great administrative skill and talent in dealing with people." That was why the board hired Munns. "It was with consternation, therefore, that I learned a few days ago that Mr. Fell was apparently unwilling to adjust to the situation."

Board member F. Raymond Fosberg mailed a toughly worded note to members to undercut Fell. He cited the old friction Fell had caused with Pough, fresh conflict with the board, interference with board policymaking, and alienating a promising early candidate interviewed by the board for executive director (who then declined the job). "The Board has until now taken the position that these difficulties could be solved without publicity and without harm to the organization," he wrote. But events now compelled a public airing.

The rest of the summer turned into a grueling campaign for proxy votes. Fell and Goodwin flooded members with a tit-for-tat series of letters arguing their points of view. In one rebuttal, Fell wrote, "Fosberg has taken undue liberties in using his status on the nominating committee as a platform from which to launch a personal attack on me." Fell refuted every charge Fosberg leveled against him.

Fell's appeal won many people over. "It is . . . easy to notice in the solicitations I have received that Mr. Fell's statements are the freest from personal characterizations and the most concerned with the issues," wrote one member to Goodwin. "I therefore feel that the majority will react as I do, and instinctively recoil from personal attack, and vote, so to speak for a stewardship as we have had to date."

Another board member warned Goodwin, "You are going to lose this fight. George Fell got out his solicitation material fast and made out a good story. . . . Only by such personal solicitation will you overcome this handicap." Two weeks before the vote, the treasurer notified Goodwin that Fell already had four hundred proxies—a huge head start in a membership of only about three thousand.

Goodwin worked all summer to line up votes for the coming showdown. He pressed his allies to solicit proxies. He lobbied inactive board members. He wrote and visited friends and neighbors and asked them to join the Conservancy to provide fresh votes for his side. He spent $479.05, mostly his own money, on a proxy mailing to compete with Fell's.

Goodwin had no idea if he could win. He did know, though, that Fell's slate was shaky. In early August, two of the candidates on the slate pulled out. They complained they had been duped into thinking they were nominated by the board, not by an opposition group. "I had written off and on to George for about three years and found him very helpful and encouraging," wrote a woman from Cincinnati who withdrew her candidacy. "I just felt he was 'tops' and all this has been a shock."

"It was a hard decision for me to make [to withdraw]," she added. "Once made it did not give me peace of mind for I felt that I had stabbed a friend in the back."

In the final two weeks, Goodwin worked feverishly to secure votes. On the day of the meeting, forty-four members met in Room 129 at the Indiana University education building. Many came with piles of proxies for absentee members. At roughly 3 P.M., the election procedure was read—but no votes were cast.

Instead, a drumroll of objections hit the floor.

The first came from Victor Shelford, a pioneering ecologist—the man who had organized the predecessor Ecological Society of America in 1915. Shelford, the elder statesman of the movement, was no longer a governor. He claimed himself neutral on the vote. But he believed the proxy procedure wrong.

"Because of the doubtful legal validity of the proxies," he announced, "I ask the president to declare them invalid and that they not be counted."

Goodwin, who had worked all summer to secure proxies, was stunned. But Shelford was not speaking off the cuff. He had brought with him Richard G. Davis, a tall, authoritative law professor from the university. The attorney explained that District of Columbia Code, section 29–603, would not allow the proxies to supplant a live vote. He objected to the ambiguity of the proxy form and procedure. He did offer a caveat, however. If the meeting chairman (Goodwin) interpreted the bylaws as allowing proxies, and if the membership agreed, a court would probably uphold the decision.

The professor thus tossed the ball to the general membership. And the ball went round and round in both zany and ironic fashion. Richard Pough, also at the meeting, agreed with Shelford. Another member, who agreed too, complained that few members had actually received campaign literature from both sides. Goodwin, thunderstruck by the professor's testimony, tried to regain control. He argued that people who had given proxies to either side would be unhappy if they were thrown out—and so as meeting chairman he would simply overrule Shelford's point of order.

But Goodwin couldn't quiet the dissenters so easily. Another member moved to overrule Goodwin. The discussion went on and only ended when members agreed to vote on the proxy matter—in a written ballot.

The vote was 25 to 21, Goodwin sustained. But that was not the end of it. Another member asked that proxy votes be counted separately from live votes. There would be two vote counts! The membership agreed. In this way, any further dispute over the validity of the proxies would not invalidate the live vote.

Fell, who had been quiet to this point, raised another issue. He challenged the voting by anyone whose membership began after July 12, a date preceding his proxy challenge. The members voted against his challenge initially, but then one moved to vote on the issue again and Charles Kendeigh, a protégé of Shelford's and another patriarch of the natural-areas movement, seconded. Goodwin was in a jam. Many of his proxies came from after July 12.

Ross, however, the governor up for election as president, jumped in with his own ruling on Conservancy procedures: There are no "second-class memberships" in the Nature Conservancy, he said, so everyone should vote. Goodwin, recognizing a good line when he heard it, quickly used Ross's reasoning to rule the Kendeigh motion as contrary to the bylaws and thus invalid.

Goodwin held his breath. Nobody appealed his ruling.

So Goodwin won the procedural battle. The ballots were then cast and the tellers and election overseers left the room to start counting. The members adjourned for dinner. Neither Goodwin nor anyone else knew what lay buried in the proxies. When the board of governors convened for an evening meeting at 7:25 P.M., nobody was sure what to expect.

The results: 1,429 votes were cast. Ross won the live vote 39 to 5. He won the proxy vote 723 to 662. Goodwin's side had carried the day.

Goodwin, over more than eighteen months of work, had finally succeeded in setting the stage for the Conservancy's next phase of growth. He had spent nearly his entire two-year term as president wrangling with this one challenge to replace executive leadership. But he now was assured that the Conservancy would consolidate leadership under a new executive with the stature and skills to run a growing organization.

As for the Fells, they resigned. They and others maintained Goodwin stole the election—and he certainly turned the tide by gathering proxies over the summer. But the Fells did not dispute the results. They returned to Rockford, where Fell went on to found the Natural Lands Institute. Although driven from the Conservancy, he would remain a guiding spirit in the natural-areas movement and become an icon of land preservation in Illinois and among professional conservationists everywhere.

THE RENEWAL

The Conservancy grew steadily after the Fells' departure. In 1958, the organization had four employees, a budget of $15,000, 15 projects, and capital assets of $200,000. In 1964, when Goodwin took over in a second term as president, it had eleven employees, a $180,000 budget, 125 projects, and assets of $1.3 million, plus $2 million worth of land and $100,000 in endowments. To Goodwin and others, the growth was gratifying. By 1961, Oceanside, New York, school superintendent Walter Boardman became the fourth executive director and was a steady hand on the tiller.

No crisis faced the Conservancy in 1964. But the ongoing loss of the earth's biological treasures haunted Goodwin and the other governors. Every day thousands of acres of land would spring up in houses and stores and offices. Goodwin and his colleagues, ever impatient, wanted to see faster conservation to match that development.

One of Goodwin's closest colleagues was Alexander Adams, Conservancy president from 1960 to 1962. Adams, a friend of Goodwin's in

Connecticut and formerly with the Mellon Bank and FBI, was a writer and public relations man. He was perhaps the most impatient of all.

"Today's conservationist is a man in a hurry," he said in a speech in Wheeling, West Virginia, in 1962. "If he is to make any contribution, he must remain one jump ahead of the bulldozer, the highway engineer, and the real estate developer. He must act quickly, decisively, and effectively." Like many conservationists, Adams believed the next five to ten years were pivotal. "Success or failure during that period may very largely spell success or failure over the next hundreds of years," he said.

Adams believed the Conservancy could be more effective if it were more businesslike. "The effective conservationist today is not likely to be a man living by himself and striding the salt meadows in hip boots," he said. "We need the lawyer, who may be clumsy in differentiating between a chickadee and a nuthatch, but who knows the inheritance laws. We need the accountant who may confuse an oak with a maple but knows how to set up a set of books that will satisfy the Internal Revenue Service. And we need thousands of others like them."

Adams was one of those men "like them." And though he stepped down from the presidency, which he held between Goodwin's two terms, he hired on as a consultant to examine Conservancy effectiveness. Adams would be the man to force Goodwin to face the question of leadership again. As Goodwin took the reins in his second presidency, the challenge before him was in many ways the same as six years before: How do I raise the performance of the organization to yet one higher level?

In January 1964, Adams delivered the first of several reports that described just how big the challenge was that Goodwin had to deal with. Adams wrote that the governors were too enmeshed in details, meetings were too long, procedures too burdensome, reporting lines too unclear, people too often ineffective. The volunteer president was like a CEO, he said, and grossly overworked, requiring 1.5 to 2 days on the job per week, not including time for speaking or publicizing the cause.

The report set off a round of debate. Adams was exposing the roots of Conservancy weaknesses, and putting his finger on the roadblocks to further growth. As for leadership, he recommended hiring a paid president and eliminating some vice presidents. He urged reducing the board size and soliciting the resignations of failing board members. To Goodwin and other veterans, the criticism was biting, an indictment of their earlier work. Still, the governors admired Adams's analysis, recognized the truth of it, and in a special meeting blessed his recommendations.

No sooner had the board digested the first report than Adams handed out another—125 pages on everything from refining the Conservancy's mission to raising membership dues to handling chapter parochialism. Adams had interviewed governors, staff, and outside conservationists. As for the average member, he found a consistent opinion: "He believes it [the Conservancy] to be 'an action organization' and 'very useful.' However . . . it is only 'moderately effective.'"

"The trouble with the Conservancy," one outsider told Adams, "is that its horizons are always too low." Another said, "It does not yet have the stature [to be nationally effective], and I do not know whether it ever will have."

Adams issued fifty-three recommendations. He urged the Conservancy to adopt an ambitious new strategy. "To become an important, influential organization," he wrote, "it must be organized as an important, influential organization would be." The future of the Conservancy, he wrote, "lies, not in saving thousands of acres, but millions of acres. . . . It must think—and act—big."

The governors did not disagree with much of Adams's analysis, but they disagreed on how to proceed. One governor thought so highly of the work he proposed endorsing the reports right off. Old-timers like Fosberg sought to table any decisions until the board went point by point through the hundreds of pages of analysis. In the end, the board decided to make a checklist of Adams's recommendations, ask everyone to give his approval or disapproval, and circulate the tally at a later meeting.

That put an end to the discussion, but the message to Goodwin from the whole analysis and discussion was clear: The Conservancy had outgrown its systems and structure—the same ones Goodwin had put in place earlier. The key problem, the same as years before, was that the current leadership structure was holding back future growth. It was time to make changes—and the man with the designated responsibility for making them was Goodwin, the incoming president.

In looking over the reports, Goodwin favored most recommendations. He respected Adams no end. But he vacillated on one critical recommendation—the old question of whether to hire a paid president. Although he had suggested the measure himself in 1956, he had to admit he wanted to keep the top of the organization in volunteer hands. The volunteer tradition was strong. He was a part of it.

When he came to fill out the survey question on the issue, he couldn't check off his approval or disapproval. He abstained and penciled in a comment: "I find the greatest difficulty answering this question. If the administrative staff has been properly set up in running order, the presidency—tho arduous—might still be filled by a volunteer."

The governors received a two-page tally on all fifty-three questions, along with twenty-eight pages of comments. Goodwin learned that most of twenty governors approved of most recommendations. Among the points of contention was the paid presidency. Only eleven of the twenty directors approved it. Four disapproved outright, including Fosberg. Five others, including Goodwin, didn't vote.

"I see no case made for a paid president," wrote Fosberg. "The only conceivable reason I could see for a paid president (in addition to an executive director) would be if he were strictly a fund raiser and had nothing to do with running the Conservancy."

"I think the result would be a sort of two-headed monster," he added. That of course was the problem with Fell and the executive hired to replace him, Edward Munns, six years before.

But Adams discounted the dissent by the minority. In fact, he was exultant. Notwithstanding voices like Fosberg's, he believed Goodwin had a mandate for change. Adams wrote in a letter to Goodwin, "What surprises me most of all is the fact that they are over-whelmingly in favor. Indeed, practically all of the negative comments we have received are from a small minority."

As Goodwin took over the reins of the presidency in the fall of 1964, into his hands came the most important decisions about organizational change in years. These decisions concerned a Conservancy that was not the same as it was in 1958. It was a bigger business, and its potential was bigger still. Goodwin was obliged to help realize that potential, to think—and act—big.

LEADERSHIP REDUX

The central question for Goodwin was how to implement the second leadership renewal in ten years. Goodwin embraced Adams's basic premise: To tap the potential of the movement, the Conservancy had to have more people and more money and a different structure. Ever the politician, Adams recommended how Goodwin should proceed. In a letter, he suggested Goodwin not impose his will all at once. "You should 'give' a little here and there while still getting on with the big job," he wrote. Start out, he counseled, by urging the board to adopt the uncontroversial points. Refer the contentious fund-raising and other issues to special committees. Ask to reserve the paid-president decision for yourself as you craft an organization you think will excel.

"This ought to protect you from any charges of having railroaded the report," wrote Adams, "and, at the same time, let you move ahead with whatever you want to get going first."

Goodwin followed Adams's advice when the board met in October 1964. "The section on internal organization is one which was intended as a guide to our organization structure," Goodwin wrote to the board in advance. "Since I am to be your President for the coming year I would like to work on this section in collaboration with the officers and staff."

If Adams was the Conservancy's Machiavellian architect, Goodwin was its Churchillian statesman. The two would work together to manage the next transition of the organization. One of Goodwin's jobs was to topple the key symbol of a volunteer-driven organization—an elected volunteer president. The chief executive had to be a full-time professional leader hired by the board. This change, Adams anticipated, would cause the biggest stir on the board.

But at the meeting, Adams's ploy worked. The governors, deferring to Goodwin as suggested, did not even formally address the presidency topic. They left it to Goodwin to handle it himself. The runway was clear for Goodwin to remake the organization into a more sophisticated, high-performing conservation engine.

The first order of business was finding the money to fund the change. Just three days after the board meeting, Goodwin, executive director Boardman, and another board governor held a get-acquainted session with

Gordon Harrison of the Ford Foundation. The Conservancy contingent had received word that the foundation was considering funding conservation for the first time. The Conservancy wanted to be in on it, and Harrison was the contact.

Goodwin brought Harrison a copy of Adams's work. Calling it a "planning report," he explained how the Conservancy was positioning itself for the future. Goodwin and Harrison met a second time in January 1965 and a third in February, allowing time for Harrison to pore through Adams's massive backup appendixes. Goodwin was grateful that, thanks to Adams, he could argue that the Conservancy was not just some lightweight environmental group. It was an outfit with a solid growth plan, detailed in Adams's commanding analysis.

The decision to position Adams's report as a plan for the future paid off. Ford invited the Conservancy to submit a proposal—with the caveat that the Conservancy carry out practically all the recommendations in the Adams report. So Goodwin, Adams, and another governor outlined in a proposal how the Conservancy would operate with three departments—projects, development, and administration—and how it would hire a paid president. As for money, they asked for $115,000 in fresh operating cash as well as $500,000 for each of two land-acquisition funds. The total request: $1,115,000—enough to double Conservancy funding, raising the annual budget to $277,250.

In June 1965, Goodwin revealed details of the Ford negotiations to the entire board for the first time. He also revealed he had gotten comments on the draft proposal. The Ford Foundation's Harrison—troubled by the Conservancy's slow pace in making changes—wanted a new proposal with a slew of revisions: a plan for less capital funding; a smaller board of governors (cut to twenty-one from thirty over three years); a standing, rather than ad hoc, executive committee; a proposal for fundraising strong enough to make the Conservancy self-sustaining; and of course the hiring of a high-caliber paid president—and pronto.

When Goodwin presented the plan to the board, all went smoothly at first. The Conservancy would have to change its bylaws to provide for the paid presidency. The top volunteer post would be chairman of the board. He sought the board's approval to submit these changes for a vote of the membership in the September 1965 annual meeting in Buffalo. Without the changes, the Conservancy could not accept the Ford money. With them, it could execute the broad restructuring at the heart of Adams's plans.

The board voted in favor of putting the bylaw change on the ballot.

As the summer wore on, however, Goodwin was beset by obstacles. The first one came after he spoke by phone with Adams, who said he would take two vacation weeks to work beside a new president to speed the transition. Knowing that some people resented Adams's forceful manner, Goodwin told him the board might object. To Adams, much to Goodwin's surprise, this was the last straw in a series of behind-the-scenes affronts. In early August, Adams mailed Goodwin a three-page resignation letter.

Goodwin was aghast. Adams was the organizational mastermind. He, with Goodwin, was the head negotiator with Ford. And yet Adams was throwing in the towel in the final stages of the grant talks. Adams groused in his letter that while he had donated an extra month of time to complete his 1964 report, some governors called parts of it "ridiculous." They grilled him "like a prisoner at the bar" over its details—even though the report went on to become the basis for the Conservancy's grant request.

"What disturbs me is the continued animosity of a small minority of the board," he wrote, "an animosity whose virulence is underlined by your comments the other afternoon on the phone."

Esther Goodwin, as astonished as her husband, was this time more sure than he of what to do. "We're going to see Alex, *now!*" she snapped. So Goodwin, with his wife and perennial partner in conservation, drove from New London to Adams's home in Westport. Perplexed by the tempest he triggered, Goodwin wooed Adams back to his side—and into acting as emissary for taking the final grant proposal to Ford three weeks later, on August 24.

The second fire of the summer came from an upset Walter Boardman, the executive director. While honing the proposal, Goodwin tried to keep Boardman on the team, even though the impending game of organizational musical chairs would leave Boardman out of the top seat. (Boardman, whose work and skills Goodwin admired, would become executive vice president.) In June, Boardman had seemed prepared to go along with the plan. This was crucial, because several governors told Goodwin they wouldn't vote for the bylaw change if Boardman didn't agree. Some even wanted Boardman to have the top job.

But in August, Boardman told Goodwin he couldn't stay on under a paid president. In response, Goodwin phoned a group of board members to set up an emergency meeting. The governors talked Boardman out of his misapprehensions. Boardman thought Adams was eyeing the presidency—but this was not the case. Swayed by the board's appeal, Boardman again said he would promote the program, and the next day Goodwin visited Ford to hear that the Conservancy's new proposal looked about right.

The final proposal was more modest but still hugely significant. The Conservancy was asking for $1,050,000 to hire a paid president, two vice presidents, and three field reps, and to pour $500,000 into a capital fund for land projects. With Adams back on the team, Boardman going along, and a proposal getting favorable consideration, Goodwin thought his restructuring was in sight.

But the tables turned on him again. Boardman phoned him the next day to say he had changed his mind. He couldn't go along with either the bylaw change or the grant proposal. What's more, Goodwin started to find his support on the board wavering. In late August, he drove to Boston to see Conrad Chapman, who with other governors had authorized but had not been involved in negotiations with Ford. Chapman was a long-time friend of Goodwin's; in July 1958 he'd been so much behind a leadership change that he had written a letter urging the firing of Fell.

But Chapman was not behind Goodwin this time. He was irked that Goodwin promised so many changes to Ford without board approval first. He felt too much had gone on in secret. He began agitating against both the bylaw change and taking Ford money. Chapman feared that Ford—which many at the time accused of having overly leftist political leanings—would subvert the Conservancy's program. "The Ford negotiations have involved not only the possibility of a grant," he warned in a letter, "but also the control of N.C. policy by Ford."

Goodwin became exasperated. The day before the annual meeting, he handwrote long-time ally and governor Fosberg a speed memo outlining the issues. The implication was that Boardman and Chapman could turn a number of governors against the Ford grant and abort the coveted lead-

ership and management restructuring altogether. "All I can say is it is a H—
of a juncture [for Chapman] to bring this up," wrote Goodwin. "If the
Board should withdraw its support of our application RHG has *HAD* it."

The day before the official annual meeting proceedings, the board met
at the Buffalo Museum of Science. The meeting, on September 10, unleashed such contentious debate that the group couldn't reach consensus.
Several governors, including Chapman, voted against the bylaw changes.
But a clear majority emerged to support them and the Ford grant. Goodwin, though embattled, won the board vote he needed.

One essential hurdle remained, the membership vote. Goodwin appealed to members the next day in his annual speech. The Conservancy
membership, he said, was now 7,500 strong. The task of the presidency,
overseeing work in seven states, and to some extent in twenty-six others,
was far greater than anyone could expect of a volunteer. "An expansion of
our program requires the aid of additional personnel, highly sophisticated
in fund raising, and public relations techniques," he said. "It is for this
reason that your Board has recommended a change in the By-laws to per-
mit the appointment of a professional president."

Goodwin ended: "Can we build a potent and hard-hitting agency of
a size commensurate with the task, one that can cope with the present
need for establishing the land use pattern and one that will be solidly there
in the future to protect from encroachment the natural areas that have
been preserved? I like to think that we of today will have the courage,
energy, and imagination to meet this challenge."

When the vote was tallied, the membership approved the bylaw
change.

Goodwin and the Conservancy were now free to name a professional
chief executive. With board support for a paid president, Walter Boardman
said he would resign, and soon after the meeting submitted his resignation,
to be effective January 1, 1966. Goodwin, though strained by the meeting,
prevailed, able to take the steps needed for the Conservancy to grow.

Turmoil persisted in the fall. The chairman of the Conservancy's Southern California Chapter wrote the entire board on October 28:
"Dr. Boardman's ability and experience, his timeless devotion to the Conservancy, and his stature in the conservation field are invaluable assets to
our organization. We feel strongly that in making any plans to enlarge the

headquarters office, Dr. Boardman should be retained as the chief staff executive, regardless of title."

But as Christmastime approached, on December 14, the Ford Foundation notified Goodwin that the Conservancy was awarded a four-year $550,000 grant, starting with a first-year payment of $90,000. Boardman followed through and departed. The money gave the Conservancy the cash for a paid president, a fundraiser, a finance officer, three more field reps, an employee benefits program, and even a provision of expense reimbursement for governors' travel to meetings.

Given his skill at guiding the organization, Goodwin was asked to be the paid president himself. He certainly was among the most dedicated of volunteers. He had sacrificed his career as a research botanist to the cause of the Conservancy. He had donated two consecutive sabbaticals during his two presidencies to revamp leadership twice. And he and his wife even donated land to establish a nature preserve.

But he could see the organization was growing beyond even his skills as a leader. Trained as a teacher and scientist, he did not see himself as the man for the job, and he bowed out. By the next September, the first paid president started: Charles H. W. "Hank" Foster, the former commissioner of natural resources for Massachusetts.

Goodwin stayed on the board for fifteen more years, always a volunteer, watching with awe as the accountants and lawyers and professional managers took the organization to new heights. The Conservancy outgrew Goodwin, but it would never outgrow the need he demonstrated: To periodically take the agonizing steps needed to transform leadership to further the growth and impact of an expanding organization.

3

MISSION FOR LIFE: On Being Systematic, Not Opportunistic

WHEN ROBERT E. JENKINS JR. JOINED the Nature Conservancy in August 1970, he walked into an office with a simple motto stenciled on the door: "Land Preservation Through Private Action." On his first day at the 1800 North Kent Street high-rise in Arlington, Virginia, his boss, president Thomas W. Richards, gave him a simple job description to match the motto: improve the scientific significance of land-preservation projects.

Jenkins came well qualified to do Richards's bidding. The top candidate in a field of forty-seven applicants, Jenkins wielded an encyclopedic knowledge of biology, ecology, and natural history. He'd taken his Ph.D. at Harvard a year earlier, student of the celebrated evolutionary biologist Ernst Mayr and ecologist Edward O. Wilson. He had leadership skills to match. He'd helped found Zero Population Growth in Massachusetts, and on Earth Day in April 1970, he personally spoke out on population control—giving seven speeches in one day.

But Jenkins, a big, burly former Rutgers football player with a broad forehead and red beard, quickly found that Richards's charge was not so simple. He would soon learn the organization was guided by a mission that had drifted since the days when George Fell and Richard Goodwin presided. While the conservation ship once had orders to sail along a precise bearing, it now had the habit of sailing whichever way the winds of deal making blew.

Instilling a focused mission and the discipline to follow it would be Jenkins's work at the Conservancy. Whereas the crew members in 1970 had an unreliable and inconsistent sense of destination, they later had a crisp one. Whereas dealmakers initially closed transactions of questionable significance, they later moved to close only those of global significance. Whereas decisions at first were mainly opportunistic, they became steadily more systematic.

Soon after he started, Jenkins began to get hints of how much the crew had zigzagged toward an uncertain destination. When the staff attorney quit a month into Jenkins's tenure, he first treated Jenkins to a bit of bellyaching about the organization's direction.

After listening to a diatribe, Jenkins objected. He insisted that the organization did a lot of good.

The attorney replied that, well, it probably did, but it was an accident.

An accident! Jenkins couldn't grasp what that meant. But in the following weeks, he started to figure it out. Scores of project files crossed his desk—Sam's Woods in Connecticut, Lichen Glade in Missouri, Fairy Chasm in Wisconsin, Neahkahnie Beach in Oregon. Each appeared with a cover sheet printed with boxes for the ecology adviser and others to sign. But he had no idea how to assess any of them for significance. He knew his biology well enough. But the reports gave no organized ecological data for decision making, and they reached conclusions based on no criteria for quality.

The motto did seem simple: "Land Preservation Through Private Action." The question was, Preservation for what?

Jenkins became more concerned when he and his wife loaded their two kids into the car to look for preserves on the weekend. Jenkins wanted to get an on-the-ground feel for the properties the Conservancy protected. But as he crisscrossed Virginia and Maryland, he didn't find the exceptional jewels of nature he expected. Almost none were scenic, biological, recreational, or even open-space treasures.

Sometimes he couldn't find the preserves at all. When he searched for Hellen Creek Hemlock Preserve, the one acquired when Goodwin became president in 1956, he couldn't find it on the first trip. The plastic-wrapped signboard, on a tree trunk along the road, was eaten to pieces by termites. When he tried to call the volunteer caretaker of record, he found the man had died two years earlier.

The field trips didn't inspire confidence. They suggested the Conservancy spent a lot of time snapping up available opportunities, not snapping up choice biological treasures. When he queried the Conservancy's office manager about the organization's purpose, he got the quick response: "We're saving land; they're not making any more of it."

Again the question: Saving land for what?

What was the significance of Hellen Creek Preserve, the southernmost stand of hemlock on the Atlantic coast? What would be the significance of twenty-one similar acres in Ohio? Jenkins just couldn't say unless the Conservancy had more precise goals, more ecological data, and had a yardstick to measure how well the preserves met the goals. Without a decision-making structure, the best he could do was to apply his general knowledge and veto projects if something didn't ring true.

Jenkins wasn't sure anyone in the office knew why they were saving land. Without a crisper statement of the mission, he couldn't advise the staff on which way to proceed. He couldn't tell people whether their chosen projects were significant, let alone among the most significant. He had the sinking feeling that a lot of Conservancy acquisitions were no more than random acts of charity.

FIGHTING FOR CLARITY

Jenkins would be the navigator to systematically rechart the conservation course. His first job was to clarify the muddled goals. The problem wasn't a lack of action. Under the business-minded team assembled by Richards, a former IBM manager and county supervisor of Arlington County, Virginia, the Conservancy was striking deal after amazing deal. But Jenkins wanted to answer two questions: What is it that the Nature Conservancy *should* be doing? And what is it *able* to do—so that it makes a real difference in the world?

The goals of the Conservancy were originally laid out by the founders, mainly scientists from university biology departments. Victor Shelford, of the University of Chicago and the Ecological Society of America's Committee for the Preservation of Natural Conditions, publicized the natural-areas movement with his *Naturalist's Guide to the Americas* in 1927. He, and later Goodwin and others, had one thing in mind—saving the surviving vestiges of wild land for research and teaching.

George Fell crystallized the mission in later writings. In 1952, he wrote in a proposal for a national nature-preserve system: "We must systematically seek out unchanged remnants of the natural features not now preserved and see that they are given perpetual protection." Although Fell felt the Conservancy should promote protection of all kinds, it should give "first attention" to places "never seriously modified by man."

Jenkins felt he knew what the founders were driving at—preserving biological value. Some of the veteran scientists from the 1950s were still around to speak up. Three years earlier, Goodwin and five others voiced concern over the business culture they had cultivated. It was driving out science. They issued a report urging the board to hire a scientist. Goodwin's friend Raymond Fosberg insisted the board restore the Conservancy's original purpose, and even its slogan: "Living Museums of Primeval America."

"The paid administration seems determined to run the organization according to its own lights without regard for the original purposes or for the desires of the membership," Fosberg wrote in a memo to every governor. "We are concerned now that money value of land preserved, or even simply number of acres acquired, may become to be regarded as the measure of success. This . . . leads us directly out of the field of natural area preservation and into that of open-space preservation."

Reports coming from the staff seemed to bear out Fosberg's concern. In January 1969, president Richards singled out one project for detailed review: the sixty-acre Farmington Apartments in Farmington, Connecticut. The owner had leased the land to a developer, who had built garden apartments worth $2.5 million. The owner was giving the Conservancy a 14 percent interest in the land, with the remaining 86 percent to transfer over a number of years. In the meantime, the Conservancy would earn monthly lease payments, and in ninety-nine years receive title to the land.

In a report to the board, Richards called the project "an imaginative new concept." But the concept, focusing on money and acres, was not what Fosberg had in mind. The Conservancy seemed to be reversing the course of the founders. It had even rewritten its brochures to reflect a membership poll. Members chose "maintain the natural beauty" as the number one reason to protect land; "preserve fauna that might otherwise become extinct" as number two; and "provide areas for scientific research" as number three.

Richards called for a change in the Conservancy's bylaws to "include preservation of recreational lands and general open space objectives" to "bring the statement more in line with our actual operations."

Fosberg was appalled, and he spearheaded a campaign to rededicate the Conservancy to the original natural-areas mission. Along with veteran governors like Goodwin, he urged the addition of a scientist to the staff, and this led to the hiring of Jenkins. Jenkins was cut from a different cloth. The Conservancy was busy hiring people who had spent a few years in business or real estate or similar fields. Jenkins had spent two of his six Harvard years in Costa Rica studying the co-evolution of fruit-eating birds and fruit-bearing plants.

Jenkins was not one to overlook history, and as he sought to clarify the mission, he read the record of the past. The wishes of the founders were clear enough, repeated endlessly in the archives. He honored that legacy while he tried to fit the mission to the circumstances of the organization and to current thinking in ecology. As an ecologist, he reasoned that in pursuing a biological mission, whatever it was, the Conservancy could take one of two directions, the qualitative or the quantitative.

In the quantitative, the organization would preserve land as a way to keep nature healthy—preserving the watersheds that build forests, the forests that build soils, the soils that filter water. The Conservancy would become an agent for keeping the great ecosystem engine of the earth running smoothly, assuring a continued flow of the "free works of nature" for human use. In this way, the Conservancy would help prevent the human species from destroying the life-support apparatus it depends on.

In the qualitative approach, the Conservancy would preserve only choice parcels of the nation's land. In a country where the march of progress was steadily obliterating the inventory of biological treasures, the Conservancy would stockpile unique parts—species, genomes, plant communities, habitats. By preserving choice parcels with their precious components, the Conservancy could protect natural diversity forever.

Jenkins leaned away from the quantitative approach. For one thing, it was inconsistent with the founders' wishes. For another, in a nation developing a million acres of land a year, a small organization simply couldn't make a significant difference. Its acquisitions would be a spit in the ocean of need. But through the qualitative approach, the Conservancy could have an impact of global significance in preserving genetic material or uniquely functioning ecological systems. The Conservancy could become the guardian of irreplaceable pieces of nature's puzzle.

To the general public, and to most in the Conservancy office, the notion of natural diversity was abstract. But to ecologists, diversity was sacred, and it was what Jenkins felt the founders wanted to save. If asked, he would elaborate on the theory behind this notion,—explaining how diversity holds life together as we know it. Diversity promotes natural stability, for one thing. Monocultures—of elm, corn, cotton, potatoes—succumb en masse to diseases. Diversity offers insurance against catastrophes. Landscapes ravaged by human or natural action will reseed from the "parts store" of neighboring land. And it promotes efficiency. Mixes of native animal species occupying unique niches produce far more protein than herds of livestock.

Jenkins also believed that diversity furthered the mental well-being of humanity—we evolved within and are wired biologically to relish ecological richness. But acquiring land for that purpose took second billing in significance. Jenkins believed buying land based on beauty or recreation or merely "open space" might work for the federal government. But preservation on a significant scale for scenic or mental benefits was beyond the Conservancy's ability.

So Jenkins succeeded in answering his questions: What is it that the Nature Conservancy should be doing? It should be protecting the diversity of life on earth, in particular lands rich with rare species and habitats. What is the Conservancy *able* to do—so that it makes a real difference? It can zero in on the unique; it can assemble a select collection of the diverse. In short, the Conservancy can preserve a "Noah's Ark" of biological components. Jenkins reasoned the Conservancy could make a difference, globally, in protecting biodiversity. So biodiversity was the goal, the measure for defining the significant work as desired by president Richards.

Jenkins tried to devise a way to institutionalize this thinking. In 1971, he came up with a scheme to classify Conservancy properties. In the top class were "ecosystem preserves"—mostly pristine, undisturbed lands big enough to save many components of a diverse system. In the second were "species and special features preserves"—lands populated with endangered or rare species. In the third were scientific preserves; in the fourth, open space preserves; and in the fifth, "trade lands," or lands lacking significance but tradable for better property (or cash). The scheme called for Conservancy dealmakers to devote their time and money mainly to the top class.

Ironically, Jenkins's job of convincing Conservancy staff of his ideas was complicated by the organization's success. The Conservancy had grown into an effective, fleet-footed, opportunistic real estate deal-making machine. Its prowess stemmed directly from the 1965 $550,000 Ford Foundation grant and businesslike emphasis urged by Alexander Adams in the mid-1960s. Whereas in 1960 it completed a handful of projects in a couple of states, in 1970 it completed 113 in twenty-three states. When Jenkins came on the scene, the Conservancy hummed, closing two to three transactions a week. The deal flow looked like a blur.

With the organization in high gear, many people didn't want to listen to Jenkins. He came with a message that made many dealmakers howl. Setting priorities hampered deal flexibility and slowed transactions. If Jenkins had been a smaller man, if he had been timid, if he held his opinions in reserve, the dealmakers would have ignored him entirely. But he held his imposing frame above most others; he debated like a Harvard lawyer, with an intellect few could match. Nobody interrupted him once he got on his soapbox. Some people were intimidated.

Jenkins established himself as the intellectual force at the Conservancy. He would pace back and forth in his office, tossing his pearl-handled knife in the air, scratching ideas on the blackboard, explaining to anyone the underpinnings of his thinking. Few people tried to compete with his quick recall, analytical powers, or argumentative might. Jenkins was a man who, as an eighth grader, read every book in the syllabus before the school year

started. He then sat in the back of the room and read the encyclopedia—
and became known as someone who seemed to know something about
everything. On graduating from Rutgers, he earned a perfect score in the
graduate record exam for biology. He wowed Conservancy staff by finishing *New York Times* crossword puzzles in fifteen to twenty minutes.

And then too he was funny. And if not funny, outrageous. "In the past,
mankind has treated his world with about as much imagination and
understanding as a bullfrog," he said in opening a talk at the American
Institute of Biological Sciences. "Male bullfrogs, as most of you know,
treat objects in their environment according to a simple formula: If it
doesn't eat you, and you can't eat it, then copulate with it."

Through an alternating current of humoring, reasoning with, educat-
ing, proselytizing, and browbeating, Jenkins indoctrinated people with
his message about the primacy of natural-diversity protection. To the scientific crowd, the bullfrog was a metaphor for human rapacity: "Our
actions have not been especially different," Jenkins said. "We have de-
voured whatever landscape proved productive, and have wantonly raped
most of what was left."

Jenkins had to be outrageous to persuade Conservancy staff diversity
mattered. He was the sole voice of science. He pressed people to understand the urgency of what he said. Many Conservancy properties were
substandard. They were too small to support viable populations of rare
species, too heavily worked over to have anything of value, or too poorly
configured to enable the Conservancy to sustain their quality. In 1971,
half of all land projects fell under twenty-five acres in size, 30 percent
under ten acres. To Jenkins, even twenty-five acres was too small to maintain ecological integrity.

Jenkins maintained that buying the wrong lands could be worse than
buying none at all. Because development was inevitable, protecting land in
one spot actually drove developers to other spots. If the Conservancy
locked up low-grade lands, it could deflect the bulldozers to high-grade
ones, thereby intensifying rather than alleviating environmental harm.
"Unplanned conservation and unplanned development go hand in hand,"
Jenkins would say.

Although standard operating procedure at the Conservancy was to buy
easily available lands, Jenkins's new religion of selectivity according to

quality criteria began to take hold at the Conservancy. Richards reported to the board in October 1971, "The last several months have . . . witnessed major progress in the shift away from acquisition by opportunity to planned acquisitions."

The acquisition of Finzel Swamp, a tamarack and blueberry wetland in the Allegheny Mountains in western Maryland, demonstrated the shift. Though work on Finzel, at the headwaters of the Savage River, had started a couple of years earlier, Jenkins pressed the deal-making staff to create a "defensible" preserve, where human impact from water flow, traffic, and building wouldn't harm the targeted habitat. Jenkins drew "take lines" along the crest of the watershed, and the staff identified an assembly of seven parcels within the designated boundary. The Conservancy then acquired them all, a total of three hundred acres.

Finzel was the Nature Conservancy's first planned preserve. It marked an abandonment of opportunism for the sake of systematically saving top-priority pristine land. Though based on the thinnest of data, namely off-the-shelf topographic maps, the boundaries of Finzel delineated a commonsense preserve outline, not a convenient one based on property lines. This was a milestone.

Jenkins got the chance to further inculcate his thinking when, in 1971, board chairman Warren Lemmon asked for a long-range plan. Working with other top managers, Jenkins took the lead and poured his thinking into a document that ran seventy-five single-spaced pages. He stated his goal in the plainest terms: "We are trying, by encouragement and by example, to get everyone to actually plan acquisitions."

The top staff embraced Jenkins's core recommendations. In May 1972, the board received an operating plan incorporating his most cherished objectives: land categorization, better management systems, higher-quality preserves, and better overall effectiveness. Jenkins had narrowed the Conservancy's aim to a single cause: preserving "the vanishing heritage of wild plant and animal species, their habitats, natural vegetation associations, biotic communities and other features."

The Conservancy now had a more precise compass bearing. It would no longer aim to just buy hot properties dangled before it. It would acquire wild remnants based on a set of science-based priorities. By including Jenkins's work in formal planning documents, the Conservancy committed

to embarking on a new direction, using systematic decision making based
on ecological facts.

FIELDING THE SYSTEM

Although Jenkins had swayed opinion in headquarters, he had not swayed
the operating practices of many dealmakers in the field—far from it. He
had a theory and a mission to guide systematic decisions, but he didn't
have enough facts to supply decision makers nationwide. He needed ecological data for people to use in every decision on priorities, as they figured out which natural areas should become targets for preservation. The
lack of knowledge formed the next target of his work.

For many years, scientists had built inventories of unique natural areas.
In 1950, the Conservancy published *Nature Sanctuaries in the United States
and Canada.* The document, twelve years in the making and the work of
more than 250 scientists, identified 691 major sanctuaries. It kicked off a
series of other publications, which Jenkins compiled. He then encouraged
more, designing an inventory for the coast of Maine and collaborating with
colleague Dale Jenkins (no relation) at the Smithsonian Institution to
inventory natural areas in the 12,600-square-mile Chesapeake Bay region.

Jenkins urged Conservancy staff to read these reports. And he urged
the board to support more of them. "It is a remarkable thing that the
smallest library generally will have a card index, a file, a retrieval system,"
he told the board in October 1971, "and yet the largest information storage library we are ever likely to see, that is the national and international
system of natural areas, has no such present retrieval system. We don't
know what is out there."

To rectify the vacuum of data, he proposed a computerized data bank.
He and the Smithsonian's Jenkins adapted the Smithsonian's museum-
collection software to prototype the first computerized natural-areas data
system. He also suggested the idea of a national system, and in 1972 wrote
a proposal for a national natural-areas inventory and data bank, request-
ing $154,730 from the Allegheny Foundation to fund it over three years.

"The information on natural areas is so scattered, incompatible, and
incomplete as to be of very limited utility to the action-oriented preservation movement," he wrote. "Synthesis of this information into a

national natural areas inventory and data bank would fill a widely-felt need, involve the cooperative efforts of all the key natural areas organizations and agencies, and produce an organized body of data which could be maintained and used for a variety of purposes."

Jenkins hit endless snags in trying to get politicians and donors behind a national project—despite his proposals and repeated introduction of federal legislation. Nobody would fund a comprehensive effort. In September 1972, he told the Conservancy board that funding was probably on the way. But that was wishful thinking. He came up empty-handed—in spite of the need, his vision, and his work at the Smithsonian on data formats and computer hardware.

He tried to whip up concern over the slow pace of progress. At a Virginia conference of conservationists in March 1973, he noted that even the Army Corps of Engineers—long an environmental stick-in-the-mud—had started a natural-areas study. "I am . . . frustrated with the way things are going at the present," he told the gathering. "I think we have some serious problems."

Some people did respond to those problems. In 1972, Jimmy Carter, governor of Georgia, approved a program for inventorying Georgia's natural heritage. In 1973, Carter was so pleased with the system he wrote neighboring governors to talk it up. He marveled at how, with the best properties flagged, the nonprofit Nature Conservancy swooped in to save Georgia big money through bargain-sale purchases.

But Jenkins largely ignored this work, at least at first. The state program struck Jenkins as just one more piecemeal effort. It distracted him from promoting the national system. He began to change his tune only when encouraged by Patrick Noonan, the Conservancy's new president, who was working in South Carolina with the chairman of the Wildlife and Marine Resources Department, Joseph Hudson. Together, Noonan and Hudson had arranged for the donation to the state of the Santee Coastal Reserve, a landmark 24,000-acre plot with a freshwater cypress lake and cypress-gum swamp. Hudson wanted to know if South Carolina didn't have more nifty lands worthy of preservation, and he told Noonan he would put up the money for an inventory.

Noonan, president since June 1973, urged the hesitant Jenkins to cooperate. Jenkins acquiesced to the appeal, and contracted with South

Carolina to start the inventory. He soon realized this was a chance to control the creation of a brand new system, using all that he had learned from efforts to date. He saw that while he beat the drum for a national program, he could start building a state one.

In April 1974, he sent Yale Forestry School graduate Thomas Kohlsaat south to Columbia, South Carolina, with an American Express card and instructions to get going. Kohlsaat set out to acquire all the knowledge he could about diversity in South Carolina. He searched the literature and picked the brains of renowned botanists. He hired a field biologist to check for rare sites on the ground, using field-survey forms he and Jenkins made from scratch. He put all that he found into the new system.

The systematic approach Jenkins wanted took discipline. In 1974, two of South Carolina's natural treasures came up for sale: Congaree Swamp and Kiawah Island. The first was a breathtaking intact old-growth floodplain with loblolly pines over 150 feet tall. The second was a forested barrier island off the Charleston coast. Kohlsaat had just started his work; he didn't have enough data to systematically assess rarity. So he and the Conservancy sidestepped any action on the sites.

The inaction stirred contempt from environmentalists. This pained Kohlsaat. He, after all, had joined the Conservancy to save land, and he seemed to be missing once-in-a-lifetime opportunities. The federal government ended up with the 22,000-acre wilderness of Congaree Swamp, but a developer bought 10,000-acre Kiawah Island for $18.1 million, and resort developers started building houses and golf courses on it in 1974. Kiawah was a big loss.

Jenkins was looking to the long term, though. He kept telling Kohlsaat: Don't be opportunistic, be systematic. We've already acquired too many duplicative natural areas—the proverbial hemlock ravine so common in the Northeast—while missing the chance to acquire rarer, if less scenic, sites like Carolina Bay wetlands. So Kohlsaat set his sights on spending a couple of years getting a reasonable database in place.

Jenkins planned from the start that someone else—not the Conservancy—would run the computers. In South Carolina, he proposed using the same hardware and software under development by the South Carolina Department of Archives and History Bureau to track historic sites. This fit in well with his notion that state government could provide a stable, well-funded institution to husband permanent, and costly, data storage and maintenance operations.

But six months after Kohlsaat began, the state decided against developing a computer database. That's when Jenkins realized *he* had to run the system. He would have to develop the data storage methodology, and he would have to find the hardware to run it on. This was a surprise. But he realized there would not be a natural-areas system unless he and the Conservancy took charge. He entered a whole new field of operations: managing a data-system operation. He bought time on an IBM System/360 in Arlington and got rolling himself.

WORKING WITH FACTS

Jenkins's sense of urgency in getting a system going increased as ongoing work at the Smithsonian revealed an ever-lower quality of decisions. Jenkins had asked the Smithsonian—in a whole separate effort—to build a database of the Conservancy's own preserves. As that work neared completion in 1974, the results were dispiriting. They showed the Conservancy operated even more opportunistically than he thought. The need for systematic decision making was extreme.

The Conservancy saved scores of properties with flimsy justification. Some were bought as good opportunities to study ecological succession—from which Jenkins surmised they were formerly farmed, cut over, or otherwise disturbed. Others were bought simply to show local groups how to carry out land conservation. Yet others were acquired to win the gratitude of donors or neighbors. On many parcels, the Conservancy had not clearly preserved anything of biological worth at all.

Exceptions stood out. Mianus Gorge, on the New York–Connecticut border, was a coherent, viable preserve. It was the Conservancy's first, a flagship. Goodwin had walked it in 1954, and a group of committed local volunteers, some pledging their life insurance policies to raise the money, bought the site in 1955. But the exceptions were just that, and Jenkins came to a cheerless conclusion: The good intentions of staff and volunteers had channeled untold time and money into projects that didn't further the cause of natural diversity.

All the while, Conservancy's dealmakers continued to eye projects of dubious biological value. In one notorious case in 1974, the field staff

negotiated to buy a fourteen-acre New Jersey plot distinguished only by
a horticulture collection of daffodil varieties. The piece had no ecological
merit as a preserve for rare species. The asking price was roughly $35,000
per acre. Jenkins raised a ruckus. He felt the project was a brazen challenge to his work to encourage science-based decision making. The board
eventually rejected the project.

Faced with the threat of more decisions based on opportunism, Jenkins
became eager to extend his inventory program, now officially named the
Natural Heritage Program. In 1974, he started a program in Mississippi.
In 1975, he started two more, in West Virginia and Oregon. With the
state programs taking shape, the world began to look different to Jenkins.
Stymied in giving birth to a national system, he saw the state programs as
an interim step. The states, after all, were the site of most decision making. The states, in short, were springboards to the nation.

As Jenkins felt better and better about the state programs, he felt worse
and worse about the utility of the system. The harder he tried to collect
data, the weaker it looked. In Mississippi, he gathered two hundred of
Mississippi's best field biologists in Jackson and broke them into groups
to document all they knew about rare species, communities, and exceptional sites—and pour it into the Heritage system. The biologists threw
themselves into the work with enthusiasm. And their collective intelligence promised an invaluable foundation of data.

But Jenkins learned a lesson. The intelligence returned had far less
value than expected. The reason: information lacked rigor. It was not a
good basis for systematic decision making. The biologists often pointed
out their pet teaching sites, or sites near their offices, or sites not far from
roads. The top pick by the scientists in Jackson was the Pascagoula River
corridor—not a very helpful insight because from the air the pristine river
stood out like an oasis in the Sahara.

Jenkins began to realize that expert observation was a poor instrument
for comprehensively, definitively, and even-handedly measuring natural
diversity. Human beings don't see enough, remember enough, or have a
broad enough perspective to accurately detect significance. Their knowledge is fragmented, disorganized, and biased by their interests. Their opinion, however helpful compared to nothing at all, couldn't form the basis

for objective decisions. Jenkins wasn't even sure the experts identified all the most valuable sites in their own state.

The upshot was that Jenkins's entire inventory system was based on a flimsier basis than he had thought. It was flawed—flawed more than he could accept.

As it happened, Jenkins hired a man who triggered a change in his thinking. Frank Pelurie, a Pennsylvania State University graduate who had worked on inertial guidance-systems and weapons-systems computers for military aircraft, arrived at the Conservancy in early 1975. Jenkins had hired him to open the Natural Heritage program in West Virginia.

In one conversation, Pelurie overheard Jenkins and others wrestling with how to reconfigure the database. What caught Pelurie's attention was the group's effort to compare different natural sites. His computer background bubbling up, Pelurie couldn't help but join the meeting of the confused scientists. Comparing sites is not possible, he said. You're talking about apples and oranges. You can't do that; you've got to compare like things.

Of course, Pelurie was right, Jenkins realized. They couldn't compare two sites for rarity. That was like putting two fruit baskets side by side and asking someone to rate the relative rarity. Who is to say which is the rarer if each has different rare fruits—one, say, from Florida, the other from California?

In another encounter, Pelurie complained to Jenkins about the cost of running a computer query. It was cheap to get a printout about a natural area. But what if you wanted to ask how uncommon something was—that is, ask if Fraser's sedge, a grass in one West Virginia site, was rare at every site across the state? Such queries cost a budget-busting $26 each—the price of nearly three Conservancy memberships in 1975. The system made decision making based on rarity prohibitive.

The conundrum of comparing sites and rarities led Jenkins to an insight, and he blurted to Pelurie. "I know, we'll invert the files!"

And as quickly as he said "invert the files," he realized his biggest folly in four years of work. The Conservancy shouldn't have collected information by site in the first place—by Finzel Swamp or Hellen Creek or Pascagoula River. It should have been collecting information about individual rarities. "Holy shit," he thought. "We got it!"

Jenkins started scribbling. "We're changing the whole thing," he told Pelurie. We're going to store data on the "elements" of nature, and on "element occurrences," or where they appear on the land.

It was a eureka moment for Jenkins. He decided right then that the main inventory would henceforth store data element by rare element. The Conservancy scientists could then compare rarity to pinpoint the most valuable sites, rather than just asking well-traveled scientists to name their favorites. He and everyone else working on the Heritage inventories had been blinded by the status quo—the way inventories had been done starting with Victor Shelford and other scientists with their landmark book in 1927. The way it had always been done in the past no longer made sense at all.

In the spring of 1975, Jenkins hailed the new approach in the *Nature Conservancy News:* "Direct comparisons can be made on the basis of real data (as opposed to subjective judgment)," he wrote. With the old method, in which people's opinion governed which fruit basket was more critical, "prettiness" could outweigh rarity as a criterion for protection. "This often leads to the gully and hemlock syndrome, in which habitat types or elements are preserved redundantly while others are not preserved at all."

"It might seem absurd that the last, best examples of ecosystems close to extinction could be rejected as 'not good enough,'" he added, "but this is exactly what can happen."

Jenkins's decision meant tearing apart a year's worth of work in South Carolina, and the new systems in West Virginia, Mississippi, and Oregon. So be it, he thought. The Conservancy's goal was to protect the entire spectrum of natural diversity, and Jenkins wasn't going to fail on that account just because of earlier defects in the way they gathered and inventoried information. The new system would provide a truly systematic and fact-based way to assess significance and assign priorities.

A LIFETIME'S JOB

In the ensuing months, Jenkins pursued his newfound vision with the certainty of a man who had a road map for making his mark in the world. In 1974, the Conservancy had secured a contract with the Department of the Interior to study natural-areas conservation. Jenkins turned the 1975 report,

The Preservation of Natural Diversity: A Survey and Recommendations, into a manifesto for a revitalized natural-diversity movement.

Though colleague John Humke was the lead author, Jenkins penned the foreword, restating what was essentially the Conservancy's mission. He began by paraphrasing Aldo Leopold, who wrote in the 1949 book *Round River,* "If the biota, in the course of aeons, has built something we like but do not understand, then who but a fool would discard seemingly useless parts. To save every cog and wheel is the first precaution of intelligent tinkering."

"We need to set aside, in viable units, adequate examples of the full array of extant ecosystems, biological communities, endangered species habitats, and endangered physico-chemical environmental features," wrote Jenkins. "Only in this way can we maintain the full diversity of genetic variability, ecological relationships, and special processes and elements."

"If nothing is done about this situation, it seems certain that species after species, community type after community type, ecological component after ecological component is going to be unnecessarily snuffed out of existence," he added. "The natural ecological fabric of the whole continent will be eaten away thread by thread right before our eyes."

Jenkins used the report for a renewed pitch for a national inventory. He, Humke, and others lobbied for nine months to get an act passed— but again he failed. Wisely, he was no longer waiting for the Senate and Congress to understand his drive for data to support systematic decisions on natural diversity. He kept pushing his vision in state capitals. In 1976, he launched three more state Natural Heritage programs, in North Carolina, New Mexico, and Ohio. In 1977, he christened two, in Oklahoma and Washington. And in 1978 he launched six more, in Wyoming, Arkansas, Indiana, Kentucky, Massachusetts, and Rhode Island.

Inside the Conservancy, Jenkins battled constantly to nudge decision makers and dealmakers into making disciplined, scientific, fact-based decisions based on the new data. Everyone was tutored in his approach, and instructed to toe the party line. But at every turn, he had to fight people who put opportunism above objectivity, who believed that doing good counted more than doing the greatest good.

One example arose in South Carolina, where Kohlsaat's politically sensitive boss wanted to involve citizens in the choices of which natural areas to give priority. Jenkins would have none of it. He told Kohlsaat: "The last thing we want is a room full of people trying to decide what their heritage is."

David Morine, the Conservancy's dealmaking mastermind, who joined the organization in 1972, often disagreed with Jenkins. The two would argue so loudly the staff thought they would sock each other. Morine, who closed a landmark deal to acquire the Pascagoula corridor—in a triumph of opportunism, politicking, and dealmaking—told Jenkins the last thing he needed was an inventory to show him where to find the greatest places on earth. Morine's rule was simple: "If it's wet, save it." And he felt such a rule of thumb worked well in practice.

The ongoing debate hampered Jenkins's progress in upgrading decision making. The 1976 long-range plan acknowledged as much: "The Conservancy clearly needs to improve the ecological quality of its acquisitions. Basically, we are still reacting to opportunities brought to our attention; in most states we are not yet systematically protecting areas identified by inventories. Only about half of TNC's projects are viable, significant ecosystems or habitat for rare or endangered species."

Conservancy president Noonan, although cultivating debate, supported Jenkins. The clan of top managers would grumble, argue, twist arms, and pound the table about the issue—and then go have a beer. Through it all, Jenkins gained total—if disputed—intellectual hegemony. His vision became the Conservancy's strategic thrust. In 1976, the Conservancy's first two goals were to develop a national natural-areas inventory system and install Natural Heritage programs in twenty-five states.

In the field, some Conservancy staff rebelled against the strictures Jenkins set forth. One of them was Geoffrey Barnard, regional director of the Conservancy for the Great Plains. In 1977, when the two strong-willed men met in Chicago with other Conservancy staff, they hijacked the meeting with an argument that turned into a three-hour shouting match.

Barnard, as secure in his view as was Jenkins, argued the Conservancy could get 90 percent of what it wanted without any Heritage data. His key question: Why burden dealmakers with all this data to get the final 10 percent? He argued further that the Heritage program was raising operating costs 30 percent for a 10 percent gain in decision-making accuracy.

As far as Barnard was concerned—and he was far from alone among Conservancy staff—the Heritage operation was a waste.

Jenkins found such reasoning nonsense. If followed over and over, it would sacrifice untold rare species. The Conservancy would repeatedly protect lands with obvious significance in preference to those with hidden or undocumented significance—and it would be back to the old gully and hemlock syndrome. The only way to capture all significant lands was to catalog expert knowledge and reports, send biologists into the field, document occurrences of the elements of diversity, compare the rare finds, and rank targets with a priority for protection.

Jenkins felt the truth of his logic was inescapable. There simply was no substitute for a systematic, ongoing process of knowledge amassment, with incremental subsequent acquisition of targeted information, with continuous refinement, reanalysis, and successive approximation. He could sound awfully jargony when he expressed his opinion in this way, but his thinking took hold. The difference between decisions based on early inventories and those based on Nature Heritage systems was the difference between opinion and fact.

By the mid-1970s, the systems were up and running in many places and yielding data dealmakers could use. By 1976, Jenkins had developed a model for expanding the state network: Go to the states and offer to hire and train a staff of biologists, establish an operating center, set up the computers, kick off data collection, and in two years let the state take over the whole shebang.

The new systems did make life more complicated for everyone. After Natural Heritage systems revealed a target for preservation, dealmakers had to research who owned the lands and then start from scratch to devise a plan to acquire them. This raised all kinds of problems. The first one was just figuring out how to meet the landowners—who might or might not like conservationists.

In North Carolina, one of the early sites emerging from the system was Nags Head Woods, a maritime forest with freshwater ponds and barrier dunes on North Carolina's Outer Banks. Faced with the rarity of the site, state director Thomas Massengale worked directly with Natural Heritage scientists to plot the boundary needed to protect it. He then cross-checked land ownership and found nine property owners. Massengale had his work cut out for him. He had to figure out the order in which to contact landowners, and make offers without calling attention to himself, lest remaining landowners raise prices on their property.

Massengale, like many dealmakers who followed Jenkins's approach, wasn't dealing with just willing sellers. At Nags Head Woods, one owner said she was waiting for a sign from God to sell (she eventually received it). Another was a felon, who Massengale had arranged to meet at a café. When the man showed up, he looked so rough that Massengale slipped out and phoned a lawyer instead. The lawyer bought the property while representing a "client who wished to remain anonymous." It took several years, but Massengale acquired all nine parcels.

At Nags Head Woods, for the first time the Conservancy acquired a preserve designed entirely from data from the Natural Heritage system. The preserve would remain for years a model of systematic, science-driven Conservancy acquisitions. It and other successes would also encourage Jenkins, in the face of constant pressure by dealmakers to go away, to keep opening new state offices and keep installing his system.

Jenkins and his staff recognized that the Natural Heritage system was not easy to use, especially early on. It produced a lot of data, far more than many dealmakers wanted. So they offered one refinement after another: ranking systems, natural diversity scorecards, mapping systems, standardized procedures, and manuals to describe it all. Jenkins never succeeded in establishing a national inventory. But he did manage, over fifteen years, to establish systems in every state (and several abroad). He kept going partly because he enjoyed a devoted following in the field, both in Conservancy and state agency offices.

Jenkins also enjoyed a devoted coterie of like-minded staff. He himself stimulated a legendary esprit de corps with joking, game-playing, and shenanigans. Phillip Hoose, a Natural Heritage planner and songwriter, bet constantly with Jenkins over any number of disputed facts, like song lyrics or quotations from *Catch 22*. Jenkins one day boasted that, as a college football player, he was so limber he could kick the bottom of a basketball net with his toe. Hoose howled with disbelief, and bet Jenkins that he (Hoose) could jump higher with the top of his head than Jenkins could ever kick.

The two scheduled a competition. People from around the office came. One of Jenkins's people climbed onto a file cabinet to mark the height of the two men's attempts. Hoose went first, his height was marked, and he refused to go again until Jenkins did better. Jenkins then ran forward and let fly a kick so high that he fell back flat on his back.

But he fell short.

So he made another half dozen running attempts—short each time—and finally called off any further attempts, convinced he was too old and out of shape to measure up.

Early the next morning, Hoose taped Jenkins's body shape on the floor, as if at a crime scene, delineating Jenkins's hapless outline. Jenkins roared with laughter when he came in the door.

By 1989, when the Natural Heritage program was installed in the last of the fifty states, many Jenkins colleagues and adversaries referred to him as a "genius." By then, the Natural Heritage software had graduated to its sixth generation and ran on personal computers. Jenkins had a staff of about 70, not counting about 350 people employed by state-based Heritage operations. But what awed people were his organizational abilities—creating a system of more than fifty state bureaus, paid for by the states, coordinated with central support from the Conservancy, running software for consistent, fact-based decision making. There was no parallel, not even close.

In 1988, Jenkins was lauded in an outside report assessing his system: "The TNC biological diversity information system has been the keystone. . . . It has been responsible for changing the whole explicit approach of TNC's land acquisition from a 'catch as catch can' activity to a program for saving biological diversity that is based on systematic collection of information regarding the abundance of species."

To be sure, Jenkins continued to clash with people who sought to buy properties as "program builders"—jargon for flashy properties that whipped up popular support or spurred people to make big donations. Conservancy staff saw these projects, even if they didn't have much natural-diversity value, not just as fair game but key to the institution's health.

Sometimes Jenkins would agree. The Conservancy had to raise funds to run programs and open offices, after all. But often he would explode over the wasted opportunity to use the same money to save the diversity of life elsewhere. He achieved pariah status in Colorado in the 1980s by opposing the 1,700-acre Phantom Canyon acquisition northwest of Fort Collins. Phantom Canyon was one of northern Colorado's last roadless canyons, through which flowed a pristine trout stream, the north fork of the Cache la Poudre River. But Jenkins didn't care about the beauty—not in his post as don for systematic, science-based decision making. When the Conservancy bought the canyon in 1987, he considered it a perfect transgression of the diversity mission—in a state where data gave other sites higher priority.

People would have sympathized more with Jenkins if he didn't let his antipathy for opportunistic decision making get the better of him. Opportunism could work out just fine. Following the Phantom Canyon acquisition, field biologists discovered a rare member of the parsley family there. But Jenkins could not let his focus rest. After a talk on biodiversity preservation at another time in Colorado, he rebuked a wealthy donor for her preference for a "yummy" piece of property—he told her she belonged to the wrong organization. He received a thank-you letter for his talk from the Colorado chapter chairman with a message that said essentially, "Your speech elicited much comment and discussion, all of it negative."

Jenkins regretted such dunderheaded moves. Yet they reflected his zeal and dedication. He had always gone to exhausting ends to fight for his ideas. During one of his attempts in the late 1970s to get Congress to pass a national natural diversity act, he couldn't get a hearing with California Congressman Philip Burton, a powerful member of the House Committee on Interior and Insular Affairs. Jenkins booked a seat next to Burton on the lawmaker's flight back to Washington from San Francisco. Jenkins lobbied Burton all the way.

When asked, Jenkins would tell people that his function at the Nature Conservancy was like that of the Pope. He was a moral nag. He didn't have a lot of power outside the priesthood of the Natural Heritage operation. When he enunciated a moral precept, people felt obliged to follow—but they didn't have to. In the end, Jenkins's precept would be simple: Master the facts, and make systematic decisions based on them.

4

WE CAN WORK WITH YOU: The Care and Feeding of a Dynamic Culture

AT AN APRIL 1973 BOARD MEETING of the Nature Conservancy, President Everett Woodman spoke of a sea change in thinking in America: a new mood in the nation, a questioning of unrestrained growth, a suggestion that industry and interest groups can devise new models of environmental betterment. "There is a national need now for some brave environmentalist organization, maybe small, private and quiet," he wrote in his report, "to sound a new tone and set a new attitude for the environmentalist fraternity toward itself, and toward the people it must deal with in the total national environment."

To the surprise of the board, Woodman apparently didn't believe he was the man to lead that organization. He resigned just a couple of weeks later. Into that void stepped Patrick F. Noonan, vice president of the Conservancy since 1972, a stocky former footballer, planner, and MBA, and the organization's star dealmaker. Noonan would be the man to lead that brave organization. He would be the leader to sound that new tone and set that attitude.

Noonan would make many contributions to the Conservancy, but among the most enduring would be a cultural foundation. Although not one to seek the limelight, he would set the example everyone would follow. His manner, his flair, his sense of propriety, his exploits—they would contribute to a lasting collection of principles and customs to guide the thought and action of Conservancy staff. To the legacy of Noonan, the staff would turn again and again to develop daring plans and deliver stellar results.

Noonan's rise to the presidency came at an uncertain time. Inside the Conservancy, leadership was splintered. Just nine months earlier, Noonan and three other vice presidents ran the organization—in the six-month interval between president Thomas W. Richards's departure and Woodman's arrival. Noonan, Christopher Dann, Robert Berner, and Robert Jenkins were ostensibly co-equals. Although Noonan had the top hand, all four were strong-willed and talented, the twenty-something Young Turks who ran the show. They all had their own ideas.

The organization operated at a blistering pace. The four vice presidents moved fast—so fast that the board threatened to pass a resolution to slow them down. It proposed barring projects from consideration that had not reached headquarters at least ten days before board meetings—lest a "climate for breeding future problems" arise. So worried about runaway entrepreneurship was the board that Chairman Wallace Dayton asked California board member Alfred Heller to start long-range planning meetings aimed at developing a tighter, goal-oriented organization.

As if to signal just how uncertain everyone was, the planning group at the October 1972 kickoff meeting felt compelled to go back to management ABCs: Woodman posed the fundamental question: What is the basic purpose of the Conservancy? What do we want to do—by what time, and for whom? In spite of Jenkins's initial work to firm up the mission and move the Conservancy toward systematic decision making, Woodman felt the organization was adrift.

Truth be told, the Conservancy was an organization in adolescence, struggling to find its way, and despite publicized victories as "the real-estate arm of the conservation movement," Conservancy staff knew they represented the smaller kid on the block. The staff, some burdened with a sort of organizational inferiority complex, talked with envy about the better-known Audubon Society and Sierra Club. Even friends of the Conservancy staff, when told about the Conservancy, were befuddled over the unfamiliar name and would ask, "The National Conservatory?"

On the board of the Conservancy sat many seasoned veterans, but the turnover of staff was extreme. Woodman reported in February 1973 that twenty-five people had resigned in the preceding year, including seventeen secretaries. The staff was populated with young people—thirty of the fifty-two were under thirty and the median age was twenty-nine. A World War II veteran and former president of Colby Junior College in New Hampshire, Woodman worried openly to the board about how to retain Conservancy leadership. And no wonder: In February 1973, star West Coast dealmaker Huey Johnson resigned—and so did Noonan.

The uncertainty began to end when Noonan came back. The ink had hardly dried on his resignation when Woodman gave notice, and the congenial Noonan quietly campaigned for the top job. He met with staff around the country, asking things like, "What would you think of me as president?" Many staff were flattered to be asked, and they backed him. Noonan posed the same question to board members. By the June 6, 1973, board meeting, the board members embraced the idea. They hired Noonan as president.

Noonan grew up in Chevy Chase, Maryland, a sleepy Washington, D.C., community. It was the 1960s. Schools remained segregated, Elvis Presley, Jerry Lee Lewis, and Chuck Berry rocked, and baseball dominated as the neighborhood game. An athlete, Noonan went to Gettysburg College on a football scholarship, graduating in 1965, earning his MBA in night school. He entered the work world thinking people should be of service to others. At the moment of his initial hiring in 1969, he was working as a planner for the Maryland National Park and Planning Commission. He came to the Conservancy at a time when everyone reported to work in a suit, and honesty and loyalty to one's fellows were supreme.

Noonan, his round face framed with narrow lamb-chop sideburns, had a head start as a leader. He had earned huge respect in stepping up the pace of project completion by 40 percent in 1972. Everyone knew he loved deal making, loved people, and loved the idea of saving nature. He was a natural at motivating others because he worked harder than anyone else, was full of praise, rarely took credit, and always made work fun.

The men in the office loved the collegial competition he encouraged. At meetings they would play pick-up softball, volleyball, horseshoes, or flag football. The women loved how he never brandished his power, never flaunted his position, never talked down to them. If the Conservancy had to get out a fundraising mailing, Noonan stayed after hours with everyone else stuffing envelopes. He had a way of earning everyone's respect.

So when he started as president, as young as he was, Noonan had a mandate. The organization was ripe for him to consolidate the best of the Conservancy's personality into a solid organizational culture. People were eager to have him show the way. In a matter of just a few years, he would more than answer the challenge posed by former college president Woodman to set a new tone and attitude.

CREDIT THE PAST

Noonan hardly started from scratch. When it came to putting his imprint on the organization, he built on the legacy of early leaders like Richard Pough, Alexander Adams, and Huey Johnson. To the staff of the Nature Conservancy, each of these men's work transcended his era. Each of the three, in the same way as Richard Goodwin, symbolized Conservancy culture—a culture Noonan would reinforce.

Pough, a businessman turned naturalist, worked at New York's American Museum of Natural History from 1948 to 1956. As chairman of the Department of Conservation and General Ecology, he helped ban the sale of wild-bird feathers and warned of the dangers of DDT. So outspoken was Pough that his boss had to protect him from being fired after he argued, against the wishes of New York highway czar Robert Moses, to stop plans for an expressway through Van Cortlandt Park in the Bronx.

Pough, who wrote three Audubon bird guides, pushed ahead with his principled, environmentalist views in spite of Moses, who controlled the museum's funding. He got in hot water again when he argued in the name of the museum to oppose the Echo Park Dam in Dinosaur National

Monument in Colorado. "Dick," he later recalled his boss telling him, "one doesn't tell corporations what they can or can't do—their business is making money, not preserving nature."

Not to be muzzled, Pough pressed his activist views at the Conservancy, where he took on the volunteer job of president in 1952. In December 1954, the Conservancy board, attending a meeting at the museum, voted in a resolution opposing the dam. Pough soon found that he was getting himself in more trouble than he bargained for. People blamed the museum for the defeat of the dam, and the unhappy upshot was that Pough's department was dissolved, and he was thrown out of his job.

The unpleasant ouster led him to resolve that the Conservancy would never be *against* anything. It would buy and preserve land, period—and nobody would then raise a stink about its work. Pough thus laid down a key plank in Conservancy culture: be nonconfrontational. He adhered to that principle for the rest of his life—and Noonan followed his lead.

Adams, the Machiavelli to Goodwin's Churchill, lobbied all through the 1960s for a more businesslike approach. In 1967, when Charles H. W. Foster (the first president) resigned, Adams urged governors to hire an executive, rather than someone prominent in conservation or public life. The board settled on Thomas W. Richards, for nine years an IBM manager. Richards, a skilled team builder, turned around weak functions like finance, and hired strong, businesslike managers like Noonan.

Adams was obsessed with effectiveness, to the point of offending his board. "The Nature Conservancy was originally organized as a committee of scientists, who wished to preserve natural areas. It had a goal and absolutely no method of attaining it, and it accomplished almost nothing," he said in his last speech as chairman in August 1969. "It is not enough to own an airplane; you also have to have someone who knows how to fly it."

In 1967, Richards put the plane in a businesslike flight, and Noonan piloted the craft in much the same way. From then on, running like a business became a Conservancy trademark. Perhaps no plank in Noonan's cultural platform would be stronger.

Johnson, hired in 1965 by the Conservancy's last executive director, Walter Boardman, took people's breath away with his brazen land deals.

In his most celebrated deal, in 1969, he agreed to acquire without board approval seven thousand acres on Maui, Hawaii, enough to connect the crater of Haleakala National Park to the sea. Conservancy board secretary Elting Arnold, who nosed through the details of every deal, was furious. A lawyer, he wrote a letter to Johnson both reprimanding him for the deal and demanding he come up with the money to pay for it.

Johnson whipped up a series of fundraisers, the first in Honolulu. Aviator Charles Lindbergh, who lived in the town of Kipahulu, on Maui, came, and began a long relationship with the Conservancy. Though fundraisers in San Francisco and Chicago went poorly, a luncheon in New York flew past all expectations. Atop the Pan Am building, Lindbergh read a hand-typed composition, an ode to Haleakala, and Johnson then pitched the project's beauty.

The magical Hawaiian forest, the wonder of the Seven Sacred Pools, the 400-foot Waimoku Falls, the discovery of the Maui nukupuu, a curve-beaked honeycreeper presumed extinct for more than seventy-one years—these all fascinated donors. Pledges poured in. Television star Arthur Godfrey, catching an elevator to the lobby with tobacco heiress Doris Duke, returned minutes later with a $100,000 pledge.

Johnson, in a matter of weeks, raised the $620,000. This allowed the Conservancy to transfer ten thousand acres to the National Park Service, including three thousand acres transferred from the state of Hawaii and seven thousand acres bought by the Conservancy or donated by Laurance Rockefeller. The entire transfer extended the Haleakala park from the ridge to the sea. Elting Arnold sent Johnson a congratulatory note, along with a book on Hawaii. Johnson—who was offered the presidency himself but declined because he wouldn't leave California—came to define the action- and results-oriented dealmaker of the Conservancy.

Even the *Wall Street Journal* took notice of the Conservancy's winning projects and swashbuckling style. In a March 1970 front-page story, "A Conservation Group Preserves Choice Sites by Aggressive Tactics," the *Journal* lauded Conservancy work under Richards, Adams, and Johnson. Within days, the Conservancy went from getting handfuls of mail each day to bagfuls. Apparently business readers liked the cultural style of early Conservancy leaders.

MAKING A MARK

Noonan, as if paying homage to these earlier leaders, would soon put himself on par with them. Within months of starting in 1969, he had applied the same aggressive approach. His dogged, can-do, unabashed working style would become another central plank in the Conservancy's platform of organizational culture. Nobody could fail to notice and admire Noonan's energy and pluck.

His most celebrated deal was saving Metompkin Island on what is known as Virginia's Eastern Shore. The shore is the spit of land jutting south from Maryland, the massive Chesapeake Bay lying on the west, the open Atlantic on the east. His work began when M. Lee Payne, a Norfolk banker, phoned the Conservancy about the island, a six-mile-long barrier sand flat on the Atlantic coast.

The situation was that the owners wanted to sell—but not for any price to conservationists. The owners didn't want anyone to lock up the island as a reserve forever. With thoughts of millions of dollars made in nearby Ocean City, they hoped the state would link the island to the mainland with a causeway—the first step in rapid and lucrative economic development. The 1960s was a time when people had stars in their eyes; they believed coastal land was a ticket to jobs and cash.

Noonan and Payne had a different idea. Payne invited Noonan and Richards to his Norfolk office. Payne, enamored with Noonan from the start, lifted two large conch shells from his desk and said he had found them while surf fishing on the island. "Really?" he recalled Noonan responding. "Could I have one?"

Payne, surprised, gave one to Noonan, and he would later say that one of Noonan's happy characteristics was that he never minded making requests of anybody, for anything.

In this case, the request of Payne was to set up a corporation to hide the identity of the potential buyer of Metompkin Island. Payne would set up Offshore Islands Inc. to negotiate a deal. The dummy company, based in Richmond and feigning a developer's eye for this appetizing strip of coastal wilderness, would then buy the island before anyone knew the Conservancy was behind the whole thing. In real estate terms,

Payne would act as a "nominee," a routine act for a for-profit real estate developer.

For the Conservancy, using a nominee was not routine. As a do-gooder nonprofit, the organization preferred to operate more in the open. But the situation seemed to justify the move. At the time, the Conservancy was a relatively small organization. It was the David, and it was wrestling a Goliath, the grand forces of land despoliation. As the David, it had no choice in this case but to use aggressive tactics to outmaneuver moneyed and powerful developer foes.

Noonan's boss, President Richards, was in favor of the clandestine corporation. But he did go to the board to secure permission. Richards believed that Payne was the only answer to saving the island. The board agreed. A week later, as if to signal public approval of such tactics, the *Washington Post* profiled the Conservancy. In "A Land Grabber Everybody Likes," the *Post* noted Richards maneuvered with "all the zeal of an avaricious real estate speculator."

Payne's group, part of that zeal-filled team, bought Metompkin and conveyed it immediately to the Conservancy for $105,000. The David had won one on the Goliath. The Conservancy had saved an obvious gem of ecological diversity, one of the last few unruined examples of an Atlantic barrier island, the habitat for untold songbirds, water birds, and, along with neighboring marshes, the nursery for marine life of all kinds.

The money for these deals came from another Conservancy ally in conservation: the Mary Flagler Cary Charitable Trust. With Payne often working in the background, and the Cary Trust funding real estate costs, Noonan snapped up some of the most ecologically valuable land in Virginia. On April 6, 1970, he flew the trustees along the Eastern Shore from Wallop Island in the north to Cape Charles in the south. With Noonan as their guide, the trustees, led by Herbert J. Jacobi, set their sights on saving the entire string of undeveloped islands—Metompkin, Cedar, Parramore, Hog, Cobb, Ship Shoal, Myrtle, Smith, and others.

With the help of a real estate recession that clobbered prices and forced debt-laden developers to sell for sacrifice prices, Noonan engineered the acquisition of all the remaining islands in the chain, and the Cary Trust funded every one, to the tune of $7.5 million. The Conservancy ended up owning fourteen barrier islands and fifty-one miles of shore, a master-piece of conservation. The quick, secret deals, especially at Metompkin, ignited hostility in Eastern Shore towns, however, something the Conservancy would have to pay for later.

As Noonan worked the Virginia Coast, he also worked the Virginia swamps. His biggest inland deal involved Great Dismal Swamp, a low-land ripe for farming—after clear-cutting, draining, liming, and fertilizing. The Conservancy identified the swamp, a 250,000-acre tract of evergreen shrub bogs, loblolly pine barrens, cypress swamps, and mixed forest of maple, pine, and white cedar, as a critical natural area. In 1970, with plans pending to run Interstate 64 across the northwest edge of the swamp, the Conservancy was spurred to look for a deal. If it didn't, land prices would soar with the promise of new freeway access.

Noonan approached Union Camp, the owner of the biggest tract, to talk about conservation. The 49,097-acre parcel, in the swamp's center, encompassed 3,000-acre Lake Drummond. It was the core of the swamp. The company, when approached by Noonan at an initial meeting, said that whatever happened, the best interests of stockholders would have to come first. Noonan knew right away the Conservancy couldn't buy the land. Appraisals confirmed the land was worth an out-of-reach $12 million to $14 million.

Noonan worked up three alternatives: an open-market sale, a "bargain sale" for half the price, and a full donation. The company could deduct from its taxes the gift portion of the latter two. Taking into account the company's cost basis, tax bracket, net income, and so on, Noonan convinced Union Camp chief executive Alexander "Sox" Calder that a donation for conservation was the highest and best use of the land. The favorable financial figures, along with likely favorable publicity, won Calder over, allowing Noonan to consummate an unprecedented deal.

Together with the work on the Virginia coast, the work on the Great Dismal Swamp showed how effective the Conservancy could be. The Great Dismal project created a publicity bonanza for everyone. There was no reason to keep it quiet, so the Conservancy reversed its Metompkin procedure and blew its publicity trumpets loudly. The response from the press was gratifying and alerted big landowners and corporations of how quickly and expertly the Conservancy could act in hugely complex deals.

The *New York Times* called the Great Dismal Swamp the Conservancy's "greatest success," adding, "The Union Camp Company has set an example which other industrial units can follow to the enhancement of their own reputations as well as to the country's advantage."

The deal earned Noonan a towering reputation. In many ways, it became Exhibit One in the case for the power of the Conservancy's culture at the time—business-friendly, nonconfrontational, results-oriented, fast-acting, and aggressive. The deal earned Noonan unflagging respect from his staff. He was the first among a team of "action addicts." He was the standard-bearer for the culture of a twenty-three-year-old organization.

LIVING LEGACY

In the glow of these grand transactions, Noonan became president. Whether he wanted people to copy him or not, he became the model. People watched him, they listened to him, they talked about him. His statements about dealmaking and management became articles of faith. When he uttered a bromide about management, people all around would start repeating it. "The individual isn't important; the organization is." "Bait the hook to suit the fish." "It's okay to disagree but not to the point of being disagreeable."

Noonan's protégés would joke about cloning Pat Noonans to populate offices with the master's skills. They valued teamwork, the spreading of credit, letting innovations run, treating everyone like family, giving and getting extraordinary loyalty. If Noonan had a new dealmaker in training, he took him out for a beer and personally sketched the workings of a bargain sale on a napkin. Noonan was the leader. People looked to him for cues. In his hallowed position, he became both speaker and keeper of Conservancy culture.

Faster and Faster

Noonan would say, "To the swift belongs the race." One dealmaker would later say, "We just flew. It was like a real estate office on amphetamines."

Noonan talked fast, walked fast, and thought fast, often with little preparation. No memos, no meetings, just action—that was his preference. So
distinctive was his quick gait that staff could recognize his footsteps coming down the hall.

In his clipped speech, Noonan would ask people: "How many acres have
you saved today?" He didn't want to know what they planned. He wanted
to know what they had delivered. The *Nature Conservancy News* would list,
by state, lands saved in every issue. The dealmakers in the field would worry,
"Oh my god, what if I don't have enough projects in there!" The competition for results would drive them to make sure their listings compared favorably with their peers'.

Noonan personally set the pace of the deal-making action, even after
he became president. In 1973, he closed the acquisition of the 220,000-
acre Sevilleta de la Joya parcel in New Mexico in just over two months.
The Campbell Family Foundation, owner of this arid tract cut by canyons
and bounded by the Ladron and Los Pinos Mountains south of Albuquerque, offered it on October 24 to the U.S. Fish and Wildlife Service.
The caveat: the deal had to be consummated by December 31. The service couldn't do it. It did want the land, but it had no money, too little
time, and no means to quickly execute the real estate paperwork.

In stepped Noonan. By November 20, the hard-driving deal meister
reached an agreement in which the Conservancy would put up $500,000
for the land, worth $12 million, and according to the conservation wishes
of the family, transfer it to the U.S. Fish and Wildlife Service. Conservancy
teams on both the East Coast and West Coast worked against the clock on
transfer details—surveys, title insurance binders, conveyance instruments,
environmental assessment reports, and so on. Noonan secured the $500,000
from the Cary Trust. Negotiations continued even on Christmas Day.

On the evening of December 28, Noonan completed the deal, just in
time to comply with the constraints of the controlling family, whose tax
bill hinged on consummation. The Conservancy took possession of and
transferred Sevilleta to the Fish and Wildlife Service. In one fell swoop,
the Conservancy created the newest U.S. wildlife refuge—and the image
of Noonan doing the deal, so big, so fast, spotlighted the Conservancy
culture of speed.

Scientific Decisions

As Noonan would say, the Conservancy was protecting "The last of the least and best of the rest," a catchphrase coined by Robert Jenkins to urge people to target rare and high-quality land for acquisition. Nobody was ever sure Noonan personally cared about the natural diversity sermon preached by Jenkins. He certainly was no naturalist. Scientists on the board joked he didn't know the difference between a rose and a buttercup. When he talked about bird life, he referred to this "blippety-blip bird" or that "blippety-blip bird" until the staff urged him to learn and use some real bird names instead.

Noonan would tease Jenkins about the interminable delays in getting decent ecological data for decisions. "Nothing would ever happen in conservation if we left it up to you!" people remembered him saying. Or to Conservancy scientists he would jokingly say things like: "I never understood those damn Heritage programs; nobody ever explained one to me." Sitting at the opposite end of the floor from the scientists, Noonan seemed to enjoy projecting a reputation as a biological neophyte.

But despite nursing an "us versus them" culture between the deal-makers and scientists, Noonan supported science. He was the one who pitched the value of the first Heritage program, in South Carolina, directly to the board in the spring of 1974, and by the end of 1974, he cited the science program as the area in which the greatest gains had been made in the previous year. "We're no longer a reactionary organization," he said at the time. "We're initiating priorities."

His and Jenkins's stand for science forced a painful migration. The organization, accustomed to defining itself by the tools of its trade—real estate deal-making tools—had to redefine itself by its mission. By early 1975, Noonan supported a numerical goal to this end: The Conservancy would seek to make 80 percent of its projects protect viable ecosystems of rare or endangered species. It was Noonan's support that legitimized science-based, systematic decision making as a growing part of the culture.

Creativity Without Borders

Noonan, in one of his first board meetings as president, invoked the words of Alexander Adams: "The future of the Conservancy is almost limitless. We are travelers entering on an endless sea. It has no horizons, only space where the line of the horizon should be." Like Adams, Noonan promoted creativity for more quickly and effectively meeting the mission.

David Morine, his new director of acquisition, soon ran into a deal that would show again and again the creative ways Noonan fostered. In late 1973, Morine was approached by a young stockholder of the Pascagoula Hardwood Company in Mississippi. It turned out the company owned 42,000 acres of some of the finest undisturbed bottomland hardwood lands—lands growing with bald cypress, black gum, and sour gum. The property included thirty miles of the Pascagoula River and forty oxbow lakes. It was a crown jewel of the American South.

Over three years, in a saga in which deal failure seemed more likely than deal success, Morine worked with state legislators to create a complex plan to preserve Mississippi's most prized natural land. It included drafting legislation to establish a state Wildlife Heritage Committee, launching a Conservancy-run Heritage program, and passing legislation to appropriate $15 million. This was all in a state where the Conservancy had closed on only one small project and had just four members.

The deciding factor in Morine's success was bringing the sportsmen of Mississippi into conservation. It was the department in charge of game and fish that badly wanted land.

With that new constituency working in his favor, Morine had to convince a hundred family shareholders to sell their land. It was valued at $22 million, much of that in the form of 240 million board feet of timber. In 1975, the people controlling the land told him they wouldn't part with the property. Morine then hit on another idea: buy the entire company. By buying the stock, the Conservancy would allow selling shareholders to save big on taxes. Instead of the company paying capital gains tax on the land sales, and then each stockholder paying income taxes on a share of the gains, the shareholders would pay taxes only once, on just the gains in their shares.

The notion of buying the company and then dissolving it to protect the land was unprecedented for a nonprofit group. But in March 1976, the Conservancy launched a tender offer for the company's shares. Morine then hit one deal-breaking hurdle after another—including an initial decision by the IRS to refuse giving an advance ruling on the tax consequences of the dissolution of the company. Without the ruling, Morine couldn't seal the deal. Noonan kept encouraging Morine, even calling from a family vacation in Disneyland to check in. Finally, Morine obtained three-quarters of the shares, dissolved the company, set aside land for the non-selling shareholder, and transferred 32,000 acres to the state of Mississippi on September 22, 1976.

Noonan's support for deals like the Pascagoula reinforced the staff's drive for inventiveness. Noonan was always pressing his people to rewrite the rules of the game if the existing rules got in the way of getting things done. In his office, he had a sign: "Small minds discuss people. Average minds discuss events. Great minds discuss ideas." And Noonan seemed to have an idea a minute, whether about a new deal or a new deal-making technique.

He would come back from business trips with articles and annotated scraps of paper, which he distributed to various staff. He once returned to hand one of his staff, Michael Wright, an empty, torn-open, flattened sugar packet with a phone number and these words: "15,000 acres, Canada, possible easement." Wright had to figure out the rest—and the Conservancy ended up with a donation of the oldest hunt club in Canada, worth $1 million.

Not that all the creative leads favored by Noonan panned out. In 1974, he and Morine tried selling the idea of building a "private enterprise program" inside the Conservancy. They were unhappy with how the Conservancy, upon saving a piece of land, drove up the value of neighboring parcels, only to miss out on sharing in any of the jump in value. Their brainstorm: have the Conservancy buy not just the core preserve but the adjacent, developable land as well—and create a subsidiary to rake in the profits on the neighboring sites. That would give the Conservancy a lot of extra cash for conservation.

The board balked; so did many of the staff. Aside from $1 million in start-up costs, people felt for-profit development was going too far. But Noonan, Morine, and others pushed the idea in various forms, only to finally scale it back to one innovation: a separate program to accept ecologically unimportant land parcels as donations—and then sell them for cash to spend on conservation. This came to be called the "trade land" program. It was a shadow of the original private enterprise idea. Still, it showed how creative thinking advanced the cause of conservation.

Big Plans

Noonan would say, "Make no small plans." He wanted people to think big, jump high, go over the top for conservation. He was taking a page from Machiavelli, who said, "Make no small plans for they have no power to stir the soul." And Noonan, though he was always joking and teasing, knew the power of big plans to stir the people who worked for him.

When he got together with his staff after first becoming president, he set awe-inspiring goals. At a time when the Conservancy staffed offices in only half a dozen states, the plan by 1980 was to "implement a preservation strategy for each of the 50 states." At a time when the membership was only about twenty-three thousand, the plan was to "[Expand] our membership at the rate of 20 percent per year toward a goal of 80,000." At a time when the Conservancy had a $4 million line of credit, $4 million in revolving funds, and only $1.2 million in an endowment, the plan was to "[Increase] lines of credit ($100 million) . . . revolving funds ($10 million) . . . endowment ($20 million)."

Jon Roush, executive vice president, led the staff in formal planning. He and his group met once a week, after work, often over a case of beer, immersed in memos, flip charts, and draft plans. In February 1975, after plenty of stormy meetings, the staff published the "1980 Program." Once again, the goals reflected the cultural expectation for ambitious thinking. Among the updated goals: do three hundred projects a year, 90 percent comprising ecologically significant ecosystems. Create a national preserve system. Open four regional offices and perhaps a dozen field offices. Expand staff to 135. "By 1980," said the plan, "we will be financially able to acquire any significant tract in the U.S."

Nothing Central

Noonan and right-hand man Roush understood that significant plans called for a significant organization. They had no intention of ruining the entrepreneurial spirit by building a big bureaucracy. They endorsed and advanced yet another key piece of Conservancy culture: decentralize the business. Deal making simply created too much paperwork and problem solving to run entirely out of headquarters. Better to move authority and responsibility to the field. In time, Noonan and his team realized they should decentralize deal making to the states. In a mirror image of the

Natural Heritage program, Conservancy program offices would open in one state after another.

The Conservancy would not take the route of organizations like the Audubon Society, where many state organizations incorporated as separate entities. The Conservancy would remain one corporate enterprise, and each state office would remain under the mother organization. After interim nurturing from headquarters, the states would fend for themselves, find their own projects, and raise their own money. By the late 1970s, the state-expansion philosophy boiled down to a simple goal: open four state offices every year.

Of course, decentralization had its risks. Headquarters could lose control. As if to prove this point, the staff of the Minnesota field office faked a project in the mid-1970s to see if they could run a phony proposal through the headquarters sign-off process. They weren't convinced the people at headquarters read their proposals anyway.

The Minnesotans documented the so-called Agassiz Glacier project. They described, on the Conservancy's standard "Form 13," a remnant glacier in Minnesota. Entombed in the ice was a mastodon. To protect the priceless relic, they proposed buying not only the property but securing an easement on neighboring land to protect the glacier as it moved. Form 13 included an appraisal for the value of the ice—based on the price of bagged ice at the local convenience store—and even suggested funding the project via ice cube sales.

When the project circulated in Arlington, every senior manager signed off. Some got the joke. Jenkins, one of those who didn't, maintained that the project was only slightly more ridiculous than some of the real ones that had crossed his desk. It was stopped from going to the board for review only when senior manager John Humke saw a secretary readying it for mailing.

In spite of the risks, decentralization became a mantra of the 1970s. By 1979, the Conservancy had opened more than twenty state offices, from Connecticut and Florida to California and Colorado. And even though some offices initially foundered—Vermont and Hawaii—the goal remained: Open four more offices each year. Noonan was behind this core principle: Put the brave and bold gun-slinging dealmakers in the states and let them run their own shows, devising daring deals and raising big money.

Earning Your Keep

Noonan from the start said, "Everyone in the Nature Conservancy is a fund raiser." Until he became boss, the development department brought in the money. Now, whether you answered phones, courted donors, or counted endangered species, you had a role in bringing in dollars. Everybody from secretaries to attorneys learned that, in the new culture of the Conservancy, you helped pay your way.

In 1974, Wright wangled a deal to move from his legal posting in San Francisco to his dream job in Arlington: opening an international program. Noonan even agreed to supply seed funding for the first year. When Wright arrived in Arlington, his wife and six-month-old baby in tow, he found only $1,000 in his program account. Panicked, he rushed to Noonan, saying he thought they'd had a deal.

Noonan handed him a list of fundraising prospects. Noonan told him to ask the people on the list, insisting that the listed prospects would fund the program.

They didn't, but Wright learned quickly now to raise money. He got grants from the Rockefeller Foundation and World Wildlife Fund.

Noonan was new to fundraising himself when he became president. But he set out right away to model the cultural norm he sought to establish. Each day in the "dailies"—the chronological correspondence file that circulated through the office—his schedule appeared on top. Everybody could see: He was always on the road, in the air, seeing more people in more cities in one day than seemed possible.

Noonan spent as much time as he could with each donor. He routinely left just a few spare minutes to catch airplanes. In the mid 1970s, he ruptured his Achilles tendon playing basketball and didn't adjust his timing to compensate. Rushing to a gate in Pittsburg on crutches, he missed a flight by two minutes. He hadn't factored in his slower, convalescence-imposed concourse speed.

Noonan cultivated his contacts constantly. He took his cue from Pough, who long after he served as president remained a prodigious fundraiser. Courtly and courteous, Pough carried a small notebook into which he would scribble names. He kept a three-card file in his office, one card for a donor's name and phone, another for key interests, a third for location. If he was going to, say, Cleveland, he would pull all cards with a

Cleveland label and phone people, arrange lunch, brief them on conservation trends, send articles, and so on.

Pough followed the old dictum that people give first to people, second to institutions, and only third to causes. One of the people Pough cultivated was Katharine Ordway, the 3M heiress who would ultimately give $53 million to the Conservancy, ranking her as perhaps the greatest conservation philanthropist since John D. Rockefeller Jr. People like Ordway prized Pough's integrity and dedication to the cause. They came to rely on his advice in giving. Noonan, who was fond of saying "the donor is always right," followed suit, and became a trusted adviser to Ordway and other wealthy donors.

One of Noonan's strongest fundraising traits was one of other people's weakest. During a week-long orientation for new employees in 1977, Noonan, curiously, didn't appear for the first few days. On Thursday afternoon the group was learning about fundraising, however, and all at once Noonan threw open the conference room door. He glowered from the doorway and said one word: "Ask!" Then he turned on his heel and walked out.

Through such theatrics, Noonan transmitted his fundraising style to all at the Conservancy. This was not so different from the winning approach in other organizations—getting in front of donors, giving a good story, and asking—without fail—for a gift. What stood out about Noonan was how he then used these tactics to carry out what many people believed was his biggest achievement: Launching a funding drive to put the Conservancy into a whole new financial league.

The drive stemmed from the long-range plan the staff put together for 1980. The staff figured that, to fulfill their goals, the Conservancy needed roughly $1 million more in annual operating funds than forecast. The initial solution was simple: Noonan pitched the board on raising money to bring the endowment up to $20 million, enough to yield, in interest earnings, the cash needed for half of the expected annual operating shortfall. But the board was not enthused, even after Noonan made several runs at persuading them. Most governors wanted their donations to go directly to buying land, and right away, not to fund the long-term operating costs of the institution.

Noonan actually got the endowment drive off the ground. Ten governors gave $153,984 and pledged another $234,345. But after a year, in 1975, twenty board members still hadn't given anything at all. Noonan could see the Conservancy couldn't possibly meet the time-honored benchmarks for successful capital campaigns. The board should have been giving 20 percent of the total to launch the campaign—which in this case would have been $4 million. The board should also have been giving 50 percent of the goal before announcing the drive to the public. Noonan's development chief urged indefinite postponement of a public announcement of the endowment drive. In one year, the Conservancy had completed only 2 percent of its annual goal. Only with "great good luck" could they succeed, the development chief said.

Noonan and his staff went back to the drawing board. In October 1975, they came back to the board with another idea: building a $20 million "Land Preservation Fund." Once the fund was established, people inside the Conservancy would borrow from the fund to pay for land purchases. They would then repay the loan. As they repaid principal, the Conservancy would lend it again for fresh purchases. As they repaid interest, they would supply money for day-to-day operations. The clever part was that the donations to the fund would serve double duty.

The Land Preservation Fund was an endowment by another name, and the board saw right through the new scheme. Some of the governors felt they would still have trouble convincing donors their money wasn't just going to fund Conservancy overhead. But the staff argued that the fund was more marketable than an endowment because the Conservancy could solicit money from donors to "save the land" rather than for paying office expenses and salaries.

Noonan talked up the marketing potential. He said the Conservancy could attach a corporate, individual, or foundation name to a donation. It could earmark money for special kinds of land. It could even dedicate funds by region or state. The fund offered all kinds of sales angles to please donors.

Some governors objected that the fund would turn the Conservancy into a bank. They didn't feel the Conservancy should be in the banking business. Other governors agreed. But one noted that the Conservancy wouldn't actually sell it that way, and Mrs. David Rockefeller had the last word. She said that giving money to a revolving fund had a lot more appeal than giving money for a capital drive. It may be the same thing, she maintained, but it sounded different.

By the next board meeting, in December 1975, the governors voted to create the fund, and to set the goal at $20 million. That triggered a new phase of work for the Conservancy, one of ramping up to raise sums of money far beyond what it had ever done before. Noonan, calling the fund new, bold, and exciting, began building staff to research prospects and build a case for Conservancy fundraising on this grand new scale.

When the preparation phase was over, campaign chairman Wallace Dayton immediately donated $500,000 and pledged another $500,000. This was an entirely different response by the board compared to the cool reception of the endowment. The ensuing months brought more good news, and by the fall of 1977, after the end of an appeal to the board, the total stood at $8 million, including a $4 million grant from the Richard King Mellon Foundation. The new fund was well on track with fundraising benchmarks. In fact, it looked like marketing—and financial—genius.

For Business's Sake

Corporate America, the sector of the economy routinely cast as enemy of the environment, quickly became a major benefactor of the Conservancy. In courting this sector, Noonan was often accused of taking tainted money. His trademark response: "The problem with tainted money is there taint enough."

The Conservancy had done business with corporations for a number of years. Thomas Richards, Noonan's predecessor, had foreseen Noonan's Great Dismal deal when he told the *Wall Street Journal* in 1970: "I'm anxious to work with other businesses, particularly the extractive industries. . . . It's conceivable, for example, that a lumber company could assess its massive holdings and find some areas that aren't beneficial to it but which would be great from our standpoint . . . and enhance their public image in the process."

But Noonan put the Conservancy's corporate cultivation work into high gear, making Corporate America the Conservancy's premier environmental partner. His talent for involving executives was what many people would most remember him for. He was the man who brought corporations into the conservation family. People like Sox Calder of Union Camp became long-time supporters. "We are convinced that there are times when special considerations intervene and preservation becomes the highest and best end use for certain land areas," Calder told a reporter.

Building on deals like the Great Dismal Swamp, Noonan invited corporate CEOs onto the board, courted them for money, and coaxed them to talk to their friends. The Corporate Program, begun in 1971, became one of Noonan's priorities. In 1976 alone, he recruited eighty-six new corporate members, each of whom gave $1,000 and up. People like Calder became allies in expanding Noonan's reach.

The so-called American Land Trust, a U.S. bicentennial project to save $200 million worth of land for conservation, became one stratagem for engaging companies. Run by the Conservancy in 1976 and 1977, the original idea was to create a major preserve in each of the fifty states. Conservancy dealmakers solicited donations from executives by showing a video, built into a pop-up briefcase, about corporations working with the Conservancy. CEOs like Kenneth Olsen of Digital Equipment Corporation watched the video—and paid up.

When the Conservancy phased out the trust, it walked away with lasting bonds with corporate executives. By year-end 1978, the first year postdating the trust, the Conservancy boasted 205 corporate associates. In 1978 alone, it reaped from Corporate America $15 million in preserved land and donations. Working with corporations became a cornerstone of Conservancy culture. Exxon, thought of by many as just one more big, dirty oil company, gave $300,000 in cash.

A CULTURE CODIFIED

By the late 1970s, Noonan was an icon of nonprofit success. The Conservancy was a group apart from—and in many ways ahead of—the growing band of environmental nonprofits. Nobody could pooh-pooh the National Conservatory anymore. In 1978 alone, the Conservancy attracted fifteen thousand new individual members, bringing the tally to sixty thousand. It protected 215 projects totaling 273,000 acres. Almost two-thirds of the projects were top quality, including sites like Pine Butte Swamp in Montana and Braidwood Prairie in Illinois. The Conservancy ended the year with a budget surplus of over $500,000.

Noonan's reputation as the master spread, and the staffs and chiefs of other environmental nonprofits hung on his example. Returning to their organizations after meeting with Noonan, executive directors who sought his advice would unabashedly tell their staffs, "Pat says . . . " and then pass on words of Noonan wisdom. The staffs knew the advice came from the guru of nonprofit management in the environmental community.

With Noonan and the Conservancy riding high and driving hard, the land and money kept pouring in. By February 1979, a completed Land Preservation Fund was in sight. Inaugurated in June 1977, the fund had soared to $18.3 million—$9 million had been brought in during 1978 alone. When the board gathered in Cincinnati at the art deco Netherland Hilton Hotel on September 20, 1979, Noonan announced the Conservancy had met its $20 million goal. That made the three-year effort the largest fundraising drive in the history of the conservation movement.

Noonan paid tribute at the meeting to the board for keeping the money flowing. As if taking every opportunity to reinforce the cultural touchstones of his tenure, he placed at the beginning and end of his remarks gestures that flagged two of the defining principles of his era.

At the beginning, he watched as Chairman John Andrus accepted a check for $12,500, the first installment of $100,000 destined for the Land Preservation Fund, from International Paper executive John Stephens. The executive, hailing from a company reviled by environmentalists as one of the biggest polluters of the era, said he looked forward to a long and fruitful relationship with the Conservancy—good for his shareholders, good for the Conservancy, good for all Americans.

At the end, lavishing praise on his staff, Noonan presented Elizabeth "Kiku" Hoagland, the director of the Land Preservation Fund, a dozen roses. He thanked her for her efforts, which he said in large measure assured the success of the campaign. The board would later pass a resolution lauding Hoagland for directing the most successful campaign in the history of the Nature Conservancy with exceptional dedication, consummate skill, and supreme grace under pressure.

Noonan once again made his imprint—working with others, delivering results, giving others the credit. His trademark approach led him to escape the downfall of many dynamic leaders—whose organizations create a cult around a personality whose departure they cannot survive. In Noonan's case, his people and his board soaked up and made the culture their own. This was the mark of a skilled leader, preparing the organization for working without him.

And it was a good thing. In January 1980, Noonan resigned. Although he said he wanted to write a book and contribute to conservation in other ways, people debated what the real reasons were. Many felt he was tired from the travel and pace of fundraising. He had no reason to leave because of results. In the 1970s, the Conservancy created twenty-three state heritage programs, acquired 1.4 million acres and $500 million worth of land, increased membership from fifteen thousand to seventy thousand, expanded capital funds from $5 million to $30 million, grew staff from 50 to 270, and added 275 corporations to the membership roster. At year-end 1979, the organization had a $1.5 million operating surplus.

LAST IMPRINT

Inside the Conservancy, the indelible mark left by Noonan on the organization's culture became remarkably visible. For the day of his going-away party, it was decided that every department would compete to perform the best skit about Noonan. Determined to defend departmental pride, the staff of each department set to work with the urgency and diligence of saving an endangered species.

The scientists, though a joshing crowd that enjoyed practical jokes under Jenkins, didn't have a bunch of bright ideas, but they did have one guy, Phillip Hoose, who played the guitar and wrote songs. They all turned to Hoose, who spent his days convincing state directors to use Heritage data. Hoose, inspired by the dailies, imagined Noonan bursting like a tornado on the scene of untold numbers of businesspeople.

When the big day came, Hoose and the rest of the staff, props in hand, walked from the North Kent Street office the half mile to the Marriott Hotel at Key Bridge, just across the Potomac from Georgetown. When the science department's turn came, Hoose played lead guitar and sang.

The rest of the scientists danced and crooned backup. Hoose had written a seven-verse blues ballad, "We Can Work With You." It was the story of a businessman who encountered Noonan at the end of the day:

> All out of coffee
> About out of time
> The resta the day
> Ain't worth a dime
> I said any more appointments
> Honey would you check the book . . .
> A Mr. Noonan's outside
> Shall I get you off the hook?
>
> I said who is he?
> She said I don't know
> But he's the friendliest man
> That ever walked through the door
> He says he's passing through Cleveland
> Jus' wants to say hello . . .
> I said send him in Honey
> Must be *someone* I know.
>
> I ran a comb through my hair
> Which had recently thinned
> When in burst a stranger
> Smiling like an old friend
> I said I'll give you three minutes
> He said I've only got two . . .
> But I'm here to help you save Ohio
> And we can work with you.

Hoose's song, a lazy shuffle of a tune, told the story of the now legendary Noonan converting the man's dead assets into earnings, accepting three blocks of Euclid Avenue as a donation, even inveigling the man out of his own tie—and then eliciting a personal check to allow the man "a day in the sun" for his own donation.

At the chorus, the whole department pulled out giant cardboard phones and slapped them to their ears, singing the blues harder:

We can work, we can work
We can work with you.
We can work, we can work
We can work with you.
Life estates and savings, too good to be true
We can work, we can work, we can work with you
There ain't nothing we can't do,
Cause we can work with you.

The staff reveled in the hot-shot culture their boss had imprinted on the organization. With the hard-driving, fun-loving, mission-driven Noonan at the head, nothing scared the staff. It could work with anyone, work through any problem—indeed could work wonders of creativity, fundraising, and strategy to win protection for America's prized conservation lands.

The Conservancy staff, imbued with the example of Noonan, had shed the confusion of adolescence. It was a team acculturated with a unique brand of management that put pragmatism above idealism and cooperation above confrontation. Noonan had been singing this cultural tune for years—and now his staff was singing it back.

5

WE'RE NOT IN KANSAS ANYMORE: The Road to Realizing New Ambitions

K EITH BULL KNEW FULL WELL that somebody was buying up big chunks of Virginia seashore. The administrator of Northampton County, covering the southern half of Virginia's Eastern Shore, had watched dozens of transfers posted under a Norfolk law firm's name. He had staked out cars in strange locations to write down license-plate numbers. And he had run the numbers for ownership, to find they were registered in the names of an unfamiliar corporation. At first, all he knew was that outsiders—"come heres" in the local parlance—were buying up hundreds of acres from "born heres."

It was onto Bull's turf that L. Gregory Low, a Nature Conservancy top manager, drove in early 1985. The mild-mannered, boyish-looking Low had come to an office in the town of Nassawadox to meet with Bull and J. T. Holland, chairman of the county board of supervisors. Low was an emissary. He wanted to explain that the Conservancy had just acquired all this land from a Pittsburgh group called the Allegheny Duck Club, and that it had only the long-term interest of the county at heart. Low, a drawling North Carolinian whose gentlemanly demeanor evinced his rigorous small-town breeding, was just the right person to act as diplomat.

But when he sat down he was not indulged with genteel conversation. He was subjected to a withering fusillade of complaints. Bull and Holland, burned by the Conservancy's clandestine ways of operating, were angry. "You've not acted honestly," Bull growled again and again. "You've not worked in the open." Bull reminded Low that the Conservancy was the biggest landowner in the county, but it hadn't given anyone in local government even a hint of what it was up to. "You've shut us out," he said.

For the next three hours Low endured a verbal whipping he would never forget.

So began a saga that would take Low and the Conservancy on a long, and sometimes bruising, ride into terra incognita. The Conservancy had worked for years to perfect the delivery of a specific service—saving rare species and communities by protecting habitat. That focus left untouched a broader service—saving outstanding ecosystems by managing the human uses in and around them. Low and others like Robert Jenkins realized the second—managing land uses as well as land—was elemental to the Conservancy's mission to save biodiversity, but they had done precious little about it. Low was the self-appointed front man for launching the Conservancy's transition to an organization that was master of both.

Low faced an issue that all growing organizations eventually grapple with: how to expand their work to meet their growing ambitions to have a bigger impact. As the organization grows, so does the opportunity for fulfilling the mission on a scale and scope far beyond what the founders envisioned. Low would guide the Conservancy in expanding its capabilities to match new ambitions. He would show that the transition to a new scale and scope is not just one of teaching new tricks for conducting the conservation business. It is one of changing the business altogether.

Low's unsympathetic reception on the Eastern Shore suggested that he and the Conservancy were unprepared. Low and other managers had not done enough thinking to fathom the demands of conservation beyond their traditional bread-and-butter work of buying land for preserves. They had not trained to recognize—let alone master—all the problems likely to come up from managing sites where the lives of people and nature blended together. To Bull and Holland, this was as obvious as the stifling humidity on the Eastern Shore in August. Low, though an expert in building an institution to acquire parcels of pristine nature, was a novice in this new line of work.

Not that he hadn't thought about it. He and Jenkins, neighbors in the Washington suburb of Reston, Virginia, had batted around the idea of *biosphere reserves*. This was a U.N. concept describing a core preserve surrounded by a lightly populated zone where people restrict themselves to environmentally compatible land uses. The U.N. actually named the 40,000-acre Virginia Coast Reserve a biosphere reserve in 1979. But the concept, born on a chalkboard in the 1970s, was just wishful thinking. Nowhere was it working as conceived. It didn't come with a program to make it happen. It didn't have any regulatory authority to give it teeth. And of course no one had tested any tools or techniques to put it into action.

The Conservancy had lots of real estate tools for saving natural areas— bargain sales, conservation easements, land registries, management agreements, rights of first refusal. These tools had even worked well for winning huge, ecosystem-size victories—the 32,000-acre Pascagoula corridor in Mississippi, the 220,000-acre Sevilleta National Wildlife Refuge, in Socorro, New Mexico. But these preserves were just bigger animals of the same natural-area species. Bioreserves were altogether different. They would require new capabilities—new tools for doing new things in a new way.

Low got the chance to spearhead this transition because the Allegheny Duck Club engineered the acquisition of 6,200 acres of prized lands bordering all the ocean-side deep-water ports on the Eastern Shore. The board of governors cashed in on this work by blessing, in December 1984, a land swap in which the Conservancy acquired fifty-four parcels—the same ones Bull saw transferred. The lands fronted the thirteen barrier islands acquired by Noonan for the Nature Conservancy in the 1970s. The Conservancy thus planned to shield the untouched islands from the radiating impacts of the mainland. In effect, the Conservancy was buying the makings of the buffer zone described by the United Nations.

Low, raised in Rocky Mount, North Carolina, relished the chance to work on this new front in conservation. In 1980, he lobbied for federal money to protect the Currituck Outer Banks in North Carolina and then transfer it to the U.S. Fish and Wildlife Service as a national wildlife refuge. After finishing, however, he had this empty feeling: While he had protected a big tract of Atlantic real estate, he'd saved only a sliver of the larger ecosystem slated for development. He won the battle with tactical land acquisition to control access to twenty miles of beach. But he lost a war against the grander forces of ecosystem harm. In turning to the Virginia Coast Reserve, he felt he had a chance at serving the mission on a broader scale.

Low had been smitten by that mission in 1975, when he read *The Preservation of Natural Diversity* by Jenkins. Until then, he thought of himself as one of the Conservancy's business guys. He was a University of Virginia MBA who couldn't identify any of the trees in the Mid-Atlantic forests. During his first bargain-sale negotiations after his hiring in 1974, the landowner waxed sentimental about his sassafras, hemlock, and tulip poplar trees until Low admitted he didn't know what they were. Low cut plenty of land deals across the Mid-Atlantic states anyway. He even bought thirteen holes of a golf course in Northern Virginia—later turned over to the Northern Virginia Regional Park Authority.

But Jenkins's argument to protect biodiversity struck a chord. Jenkins basically asked him, "What would you rather work on, a golf course, or something that's liable to be lost off the face of the earth?"

That was an easy question for Low to answer, and it would forever remain so. He realized at that moment he had more than a great job. He had a mission.

His passion for the mission became unrivaled. When in 1976 he sought to start up the North Carolina state office, job hunter Thomas Massengale appeared at his door. Low, then vice president of finance, didn't have the cash to pay for a new hire, but he did have the cheek to cut a deal. If Massengale could raise $25,000 by the end of the year, Low said, he would pay him his salary in arrears in January—and hire him as state director. In short order, Massengale came up with $29,000.

The job required passion. When Massengale later became regional director in the South, he often faced long odds in getting new programs established. In a meeting in Houston, William Blair, Noonan's successor as president, was talking to donors about the politically charged subject of endangered species. All at once, Blair had trouble with his projector, giving a woman irked by the nature-saving talk her chance: Oh just cut it off, cut it off, she shouted. Afterward, a man reproached Massengale, Low's point man in the South: "Boy, I want you to know that I would stomp the shit out of Bambi."

Yet while Low faced similar challenges, everyone in the office came to respect him as the rising star with a knack for cutting to the chase and delivering results. In 1977, he leapfrogged his peers to become, after Jon Roush left, executive vice president. He then spent eight years, with the help of troubleshooters like Massengale, putting Conservancy offices in twenty-five states.

When Low came to the Virginia Eastern Shore, he expected some hostility. The locals were mad as hell about earlier deals to buy the thirteen islands. At one point, the Conservancy shut them out entirely from hunting, picnicking, and taking dune-buggy tours on some of the lands they had long treated as their own. The fresh purchases on the mainland would incite the local people again. Aware of the bad blood, Low promised the Conservancy board he would reach out to local leaders and let them know what the Conservancy was intending.

That's what brought Low face to face with Bull and Holland. Attacked for the Conservancy's sins of stealth over fifteen years, Low defended recent deals. The Conservancy, said Low, wasn't going to fence out local people. It wanted the land to buffer the islands and the estuary from waterfront building. The Conservancy wasn't halting development, either. It would resell land after putting restrictions on it. Farmers could still farm. Homeowners could still build. The county could still collect taxes. Unfettered growth that would harm the coastal ecosystem—that's all that would stop.

Low acknowledged that on many counts the Conservancy was guilty. It had not been a good member of the community. It had acted as it had so many times in the past—buying land without consulting anyone locally. Its actions sandbagged county leaders, whose constituents surprised them by reading about key county developments in the newspaper first.

Bull, after venting, appealed to Low, saying that he and Low had common goals. He stressed that, for ten years, he had encouraged planning, building, and subdivision to preserve the best of the county's natural character. Low, he said, should cooperate with the county to create high-quality development, and high-quality tourism. Unless they worked together, he added, neither of them would meet his goals.

Until then, the Conservancy had partnered with many state and federal officials. But it had not dealt much with local civic or government leaders. Low was only dimly aware that familiar land-preservation skills and techniques were woefully inadequate for this new job of working locally. The message from Bull and Holland was that they fell far short in preserving landscapes alive with people, businesses, and all the trappings of a healthy community.

But Bull and Holland—even if they felt like tossing Low out on his ear—said they had common ground. They were all for controlling unwanted development. So they asked Low to involve them in Conservancy planning and initiatives. Low, who had resigned as executive vice president to take this job, lacked the experience to be sure of how to proceed. But he thought: "I'll give it a try." In fact, he probably had no choice, and neither did Bull and Holland. They were all in this together.

Holland jump-started the partnership. He basically told Low, "I'm going to drive you around the county, we'll visit some local folks, I'll get you on the radio, we'll go visit the southern tip of the shore to look at where a lot of new development is coming in." Low spent the afternoon meeting with locals, talking on radio WESR about the Conservancy's plan to buy land and leave it largely as farms, and visiting the finest sweep of landscape on the shore—the tip, Cape Charles, with its waving grassland, marsh, and bayberry and myrtle thickets.

Low was started on the trail to meeting the Conservancy's mission on a broader scope and scale. As time passed, he would learn about community relations, local land-use management, and public policy. He would introduce the Conservancy to these and other fields of expertise on a journey embracing a broader world of conservation work—work they would initially call "megasite" conservation.

EXPERIMENT AND REPLICATE

If Low didn't fully grasp the nature of the new work he was getting into, he did grasp how little he knew about how to proceed. After initiating his partnership with the Eastern Shore community leaders, he launched a start-up think tank inside the Conservancy. He called the group "four sci-entists and an MBA." He was the MBA. Among the scientists were Jenkins and recent hires Mark Robertson, a marine biologist, and John Hall, manager of Virginia Coast Reserve. It was a crack team. Low wanted to be sure that the reserve, the Conservancy's first megasite, benefited from the thinking of the best minds in the conservation business.

Low insisted the team meet every two months. They debated conser-vation design, ecology and hydrology, public relations, outreach, regula-tion, and politics. These were tough meetings, about many unfamiliar topics, driven by three Conservancy vice presidents who relished concep-tual jousting. Robertson's wife took to putting a big bottle of aspirin on the counter each time the rookie came in from a meeting. At one point, he drafted a plan. When the group met, Low began, "Now Mark, don't take any of this personally." The group then dismantled his ideas and scut-tled his work.

Low loved intellectual inquiry—including puncturing holes in trial balloons. At Virginia's Darden School of Business, his professors taught the Harvard Business School case method. They showed him how to probe, analyze, and probe some more. For the Virginia Coast project, Low started probing traditional thinking about land protection. At the first group meeting, he asked the team what was needed to protect a large coastal ecosystem. The scientists said the Conservancy had to protect the water.

Falling back on the Conservancy's time-tested tool for nature protec-tion, Low asked, "Can we buy the water?"

Robertson told him that, no, the Conservancy couldn't buy the water because it was in the public domain. But the water had to be protected because everything harmful on the mainland finds its way into the water. Paving and housing foul surface and ground water; the water overloads lagoons with nutrients; the nutrients produce too much algae; and the algae kills marine life. "Water runs downhill," teased Robertson.

Low, beginning to understand the scientists' message, shot back with the obvious answer: They would buy the mainland. The mainland—Low realized of course that wasn't feasible. Fifty miles of shore, multiplied by a mile of buffer land—the cost of buying all that was beyond imagining, even if the Conservancy already had a 6,200-acre jump-start.

Group conversations like this became a springboard for new thinking. The team would have to find some new affordable ways to promote new kinds of uses on the lands next to the coastal waters. To get started, they tried a variation on an old tool, the conservation easement. They proposed to resell the seaside farms bought by the Conservancy with easements restricting building. They would then recycle the proceeds into more conservation. A year later, in 1986, they actually sold two farms to buyers from Norfolk and Baltimore. These were the Conservancy's first "conservation buyer" deals on the Eastern Shore. The new owners still had the right to farm, and to develop land in prescribed places, at the prescribed density. But they couldn't engage in any development Conservancy scientists felt would degrade coastal waters.

The conservation buyer deals, though a milestone in the Conservancy's effort to advance conservation, caught heavy flack in the local press. In the national press, a *Field & Stream* writer blasted the Conservancy for selling land for development. Why was a conservation organization switching gears and promoting home building? Of course, appearances deceived. To those who would listen, Low countered that the land was sold for conservation—although the property itself was not the conservation target. The nearby marshes and barrier islands were.

Low no longer sounded like a traditional conservationist. Like many an innovator, he talked a line that didn't make sense to many people. If the Conservancy tries to lock up all developable land from growth, he would say, local politicians and businesspeople will stymie our work. On the Eastern Shore, the future of the barrier islands depends on guiding development away from harmful land uses and toward compatible ones. Conservationists shouldn't resist all development, he said. They should work with the community for the right kind of development.

The Conservancy had begun work with the community on the Eastern Shore a few years earlier, but for different reasons. In 1982, Edward Ames, the managing trustee of the Mary Flagler Cary Charitable Trust, which funded Noonan's string of island acquisitions, began to worry about the reservoir of resentment accumulating from the Conservancy's more secretive work. He urged the Conservancy to reach out to the community, and he funded preserve manager Hall to do so. By 1985, the slow-talking, congenial Georgian started to salve a lot of old wounds. The

Conservancy restored a historic farm home as its headquarters in 1984. It was also instrumental in helping the U.S. Fish and Wildlife Service buy Cape Charles Air Force Station to protect the hallowed, pristine view of the southern gateway to the Eastern Shore.

Building on Hall's work, Low proposed to experiment with new initiatives to promote long-term conservation. In one of the first major diversions from traditional Conservancy work, in 1987, Hall helped launch Citizens for a Better Eastern Shore. A group representing all sectors of the community aimed at promoting wise local development, CBES held its first meeting in July 1988. Its goals were to conserve the county's natural resources, preserve its rural character and lifestyle, secure economic self-sufficiency for all citizens, provide adequate public services for all citizens, and support agriculture, tourism, seafood, and light industry as the county's major industries. To Low and the Conservancy, time and money spent nurturing CBES, with the support of the Cary Trust, was an investment in shore conservation, even if no land changed hands.

In the late 1980s, CBES paid a big dividend. Northampton County, under administrator Bull, was trying to fashion a zoning ordinance to control the density of new housing. Like many poor rural counties, Northampton lacked zoning with any teeth. It allowed one residence per 30,000 square feet, or three-quarters of an acre, on agricultural land, hardly strict enough to protect water quality on buffer lands along the shore. But with the urging of CBES, the support of the NAACP, and the Conservancy, the county board of supervisors in 1989 voted 3 to 2 for a new measure. It allowed only one residence per five acres along the waterfront, with a limited number of one-acre lots.

The ordinance, though not ideal, was a big step on the way to better conservation. For Low it was a breakthrough. It demonstrated how the Conservancy could exercise a new skill: working within the local political system to manage growth. Working in this way was still experimental for the Conservancy, but Low believed it held much promise for protecting ecosystems and buffer zones. "We should never underestimate the power of a group of informed, organized, and determined local residents," he said at the time.

Low tested community-based conservation further when he sought to build relationships with members of the black community. Hall met with black leaders and learned they cared about conservation, but more about better housing. Many in the black community worked in meager-paying seafood- and vegetable-packing jobs and lived in houses without indoor plumbing. They accounted for a poverty rate that in Northampton County ran twice the national average. The black leaders wondered whether the Nature Conservancy could do anything about affordable places to live.

Low was at a loss at first. Neither he nor Hall knew anything about housing. But they did care about the long-term relationship with the black community. So they took a stab at helping out. Low was increasingly convinced that to succeed with long-term conservation, everyone who lives and works in protected areas—not just an elite few—must support conservation and compatible human uses. So he called around until he discovered that James Rouse, a big Maryland developer, had started a nonprofit affordable-housing group called the Enterprise Foundation. One staff person worked on rural housing, and he spent time on the phone with Low because they had mutual friends. He also agreed to spend one day on the Eastern Shore—if Low picked him up, drove him down, and drove him back to Baltimore.

Low and his Enterprise contact met with a number of county leaders, including Arthur Carter, a black physician. At the Conservancy's headquarters in Nassawadox, the county leaders learned that if they wanted to build more than one housing project, they would have to create a housing institution. Thus was born the Northampton Housing Trust, spearheaded by Carter. A couple of years later, the Conservancy provided about $15,000 for the trust to write a grant proposal, and the group won a $1.5 million federal grant for the improvement of substandard housing and community development.

Through it all, Low became a big believer in one of his colleagues' aphorisms: "You have to make deposits before you take withdrawals." John Hall's small deposits in CBES and the Northampton Housing Trust yielded a big return in winning local support for the Conservancy.

The promising results coming in at the Virginia Coast Reserve convinced Low that he was on to something. The Conservancy could indeed succeed at a bigger scale and scope. The challenge was now to convince other people in the Conservancy that this was the way of the future. The

Virginia Coast Reserve, after all, was just a prototype. If Low and his colleagues wanted anyone beyond his closest circle to believe in the value of
what he was doing—and look beyond their traditional work at the
Conservancy—he had to successfully replicate this work elsewhere.

Though Low had a lot of influence in the Conservancy, he was surrounded by doubters. Naysayers grumbled that the reserve worked because
it was heavily funded—and babied by several vice presidents. They talked
behind Low's back, quick to question the Conservancy's role in such a for-
eign undertaking. Launching a citizens group? Working on zoning?
Supporting affording housing? What kind of conservation was that? The
Conservancy saved land by buying it one piece at a time.

Undeterred, Low supported the launch of several new megasites. From
earlier work on state programs, he learned one lesson about spreading a
new idea: People don't believe it when they see it at first. They write it off
as an anomaly. They cite funding or staffing or location as special ad-
vantages that explain success. The second example—that's different. When
something succeeds a second time, people take notice.

In 1987, the Conservancy launched another megasite in the Florida
Keys, managed by team member Robertson. Soon thereafter it launched
projects in the Clinch Valley in southeastern Virginia, and another in the
ACE Basin in South Carolina, the ecologically rich wetland formed by
the Ashepoo, Combahee, and Edisto Rivers. In the executive ranks, Low's
work did catch attention. President Frank Boren, Blair's successor in 1986,
called this "Conservation Phase II." "We're drawing bigger circles," he
wrote in 1989.

The megasite concept had gained momentum. Using Natural Heritage
data, Jenkins and his scientists identified hundreds of candidates for new
megasites. In the United States this included places like the 500-square-
mile Gray Ranch, a dry grassland and mountain range in the boot-heel of
New Mexico, and the basin of the Altamaha River, a giant watershed that
drains into the Atlantic south of Savannah.

A critical turning point in support for megasites came with the arrival
of John Sawhill, the new president in 1990. Sawhill ordered the staff to
draft a new strategic plan, and upon its completion, blessed the megasite
concept as a centerpiece of the Conservancy's new direction. "The Nature
Conservancy," the plan read, "will commit to a significant new program

of biodiversity conservation: the protection of whole ecological systems." The plan—with a tip of the hat to the biosphere reserve program—renamed the megasites "bioreserves."

For Low, five years of experimentation and testing had culminated in the official announcement of an entirely new field of operations for the Conservancy. While increasingly relying on the help and intellectual heavy lifting of chief operating officer William Weeks, he had successfully expanded the scope and scale of projects falling under the Conservancy's mission, and he had introduced staff to the new skills needed for community-based conservation at a large scale. Like many innovators steering their organizations in a new direction, he still didn't know where this line of work would ultimately lead, but he did pass a critical milestone: obtaining the green light to proceed with his new venture with the full support of Conservancy leaders.

DISTILLING THE MODEL

The Conservancy publicly announced the bioreserve program in 1991, at the same time that Sawhill announced an unprecedented $300 million funding campaign to pay for the new reserves. In June, Low masterminded the first conference on bioreserves, bringing two hundred staff to American University to get the word out. With Low and his team in the limelight, President Sawhill told the crowd this was "a whole new approach to conservation. . . . It's about our future." Sawhill set an official goal of creating seventy-five new reserves.

Sawhill's announcement marked the dawn of a new chapter for the Conservancy. Henceforth, the Conservancy would work at a new scale to help people live in harmony with nature. The question now before Low was how to run these new projects most effectively. He had spurred lots of innovation in community relations, public policy, and limited development. Now he wondered what lessons could the Conservancy extract from all these early projects? And how could the organization distill them into steps that would stimulate rapid, effective replication by Conservancy staff across the country?

Low was particularly eager to isolate the key success factors for taking a conservation project to scale. As a start, he had several brainstorming sessions with John Cook, former head of the Florida operation and now head of the Gray Ranch project in New Mexico. Cook suggested a starting point: "Good people, good plans, 'walking-around money'—seed money for trying new things."

Low liked that as a rule of thumb. Walking-around money, after all, was the basis for experimentation. It kicked off all the test projects at the Virginia Coast Reserve—and still continued to do so. In 1991, it helped launch the Northampton Economic Forum, a partnership with CBES and the NAACP, which advocated the interests of conservation, community, and economy. With major funding from the Ford Foundation, the forum published "Blueprint for Economic Growth." The blueprint echoed the original list of CBES goals: conservation of the county's natural resources, economic self-sufficiency for all citizens, and a broad economic base including seafood production and tourism.

Good plans buttressed all of his efforts, starting with the megasite plan first written for the Virginia Coast Reserve in 1984. Following up on a long tradition of planning, Sawhill required all prospective bioreserve teams to submit plans to headquarters, where teams would then meet with senior managers for a day-long grilling session. Low wrote a new plan for the Virginia Coast. Robertson wrote one for the Florida Keys. Other teams wrote them for Clinch River, ACE Basin, and elsewhere.

Good plans became one of the most challenging elements for Low as he guided the Conservancy into this new field of operations. In fact, they emerged as a primary focus of his work. Low was eager to encapsulate the elements of success in an algorithm—a term he was fond of that suggested a neat formula for guiding action. The urgency of this task was all the greater because, as the early plans piled up on his desk, he wasn't happy with the thinking they contained. One of the most basic problems was they rarely defined exactly what the Conservancy was conserving. At a site with rare freshwater mussels, for example, was it conserving the river water, the riverbed, the riverbank, the watershed?

People also had trouble identifying the threats they were fighting— that is, the key factors endangering the health of the ecosystem. Typically, teams would make a laundry list and rate every threat as "very high." Logging, farming, housing development, road building—all earned a high-priority ranking, but none was singled out for premier treatment.

Even then, people defined threats imprecisely. "Water quality degradation," for example, was a common yet hazy threat to many bioreserves.

When Low and the senior staff got together with the bioreserve teams, the teams often became defensive as their plans unraveled. Top managers would send people back to draft and redraft the documents. People got frustrated and conservation on the ground slowed down. Low concluded he had fathered a godawful process that led to documents with subpar plans for action. He resolved to come up with something more workable. "We've got to figure out a methodology here," he thought. "We need an approach that's going to work."

About the best Low could say about the painful work on the plans over more than five years was that they forced him to see the nub of the problem. He needed a systematic way to help teams pinpoint what they were trying to preserve, what the precise threats were, and how to abate them. The trickiest part was the specification of threats. The teams repeatedly stumbled over figuring out what human actions in and around the bioreserves most threatened biodiversity.

Fortuitously, a colleague from the U.S. Environmental Protection Agency gave Low an article on human health. The parallels with ecosystem health were obvious, and when Low read how health workers distinguished between stressors and sources of stress, it dawned on him: The Conservancy also had to make this distinction—between the threats to the bioreserve and their source.

With this distinction in mind, Low's conversations with bioreserve teams were altogether different. If "water quality degradation" was the stress, he could ask a team, what is the source? Is it toxins? Is it sediment? Is it nutrients?

Sediment, the team might respond. It's smothering the freshwater mussel beds.

Then Low could ask what was causing the sediment. Is it cows in the stream? Row-crop agriculture? Timber harvesting?

Cows in the stream, the team might respond.

Okay, Low could next say, now you know what to work on next Monday.

Such thinking led Low to the algorithm he so badly wanted: a "4S" (four-step) analytical process, comprising an examination of systems, stresses, sources, and strategies. He wrote his 4S thoughts into a short white paper in late 1992 and gave it to a half dozen colleagues. He invited them to meet him at the nearby Key Bridge Marriott Hotel, where the group discussed the 4S concept. Everybody seemed to think the concept made sense. If bioreserve teams systematically walked through each of the four steps, they would come up with better plans for conservation.

As the meeting was about to break, Charles Bassett, Southeast Regional director, stopped everyone. He said that everyone was missing the most important S.

What was that? Low wanted to know.

"Success," said Bassett. The question was: "What does success look like?"

To complete the algorithm, Bassett said, they needed a step in which teams measured their success against a benchmark. Otherwise, the teams would keep working on a project forever, no matter what they accomplished.

Low conceded Bassett had a point. So the group adopted a fifth S, S for *success*. Nobody actually knew how to measure the success of bioreserve conservation, but they blessed the 5S scheme—and Low had a new approach for working at a new scale and scope. He had succeeded in extracting the lessons from the early bioreserve projects, and he had a system for helping others develop their marching orders for this new line of work. The algorithm was complete.

The 5S process was a breakthrough tool. No matter where the threat to Conservancy preserves originated, inside or outside the core reserve, the 5S review pointed teams toward strategies for mitigating that threat. The five steps would point people at the real targets of their work, whether buying a piece of land or nurturing a local civic group or influencing local land-use policy decisions.

Low was enamored of the significance of his strengthening grasp of how to use community-based techniques for landscape-scale conservation. As with so many achievements in the sweep of events, the significance wasn't at all obvious to many other people. As late as 1995, Low ran a staff workshop about community-based conservation. Before his session, his assistant drew a picture on a flip chart of Dorothy and Toto from the *Wizard of Oz.* The caption: "Toto, I have a feeling we're not in Kansas anymore." Low thought the metaphor clever. The moral, he told everyone, was that the Conservancy was in an entirely new business—no longer just a land buyer.

But his insight didn't light up any signs of recognition—in fact, just the reverse. Even the many practitioners and managers in attendance didn't follow his reasoning. Trained in the land-buying tradition of the Conservancy, they argued they practiced the same business as they always had, just more of it, in bigger pieces, with more partners.

Low argued otherwise. In the new world of conservation, the thinking, tools, and techniques of the new trade, as suggested by the 5S algorithm, so overshadowed the traditional ones that the business would never work the same again. To protect land in 1995, they had to lobby for zoning changes, advocate new ways to farm and log, assist entrepreneurs in building clean businesses, serve on local task forces to manage growth, and so on. This was indeed a new business, requiring fundamentally different skills and practices.

But the Oz metaphor was a dud. Low was amazed. He realized he had more work to do. The Conservancy was in a new business, and many people didn't realize it. You couldn't acquire land, put a fence around it, and call it good anymore. You had to support the people who lived and worked in a place so they would coexist harmoniously with the precious pieces of nature in the same neighborhood. Now Low needed a means to get people to fully grasp that this new thinking underpinned their work.

MAKING IT STICK

One man who did support the new thinking was the one who counted most: Conservancy president Sawhill. He backed Low and chief operating officer Weeks in founding a skunk works called the Center for Compatible Economic Development in Leesburg, Virginia. CCED, started in November 1995, would experiment with and advance the thinking of the new line of business. Low viewed CCED as an R&D arm of the Conservancy, inventing, nurturing, and promoting new ways to halt or mitigate threats to biodiversity.

Low and Weeks used the CCED to press ahead with programs to come up with tools and techniques that conserved ecosystems while helping local economies. Weeks wrote *Beyond the Ark: Tools for an Ecosystem*

Approach to Conservation. Low wrote *A Citizen's Guide to Achieving a Healthy Community, Economy and Environment,* and then *Pathways: Building a Community-Based Initiative for Compatible Economic Development*— a step-by-step guide for communities to create a plan for a healthier economy and environment.

Their philosophy was simple, wrote Low. "The health of each element—community, economy, environment—is tied to the vitality of each of the others."

In 1996 and 1997, Weeks and Low convened a series of intensive three-day workshops, each attended by five project directors, where they taught the 5S algorithm and explored the community, economic, and environmental threats to biodiversity at each site. The directors swapped war stories, shared lessons, and offered advice. Afterward, they raved about the sessions. They seemed to be catching on to the new work and thinking of the Conservancy.

But Low was less enthusiastic. The directors didn't come up with concrete enough action plans. He felt that he and Weeks were on the right track, though, when one project director wished out loud for the group to reconvene a year hence. That gave them an idea: What about redoubling the workshop effort? What about reconvening the project teams not just once, but twice?

Low and Weeks decided to try running the groups through three three-day workshops in a row, over half a year. In each one, they would drill deeper, and in the process drive the lessons about the new business fully into the working lives of bioreserve directors. The men believed that perhaps the key to imbuing the organization with a new line of thinking was more intensive training.

In 1998, as the Conservancy abandoned the word *bioreserve* in favor of "landscape-scale conservation," Low and Weeks brought together two people from each of five landscape-scale projects to test their three-workshop training idea. They marched every pair through all five of the 5S steps—while the other teams vetted or validated the thinking every step of the way. In the first workshop, people described the system they were trying to preserve, its stresses, and sources of stress; in the second, the possible strategies for addressing the threats; in the third, a brief plan for executing the chosen strategies.

The two men convened the first session in February in Vero Beach, Florida, site of one of the five projects, Indian River Lagoon. Among the teams was Allen Pursell, a forester and project manager for the Blue River Project in southern Indiana. Pursell, like so many landscape-scale managers, was nervous about a forty-five-minute presentation to Low and Weeks, two of the top dogs in the Conservancy hierarchy. He was concerned, too, about an hour of questioning by the rest of the group.

Low insisted on a tough-love style of peer review. Five ground rules governed the discussion: everyone participates, nobody dominates, bosses can't boss, everybody advocates, and the project team members—not the workshop group—decide what to do when they go home.

Pursell was at first on the receiving end of the tough-love experience: He was told by Low and others that he was focusing on saving too many minor plants and animals. They might be rare in Indiana, but they weren't rare globally. Next he was on the delivery end: he offended one peer by saying her decision to draw bioreserve boundaries at the state line didn't make any sense. Through this kind of give-and-take, the initial meeting had the desired effect on all of the project teams: It shook people up enough to change their thinking.

Pursell had an unwieldy list of sources—housing construction, recreation, fire suppression, and about fifteen others. The list overwhelmed him. In response, Low asked him to score each one, rating its impact on the most sensitive parts of his landscape-scale system—on rare cavefish, freshwater mussels, cave crustaceans, the Indiana bat, and so on. Low showed Pursell that threats to his ecosystem came mainly from just a few sources of stress—he called them "killer threats."

The group helped Pursell whittle his list to two: "inappropriate forest practices" and "inadequate wastewater treatment." In southern Indiana, most landowners own twenty- to forty-acre woodlots and usually cut timber without any professional forestry advice or thought for long-term ecological or financial consequences. The reckless cutting, often in haste to cash in on timber value in emergencies, destroys the forest and the foraging habitat for the Indiana bat. Failing septic systems or waste-water treatment plants, meanwhile, release too many chemical and bacterial pollutants into the ground water. Septic-system effluent seeps through shallow soils, travels along layers in the limestone bedrock, and plunges through cracks into the underground water flow, which in the Blue River region passes through an estimated one thousand caves, an average of one per square mile.

The first meeting forced every project manager to focus on killer threats, and this set the group up for the second meeting, in Colorado's Laramie Foothills, where managers presented strategies for dealing with the threats. That in turn set everyone up for the third meeting, in October, hosted by Pursell at a plantation-style home on the Ohio River. At the third meeting, every team arrived with plans for their chosen strategies to abate their ecosystem threats. By this time, Low had the group thinking in exactly the way he wanted: On coming up with the specific innovations needed back on the ground to protect biodiversity. The question was, do these plans promise success? Will they stand up to tough love?

Pursell's plans were innovative, bold, unusual, and unprecedented in Indiana. And as it turned out, they stood up to tough love. The first was to control effluent by forming a waste-water management district that would include septic systems. The district would regulate septic system maintenance for the first time. The second was to slow harmful logging by forming a "forest bank" to pay landowners an annual stream of payments for their timber. The Conservancy would run the bank, manage the landowners' timber, and cut it at the right time in the right way.

Passing the tough-love test, Pursell left the third workshop feeling like a man who had experienced a revelation. When he started out, he'd had no idea how little he knew. The third meeting seemed to have, yet again, the desired effect. The stepwise tough-love regimen—Low's algorithm—gave all the project managers a clear picture of how to move ahead as soon as they returned to the office.

Low could see the confidence grow among the directors as they ran the workshop's challenging intellectual gauntlet. He was optimistic the teams found solid strategies for biodiversity protection. When he read the workshop evaluations, he said to himself, "Bingo!" The evaluations glowed. The process of breaking the analysis into discrete parts, insisting on constant inquiry and endless iteration among a group of peers, and demanding constant improvement—all of these put together paid off in solid Monday-morning action plans.

With the new workshop format, Low and Weeks created the vehicle for bumping people out of age-old ruts of conservation thinking. They had a tool to open people's eyes to broader ways of looking at their work and delivering strategies to fit the new, bigger scale and scope of the Conservancy business.

Through it all, Low had learned that spurring the organization's movement to a new line of business would not happen through mandate, or education, or planning, or even through putting people on the ground. It demanded one-on-one prodding by internal champions and opinion leaders like himself. Even more pivotal, it required peer-to-peer coaching by fellow staff facing the same strategic challenges. Without the systematic coaching of peers, the new ideas and strategies for landscape-scale conservation would not take.

The new workshops cast peers in the roles of both doctor and patient, as one person would later tell Low. Each was a doctor to the rest as the group discussed the peers' projects, and then the patient when their own turn came in the process. The intensive doctor–patient peer review spurred the needed transition of thinking and action. Low, a student of writings of innovation experts like Everett M. Rogers, would later stress in *Landscape-Scale, Community-Based Conservation: A Practitioner's Handbook,* his own manual about community-based conservation: diffusing innovation is fundamentally a social process. The same could be said for driving the workforce to embrace a new business.

THE PITFALL

As Low came up with this new means to institutionalize the new business, another story was playing out at the Virginia Coast Reserve, where he and Weeks continued to experiment with integrating the lives of people and the work of conservation. What Low discovered was that, despite expanding an organization's capacity to fulfill its mission at a broader scale and scope, the organization and its people have their limits.

Acting on a suggestion in the Northampton Economic Forum's "Blueprint," the Conservancy announced in December 1993 that it would launch a start-up for-profit company to create jobs on the Eastern Shore. The company would be called the Virginia Eastern Shore Sustainable

Development Corporation (VESC). It would be the flagship effort for the Center for Compatible Economic Development to demonstrate once and for all how intertwined were the causes of conservation and economic health.

Low had become a booster of the idea of using market forces to preserve the environment. The Northampton County Board of Supervisors agreed that this new idea, sweeping the environmental field at the time, had merit. The board created a new county government position, director of sustainable development, a first in the nation. The Conservancy and the county were now on the same quest—doing good for the economy while doing good for nature. The notion was mostly a blue-sky theory, but Low was convinced that successful conservation depended on successful local economies—job-creating economies.

With the help of Old Dominion University's Entrepreneurial Center, Low and others developed VESC's business plan. It called for investing $400,000 to help build fifteen small businesses in agriculture, tourism, craft gifts, and real estate development. It also called for spending $700,000 for a lodge to serve nature lovers and for acquiring over $2 million worth of farm, business, and residential property. In four years, VESC would become profitable, and in year five, bring in revenue of $2 million.

In mid-1995, with $2.25 million in capital, a new CEO, and the thirty-five-page business plan, VESC opened for business. Low was chairman of the board. Like many start-ups born in a flourish of optimism, VESC didn't get off to a great start—just the opposite. It burned through its capital and didn't even begin to meet its projections of increasing revenues 15 percent per year. After year one, Low presided over a board meeting in which VESC amended its projections: It would turn a profit not in four years, but in several more.

The start-up phase continued to falter. After two years, the company lost more than $1 million—86 percent of its initial capital. Low and others remained optimistic. They had faith that VESC would soon turn the corner and hit its numbers. The CEO, in fact, saw "no threat to ultimate success." Many managers inside the Conservancy marveled at the costly experiment. They ridiculed the project, its tenuous link to Conservancy goals, and its founders' lack of financial experience with for-profit business. But Weeks and Low carried on.

By the middle of the third year of operation, business looked even worse. At the June 1998 VESC board meeting, one director wondered if the entire concept should not be reconsidered. Perhaps the company should reconfigure as an R&D operation, he said. The loss for 1998 was $755,477.

Low continued to hold out hope that the strategy would take, that the environmentally compatible businesses would turn a corner, that the experiment would prove itself after all. But in 1998, two key investors, the Cary Trust and Ford Foundation, lost faith. They subsequently ordered an inquiry into the failing enterprise to understand what went wrong.

The hard lesson for Low was this: He and Weeks had overreached. They had tried to stretch the Conservancy beyond its capabilities. The notion of mixing conservation and job creation was still sound—but making the Conservancy the operator was not. The fact was, the Conservancy didn't know how to run a for-profit business. It didn't have the skills or experience.

"The Conservancy must promote substantive, alternative economic development initiatives, or the health of the bioreserve may be irretrievably damaged," wrote Low in the 1992 Virginia Coast Reserve strategic plan. He still felt he was right. The Conservancy might still "promote" a for-profit enterprise. But he was wrong about running the enterprise himself. The whole episode was difficult and embarrassing for both Low and investors like Ford and Cary.

The experience defined for Low the scope of the new business they were putting the Conservancy in. It did include community-based conservation and economic development. It did not include business development and operations. In keeping with the program of experimentation started by Low back in the 1980s, he had continued to promote new innovations to meld the causes of conservation and job creation. But with VESC, he found he had gone to the edge, the bleeding edge, and had to back off.

THE MAKEOVER

Plenty of Conservancy managers, jealous of Low's steady supply of money to fuel his pet ideas on the Eastern Shore, gloated over the failure. To them, this was Low's comeuppance. But Conservancy president Sawhill was of another mind. Sawhill believed that community-based conservation was inevitable and indispensable. If you were going to preserve big landscapes, you couldn't avoid engaging people, Sawhill felt. At a time when the VESC experience made some people doubt the entire move into landscape-scale conservation, Sawhill pressed the organization to move further still.

Sawhill came to Low and asked him to build a Web site to broadcast the lessons of experience. Low said that a Web site would be fine, but the Conservancy needed a much bigger initiative to advance the work. Low wrote a short white paper proposing a Center for Community-Based Conservation.

Sawhill, a follower of Low's thinking, convened a meeting to talk about the idea. The other managers gave Low a hard time, questioning another skunk works solution. California State Director Steven McCormick asked why the Conservancy needed a new center to advance community-based conservation. Why not do that as a part of the Conservancy's main program? McCormick, in a separate effort, had been working on a large landscape himself in California's Coachella Valley, near Palm Springs, and he, too, was partial to community-based solutions.

Well, why not? replied Low.

Several months later, Sawhill named Weeks executive vice president responsible for all Conservancy operations and Low head of U.S. conservation programs. All at once, the bioreserve experimenters and community-based conservation advocates ruled the direction of the organization—in spite of the growing blemish on their record from the faltering VESC. Community-based conservation had moved out of an off-site skunk works and into the mainstream.

One question still nagged at Low: The scientific underpinnings for the move into this new business. From the point of view of protecting biodiversity, what was the Conservancy targeting in such huge sites?

Into Low's e-mail in-box fell the answer. He received "Functional Landscapes and the Conservation of Biodiversity," an article drafted by Karen Poiani, a Conservancy Ph.D. in conservation science. Reading the article on the bus and metro to his office, Low got chills, much as he had when he read Jenkins's paper in 1975. Poiani and her coauthors (Brian Richter, Mark Anderson, and Holly Richter) laid out the scientific basis for the whole new push. The Conservancy's job was not just to preserve rare and uncommon elements of biodiversity captured in sites and preserves.

The real goal of the Conservancy was to conserve the composition, structure, and function of nature—its complexities, interactions, and ecological processes. In this light, the biodiversity mission spanned scales as small as a spider's web hidden in the leaf litter to as large as a vast tract swept by wildfire in Yellowstone National Park. Indeed, nature operates at small, medium, and large scales, and thus, so must the Conservancy to achieve its mission.

The next day, Low phoned Poiani. He told her the paper would become a seminal work at the Conservancy. If the Conservancy was going to follow its tradition of using science to determine priorities, Poiani and her coauthors' paper explained how.

The stage was set for the transition that had been thirteen years in the making for Low. The Conservancy had experimented with new scale and scope. It had replicated its ideas in multiple large sites. It had developed the 5S model for planning this new business. It had outlined the scientific underpinning for its work. What remained was an across-the-board organization commitment to the new business.

Despite the years of work by Low, Weeks, and many others, across-the-board buy-in was still lacking. Most people in the organization, even in 1998, thought of the Conservancy as a land-buying group, conserving nature parcel by parcel. In state offices, the business of the Conservancy was still the business of creating preserves. Nothing had tipped the deal-makers in the field from that line of thinking into grasping the message Low tried and failed to convey with Dorothy and Toto in 1995. The move to landscape-scale conservation was nothing less than the transition from a business mainly defined by real estate deal making to one mainly defined by institutional deal making.

Sawhill provided the final push. Seeking a new fundraising target and a conservation goal to carry it, he redoubled his bet on this new business. At the annual meeting at Keystone, Colorado, in the fall of 1998, he announced, borrowing a phrase from management thinkers James Collins and Jerry Porras, a new "big hairy audacious" goal. The Conservancy would preserve five hundred new landscape-scale projects by 2008.

The audience of volunteers and staff was stunned. That meant adding 425 new big-time projects in a decade.

"To reach this goal," Sawhill said, "we have to open a new office every eight days for the next ten years."

And that was not all. To succeed in the new business, the Conservancy needed more money than ever before imagined. Sawhill announced a new capital campaign goal of $750 million—exceeding the previous campaign goal by an astonishing $450 million.

Where would the Conservancy get all that money? From believers in the new business. In fact, Low had worked with Sawhill, Weeks, and others to put together a proposal for soliciting the kickoff campaign donation. Weeks and Sawhill asked board member and philanthropist Daniel Efroymson for a $10 million leadership grant—$2 million for matching grants for landscape-scale projects, $2 million for running Low's tough-love workshops to implement two hundred landscape-scale projects in five years, and $6 million for building the Conservancy's international capacity, Indiana projects, and programs for testing new compatible economic development ideas.

Efroymson was a Hoosier who had heard Pursell talk about landscape-scale work. He liked the idea, and he agreed.

The Efroymson grant gave Low the fuel to power his mechanism to guide the Conservancy through the transition he had so long worked on. In the next few years, he spread the new thinking, using the renamed tough-love "Efroymson process," throughout the Conservancy, and results started to pour in.

By 2003, Low had run two hundred project managers through this tough-love workout. Pursell returned for a second Efroymson session in 2003. The septic management district was on the drawing boards—one county had built it into its comprehensive plan. The forest bank was up and running. Pursell had enrolled timber owners transferring 1,100 acres to Conservancy management.

Low had abandoned compatible-development projects in which the Conservancy acted as operator. He still smarted from a highly critical postmortem report on VESC, which cited "hubris" as a cause of failure. VESC was dissolved in 1999 at almost a complete loss. Low had to incorporate some chastening lessons of failure into his advice on running new landscape-scale projects.

But in spite of regrettable setbacks, Low had secured the future of the Conservancy in a new business. The journey had taken more than fifteen years, the time necessary for experimenting with new kinds of conservation, refining a model of the new business, and coming up with a mechanism to institutionalize the changeover. But the results were now growing as fast as the Conservancy. As the Efroymson work in Indiana and across the nation took hold, Low called an end to his journey as one of the chief promoters, guides, and midwives to the biggest transition in the Conservancy's business since its creation. In 2004, he took a new post with the Conservancy: running landscape-scale operations himself in the Sierra Nevada.

6

THE POWER OF "WE":
Engaging Every Constituency for Breakthrough Results

T HE SOFT-SPOKEN, UNASSUMING KENT WOMMACK, exec-
utive director of the Nature Conservancy in Maine, had been in his
post less than a year. Sizing up his performance, he spilled his misgivings
to Charles Micoleau, his new chairman, about the way he ran his board
of trustees. He said, in effect, "I don't feel I'm using the trustees' time very
well. I'm not getting people engaged in the action. I feel like I need a better way to tap the trustees' talents, expertise, contacts, and wisdom."

Wommack, speaking in 1991, didn't have to elaborate. Micoleau, a
board member of the Maine chapter since the mid-1980s, had been thinking the same thing. The staff spent too much time giving presentations, too
little time soliciting views. The agendas forced trustees to absorb hours of
detail on land deals—profiles of the sellers, financing, property configura-
tions, ecological significance. When the deals came to a vote, everyone—
without exception—voted in favor.

105

"Who am I to disagree?" thought Micoleau, who felt he didn't know enough about the scientific or legal facts to say otherwise.

As in many organizations, board meetings in Maine served too often to needlessly inform, too rarely to elicit initiative. Trustees spent most of their time listening or doing things that didn't make a difference. At a May 1991 meeting of the Maine board, then-chair Carol Wishcamper broke the board into groups to debate the Conservancy's new strategic plan. She was tired of the staff's pattern of lecturing. The staff, she felt, didn't trust board members to express their opinions. She later chose not to serve as chairman beyond her first term.

Wommack, thirty-six, a short man with a relentless smile, tuned in assiduously to dissonance among his constituencies. Unlike managers in many organizations, he recognized that sagging performance can often be traced to disempowered people, whether his board, staff, or any other set of stakeholders. This spurred him throughout his career to better engage each group he worked with. Over two decades, some of his most memorable moves in management would stem from a single skill: the knack, even the gift, of engaging others.

Wommack showed an early interest in this theme. At Colby College in Waterville, Maine, he studied political science—which he later described as the science of initiating and managing change in large societies and organizations. He earned a master's degree at Yale School of Forestry and Environmental Studies, where he designed his own curriculum. He chose courses from both the forestry and business schools, later calling his studies "socio-ecology," or the intersection of the human and natural world.

Wommack would turn repeatedly in his job to initiating change through others—staff, lawmakers, the public, corporate executives, peers in the environmental movement. The indomitably complimentary and grateful conservationist worked hard to improve performance by aligning his interests with those of others, and then inviting others to help realize an enticing vision. In part, he would appeal to people's self-interest. In part, he would appeal to the interests of others in realizing the best in themselves. This skill would become his hallmark.

In 1991, Wommack, always thoughtful, always interrupting himself to recast his sentences, would extend his appeal to his board. He had grown uneasy with the lack of engagement. He knew that running a board was not easy, rarely the forte of presidents or executive directors, and that his board felt marginalized. He heard trustee detachment seep through comments after meetings. "You guys are doing great work; we're proud to be associated with you," trustees would say.

"*You're* doing great work"—that phrase bugged Wommack. Shouldn't they be saying "we"?

Complicating the task of running a board at the Conservancy was an organizational quirk: The trustees of the fifty state boards were second in command to the national board. The state boards actually had no legal authority; only the national governors did. The state trustees ran their operations *as if* they had legal authority, although they couldn't take final responsibility for legal or financial matters. They were advisers, albeit often powerful ones.

Wommack questioned the obvious: Why should the state board members approve every deal—given they don't have the authority, don't have any independent deal-making details or expertise, and don't want to second-guess decisions by a seasoned staff? Wouldn't they contribute more value if they debated loftier issues—of policy, not practice, of strategy, not day-to-day action?

"It's silly to hold board meetings to ask trustees for advice where we know the right answers," Wommack thought, "and not ask about things where we don't."

Wommack recognized the lost opportunity. On too many boards, the chief executives and the staff worry far more about the board bollixing up their plans than pitching in to pump up their performance. In fact, they often craftily sideline their boards. Wommack, not one to rule by fiat, couldn't help but feel his board had matured over the years and was ready to for a new level of engagement. He thought, "These are really smart people. They have friends and contacts and know the governor. They want to help, they have something to offer, and I need to tell them what it is."

On March 12, 1992, he and Micoleau went to the board to announce a change. Micoleau noted that the trustees had expressed concerns about the role of the board and how the structure of the meetings obstructed intensive interaction and meaningful contributions. In turn, Wommack said he and Micoleau had decided to try a new format. The staff would no longer talk the whole time, and the board would no longer review, or vote on, every land transaction, unless unusually costly or risky.

The board breathed a collective sigh of relief. The trustees agreed to ease into the changes and reassess as they went along. Now it was up to Wommack. It was up to him to engage an increasingly influential but underutilized constituency. It was up to him to seek the trustees' advice and help them make more of a difference. This would be a major step in his work to engage a variety of constituencies—engaging them to contribute to the larger goals of the organization.

DEALING THE PUBLIC IN

Wommack's efforts in 1992 did not mark the first time he had faced the challenge of engaging a critical constituency. His first big foray dated to 1986, when he caught wind of the work of a commission set up by the governor of Maine to study outdoor recreation. The commission urged lawmakers to pass a $50 million bond to buy land for public use. This looked like a chance for the Conservancy to hitch its wagon to a statewide effort to get money for conservation.

In keeping with tradition, Wommack was used to controlling conservation deals by himself. He hired on with the Conservancy in 1983 in Maine as a dealmaker, saving gems of nature, like the scrub pines of the Waterboro Barrens and the grasshopper sparrows of Kennebunk Plains. He didn't involve outsiders to get the job done. As one Maine trustee joked, the Conservancy operated like poachers in his northerly home of Washington County: quick, quiet, and alone. And he, and many donors, liked it that way.

But Wommack and fellow Maine conservationists knew that to get the millions of dollars needed to buy bigger parcels of land, they couldn't depend solely on private donors. They had to engage taxpayers. All at once there emerged this recommendation by a governor's commission to pursue that very strategy. Here was an idea to capture money for buying big, lake-strewn expanses of Maine's North Woods.

Taking a crack at getting this money would require skills outside the Conservancy's expertise and traditional mission, namely, lobbying. It would also require keeping politicking at arm's length. The Conservancy traded on its nonconfrontational, nonpartisan, deal-making reputation. So Wommack consulted with Mason Morfit, Maine state director, to decide if the state bond fit two time-honored Conservancy criteria for launching any new effort: Was the work critical to the mission? Could the Conservancy make a crucial difference?

Morfit agreed the answer to both was yes, and Wommack arranged lunch for himself, Morfit, and chapter chair Ellen Wells to meet a major booster of the bond proposal, Angus King. King was an entrepreneur who worked in the alternative energy field and was one of the recreation commission members who championed the bond as a lead commission recommendation. He received from Wommack the outlines of a deal: If King supported a proposal with wording to save biologically diverse lands, the Conservancy would take first crack at drafting the legislation, along with staffing and paying for the effort to get the bill passed. King liked the idea.

King's support set Wommack on a voyage of political learning, beyond his tried-and-true craft of land transactions. On this voyage, he would learn how to ally with people far beyond his normal base of supporters and demonstrate the skills needed to initiate change by engaging a variety of stakeholders from outside the organization. Recognizing his inexperience, he decided to invite onto the scene one of the Conservancy's two lobbyists, Carol Baudler, a veteran of statehouse battles in Minnesota. Baudler would walk Wommack through a game plan, and for the next several months, coach him in visiting state officials, legislators, commission members, conservationists, and sportsmen.

Wommack and the Conservancy were out to energize a whole host of constituencies to back the Conservancy's cause. Their first step was to gather intelligence. What did other groups want in a bond proposal? Which lands did they care about? Who else would join a coalition? The Conservancy's strategy was to step forward, spend money, and devote staff to a statewide effort. It could then control the agenda while staying offstage. For the Maine chapter this was new territory.

The role of conservationist-cum-lobbyist unnerved Wommack at times. Establishing a political action committee, he worried that the work might contravene the Conservancy's operating principles and taint its reputation. But instead, reaching out had a salutary effect on him and the Conservancy in Maine. It broke down parochialism.

Still most comfortable in hiking boots, Wommack had spent his summers as a kid in camp canoeing the wilds of Canada, inspired by nature. He later tromped the backcountry of Olympic National Park in Washington as a ranger for three summers. He was not cut from the same cloth as many people who enjoyed the outdoors in Maine. But he and his staff met hunters, snowmobilers, and other outdoors people, and got to know both their personalities and their points of view.

Wommack hired a state lobbyist to work with the legislature. He and his team then drafted two bills: one for a $50 million bond, the second for rules to govern its spending. By the time lawmakers held a public hearing in spring 1987, the room overflowed, weighted heavily in favor of bond supporters wooed by King, the Conservancy, the Maine Coast Heritage Trust, and many others. The supporters—paper companies, real estate firms, sportsman groups, planning commissions, businesses, and conservationists—came from across the political spectrum. In view of such support, with King as the spokesperson, most lawmakers backed the bill.

Next came weeks of lobbying to keep fiscal conservatives from gutting the bill—which they first wanted to cut to $5 million. On June 26, 1987, just hours from the close of the legislative session, the two bills passed with only three dissenting votes. The Conservancy ended up with a compromise bond of $35 million—and scarcely a change in the wording of the bill governing spending. That was a big victory for conservation, and the first leg in Wommack's education in engaging outside constituencies.

The victory was temporary. The coalition still had to secure voter ratification of the bill in the fall election. For that effort, Wommack hired political pollster and Bowdoin College professor Christian Potholm, who polled people in August. That's when, in a September meeting in Potholm's Portland office, Wommack and Baudler learned some bad news. Despite their crafty lobbying in the spring, most of the electorate hadn't heard of the initiative. Voters didn't understand it and didn't support it.

Potholm told Wommack and Baudler that his poll showed that only 20 percent of voters supported the bill. He added that 20 percent opposed it, and 60 percent were sitting on the fence.

With such numbers, Wommack said he worried that opponents would defeat the bond. He noted that right-wing groups opposed the expense, the interference by government, and the withdrawal of land from tax rolls.

That's when Wommack learned a principle of engaging a coalition. Said Potholm: "It's not your enemies that will kill the bill. It's your friends." He warned Wommack that he had to get all his friends in the same boat. If anyone hopped out to preach his group's parochial views, the Conservancy could kiss the bond goodbye.

Potholm laid out his formula for winning. The essence: making allies of the two groups who make up 65 percent of the vote—the people who define themselves as environmentalists and the people, the hunters and anglers, who define themselves as sportsmen.

Potholm suggested running a focus group to pinpoint the pivotal issues. He would hold a day-long session with voters and then launch a campaign of television ads and direct mail to broadcast the message that emerged as most compelling. Wommack and Morfit agreed to the plan immediately. The board then backed them up.

Potholm soon found that one concern gnawed at pretty much the entire electorate: loss of access. Loss of access to woods for hunting, to streams for boating, to beaches for swimming. Since the Great Ponds Act of 1647, Maine had guaranteed the passage of people across private lands to "to fish and fowl" at "all great ponds." With landowners busy subdividing, and contractors busy building, the issue that most raised people's hackles was the loss of access to Maine's finest outdoor places. Potholm suggested the ads play to this access anxiety.

The resulting campaign, five thirty-second spots produced by Roger Williams Advertising, hit the mark. One ad showed a tranquil Maine lake with a "keep out" sign bursting upward from the water. Another showed a Maine beach with two boys and their mother pleading for access. Three of the ads showed beloved Maine sportsman and columnist Bud Leavitt, dressed in a plaid shirt and bow tie and with trout flies hooked to his hat, intoning, "If we don't make more land public, somebody else will make it private."

Viewers could just imagine their favorite haunts lost forever. The bond money, however, promised access to coveted hunting spots in the woods, beach spots on the coast, lakeshores across the state—forever.

Wommack and the Conservancy did indeed have to coax coalition members to preach the group message, not the message of their own group. When one of the ads showed a father and son, shotguns in hand, walking through the woods to hunt, an anti-gun group cried foul. But Potholm argued to retain the ad. It endeared the bond to every hunter who voted.

Potholm asked if the ad was so offensive that it was going to turn the anti-gun group's members' yes votes to no.

Not a chance, came the answer.

Then let it run, was Potholm's reply. Without hunters, he maintained, the coalition was finished.

Wommack, deferring to King's pitch for the hunting ad, knew full well that if the Conservancy had fashioned the message, it would have preached the benefits of biodiversity. The electorate would have yawned. The bond would have failed. So Potholm was right. As the $200,000, five-week campaign ran, the job became one of gently holding the coalition to a consistent message.

And hold them the Conservancy did. In November 1987, the bond passed by a landslide: 65 percent to 35 percent.

The vote was a twofold victory. It created the Land for Maine's Future program, an unprecedented pot of $35 million to buy Maine's best property. Under authority granted by language in the second bill, it also earned the Conservancy a seat at the negotiating table. The state staffers responsible for spending the money could—and would—call in the Conservancy when they were short on negotiating expertise.

In this, Wommack's first experience in the power of engaging outside constituencies to further his own organization's goals, he would tell people he learned four lessons: volunteer to do more than your share, give all the credit to others, meet others on their terms, and refrain from fretting when you don't agree on why to do something.

As it turned out, the state did ask the Conservancy and other land-conservation groups to negotiate on its behalf. Wommack, in his most celebrated deal, represented sixteen public agencies and private groups and spent hundreds of hours over eighteen months to assemble a package of land from holdings of Diamond Occidental Forest, a French company eager to log, sell, or develop 800,000 acres of Maine forest.

On the other side of the table was Daniel Christensen, Diamond Occidental vice president and general manager, point person for a group of Parisian investors most concerned with financial returns. Christensen, sympathetic to the Conservancy, gave the Conservancy maps of all 800,000 acres. He told Wommack to give him the Conservancy's wish list and he would see what he could do. But he added that Wommack had best be quick—Christensen's investors were in a hurry.

Wommack's manner kept Christensen at the table. Wommack didn't play tricks Christensen knew so well—like agreeing to a provision and later taking it back, or putting down a take-it-or-leave-it offer and walking out. The negotiations went on and on because the two men kept horse-trading pieces of property chosen from a menu of tracts from the 800,000 acres. Assembling a selection to fit both the state's and Christensen's needs was mind-numbing.

Wommack had no choice but to keep offering alternative solutions. Christensen had developers and timber buyers lined up with cash for the land if Wommack couldn't make a deal. The negotiations bogged down over the value of the land. The value to Diamond Occidental of each parcel was the discounted cash flow of timber or building lots. The value to the state of Maine was based on comparative values of other properties—a more slippery number.

In the final two months, negotiations intensified. Christensen's deal-making window was closing as his investors pressured him to sell. Finally, on a Friday at 2:30 P.M., the two men sat down at the Maine Forest Service office in Augusta, Maine. Thirteen hours later, at 3:30 A.M., Saturday morning, after too much cold pizza, Christensen and Wommack had a deal.

The entire package comprised seven sites, 40,000 acres, and cost $13 million. At the heart of the deal was a parcel of 31,512 acres around the fabled Nahmakanta Lake.

Wommack and the Conservancy had helped Maine preserve fifty miles of shoreline on twenty-four lakes and ponds. It was the largest single land conservation purchase in the history of the state. Wommack instantly won widespread praise, even if he annoyed some property-rights activists piqued by government acquisition of big woodland tracts. The state gave him the "Iron Pants Award"—for staying at the table longer than anyone else imaginable. In the process, he had learned perhaps another lesson he could pass on: A hard-working, honest broker willing to shed his parochial interests not only engages his constituencies but keeps them engaged over the long term.

BOARD WORK

When, two years later, it came to figuring out how to empower a constituency much closer to him—his own trustees—Wommack thus started from a rich background of experience. He was a veteran in reaching out and involving others in the Conservancy's crusade.

Yet Wommack found that handling his own board was tougher than almost anything he had done before. His heart-to-heart with Micoleau, and their announcement at the March 1992 board meeting, were only the first steps of a new journey. Mea culpa completed, he wasn't sure how he was going to bring out the best in his board.

Over the next year or so, he and Micoleau tried a lot of things: more ad hoc task forces, breakout sessions at meetings, shaking up the order of the agenda. Yet too often, a month or so before a board meeting, Wommack and the staff scrambled to figure out how to fill up the entire meeting time. "What will we do for a whole meeting?" they wondered. With a seasoned staff guiding a well-oiled operation, they couldn't easily decide what the relevant issues for the board were.

And the board members felt they weren't being handed any substantive issues, either. When developer Lyndell "Joe" Wishcamper joined the board in late 1993, the trustees still said hardly a word, the lack of trustee involvement frustrated people, and the meetings ran overtime besides. Wishcamper said, in effect, "You're not going to keep powerful people on the board if all they do is come to meetings and sit as if they're watching television." He told Wommack that trustees had better things to do with their time than act as passive observers. If they didn't feel like they were making a contribution, they would leave.

Wommack had set a personal goal of building a board so influential it could open any door in the state. But he was not certain how to give the wealthy, wise, and influential a better way to contribute. He did bring policy questions to his trustees that really mattered. In early 1994, he raised a topic that troubled all state directors: whether to pay local property taxes. At the time, the towns of Lubec and Jonesport refused to recognize the Conservancy as tax-exempt. As a "good neighbor," the Conservancy made a "donation" to the towns in lieu of taxes. The town of Shapleigh revoked the Conservancy's tax-exemption because at one preserve the Conservancy piled up gravel to block entry by cars and trucks—and to the town's way of thinking blocked public access.

Wommack didn't actually have an answer to the tax question—and that was the point. He asked the trustees what the tax policy should be.

Wommack was nervous about this discussion. Trustees knew plenty about taxes and town politics, and they could easily make a decision that gave him trouble. On May 12, however, the board agreed that the Conservancy should defend its tax-exempt status more aggressively, volunteer tax payments only in rare cases and in modest sums, and draft defensible guidelines so they could treat towns fairly.

Wommack was relieved. To be sure, his staff wasn't sure the trustees were right: One town manager talks to another, and surely tax-poor towns would soon cry for their share of Conservancy funds. But Wommack believed the decision fell within the bounds of what was right. Moreover, the board lifted a huge burden from his shoulders. If the policy flared into a controversy, at least the board knew about the issue.

Wommack believed there was no "right" decision. What mattered was that the staff and the trustees made the decision together. And as it turned out, as he repeatedly relinquished control of such decisions to the board, he never felt the trustees made a wrong decision. And in time, he and the staff got better at bringing them into policy discussions.

The board responded favorably to Wommack's efforts on policy, but he did not proceed apace on other aspects of engaging the board. He and the staff completely controlled fundraising. Maine launched its "Legacy" capital campaign in 1989, and Carol Wishcamper was named campaign chairman. But when Wommack took over as executive director, he never succeeded in empowering the board to do much, and performance showed it.

The campaign suffered from a classic problem: The campaign chairman, Wishcamper, remained a figurehead. Wommack didn't call on her to ask anyone she knew for money. He didn't ask her to use any of her skills or time. The campaign, scheduled to wrap up by the end of 1993, wore on and on. It ended at the end of 1994 with $5 million raised. Albeit successful, it was a campaign everyone was glad to put behind them, including Wishcamper, who by that time had left the board.

By the mid-1990s, Wommack's plan to engage the board was still a work in progress. He was feeling his way along. The answer to reaching full engagement just wasn't clear. He knew it would be a gradual process. He had to gain confidence in the trustees and they in him.

COMPACT FOR ALL

In the meantime, Wommack was drawn once again into events outside the organization. Those events would call on his skills of engagement at yet a higher level. And from them he would learn still more about reaping higher performance by empowering various constituencies. The trigger for his work with outsiders came in early 1996. Maine green activist Jonathan Carter spearheaded a drive to ban clear-cutting in the state. Carter collected fifty-eight thousand signatures to put the issue to a vote in the fall. In a state where a Sunday drive brings most motorists in sight of at least one clear-cut—with soils laid bare and ground prickling with broken limbs—a ban sounded like a dandy idea.

But foresters and timber owners were apoplectic. They argued the referendum would forbid clear-cuts altogether, which are often aimed at fostering regrowth of sun-loving—and valuable—species like white birch and white pine. It could force them to cut less wood each year than they actually grew. Given that the referendum would ban a variety of forest practices, the timber owners viewed it as a broad anti-forestry bill masquerading as a narrow measure to simply stop clear-cuts. Some landowners believed the Green Party wanted to shut down modern forest practices in Maine. They pointed to a state study that predicted the ban would kill 15,600 jobs.

Wommack recognized the ban's shortcomings, as did more moderate groups like the Natural Resources Council of Maine and Maine Audubon. The referendum would ram through flawed policy in a state where many jobs depended on forestry. But it put the groups in a bind. They hated to support the ban as written; but if they had to choose sides in the face of a tidal wave of support for the referendum—and they would have to in a fall vote—they would support it.

The Conservancy wouldn't join the fight against Carter's referendum. Taking a stand was too political. But Wommack wanted to avoid a forestry-policy train wreck. He asked pollster Potholm to piggyback a few questions about the ban onto another poll: Are you in favor of the clear-cut ban? Are you in favor if it destroys jobs? Would you favor a compromise that protected the forest but allowed responsible forestry?

Wommack wanted to know where the public stood. Potholm's answer: Ready to lash out at clear-cutters—yet easily swayed to oppose the ban to save jobs and local economies. Far and away, the third option got the most support. The public wanted more concrete measures to assure sustainable forestry.

Wommack floated the compromise behind the scenes, and he received a call from a representative of the timber industry. Worried about the prospect of a bloody campaign, the industry sought a discussion with environmentalists. Would the Conservancy act as go-between? Then came a call from the office of the current governor—Angus King, Wommack's conservation-bond ally. Could Wommack get the two sides talking?

Wommack had already earned respect from timber owners. In 1993 Catherine Johnson, lobbyist at the Natural Resources Council of Maine, and Roger Milliken, the manager of a 100,000-acre family woodland, dreamed up the idea of a forest-biodiversity gathering of people from industry, government, academia, and environmental groups. They wanted to head off a battle over biodiversity, like the one then raging between West Coast loggers and spotted-owl activists. A legislative discussion of biodiversity was dangerous, Milliken thought, and he wanted to avoid it.

Milliken and Johnson invited Wommack to join them. The threesome formed a steering committee and invited more than a hundred top people from opposing camps, and most accepted. The environmentalists agreed to come because they were eager to create ecological reserves, a recommendation of a report from the Maine State Planning Office. The forest owners came because they realized they couldn't fight regulation and lawmakers forever, and they worried that if they stayed away, something crazy could happen. They had to find a forum to influence state policy.

The Maine Forest Biodiversity Project held its first meeting in May 1994. Two professional facilitators—who had earlier run meetings of pro-life and pro-choice groups—came to keep the conversation civil. Progress was interminably slow, as they worked for hours just to define *biodiversity*. But the group, ranging from the Appalachian Mountain Club and Maine Audubon to the Small Woodland Owners Association of Maine and Sportman's Alliance of Maine, agreed to meet again. And again. Each time in a two-day conference. And by early 1996, they had met five times.

As the formal daytime talks built trust, the time between and after built even more. During a meal, over a beer, in the hall, antagonists formed friendships. They saw each other as more than someone who believed in something they didn't believe in.

Wommack learned to engage supposed adversaries on a personal level he had never reached before. One of his most important relationships developed with Milliken, who gingerly straddled the timber and conservation camps as a board member of both the Maine Forest Products Council and the Natural Resources Council of Maine. At the conferences, he and Wommack spent hours vetting discussion topics, scheming about ways to involve people who had not been talking, wording questions that gave people room to maneuver. So impressed was Milliken with the Conservancy's approach that, by late 1995, he agreed to join the Conservancy board.

When Wommack came to his board in February 1996 to discuss whether he should get involved as mediator in the clear-cut ban furor, he had contacts across the political spectrum. With his widely recognized non-threatening manner, he was perfectly positioned to engage constituencies for the Conservancy's cause. He and the board hesitated over his stepping into the fray, however. It was a highly charged political issue, and the Conservancy could not possibly control the debate or outcome. But given the call from the governor, given the civic obligation, the trustees gave approval.

In the small world of Maine, Wommack wasn't the only one driving the action. Behind the scenes, Milliken had urged the Maine Forest Products Council to meet with "mainstream enviros." Milliken argued that the industry couldn't simply oppose the ban—the fifty-eight thousand signatures represented a groundswell of public opinion the industry had to deal with. So Milliken brought together the timber owners and moderate environmental groups for talks, and the meeting at the Natural Resources Council of Maine no doubt paved the way for Wommack to get to work on a deal.

To Wommack thus fell the delicate, conflict-ridden role of facilitator but not advocate, mediator but not meddler—a fine line to walk. He had his own opinions but strove to stay neutral. He had to find common ground.

The negotiations wore on for five months. They came down to a final negotiating session at Blaine House, the governor's mansion, where Governor King had given space for the talks. Wommack was now going provision by provision through a twenty-seven-page draft document called the "Compact for Maine's Forests."

"Remember," Wommack told the group, "we have to agree on everything, or we have nothing."

So he went, in agonizing fashion, point by point, until the environmentalists—Maine Audubon, the Natural Resources Council of Maine—began to balk. The agreement was not easy to swallow. The maximum clear-cut size, for example, was reduced to 75 acres from 125, but most clear-cuts were much smaller anyway.

An aide to Governor King motioned Wommack to the side and asked whether, if the governor offered to establish ecological preserves on state lands, that would bring the environmentalists along.

Wommack saw this as a concession out of heaven. The Natural Resources Council of Maine and Maine Audubon embraced the change. They had wanted such preserves since the issuance of the 1993 state report recommending them. The provision was modest—a set-aside of a paltry 10,000 acres of existing public forest as Ecological Forest Reserves. But it tipped the balance in the talks. The environmental groups supported the compromise, and the paper companies grudgingly agreed to go along.

In the end, voters rejected the compact—twice. But joint lobbying for the measure by forest companies and environmentalists eventually led to the legislature's passing in 2000 a modest bill to authorize the state to designate up to 15 percent of Maine's public lands as ecological reserves. More important, Wommack's engagement with the people who influence the Conservancy's work strengthened the Conservancy's bonds across the center of the political spectrum.

THE $35 MILLION STORY

That engagement soon paid big dividends. In 1998, New England timber manager Wagner Woodlands phoned to suggest a bidding partnership. International Paper was auctioning 185,000 acres of woodland along the upper St. John River, the biggest, wildest whitewater river draining the forests along the border next to Quebec. Did the Conservancy want to join the bid?

The St. John was one of Maine's storied waterways, a wild whitewater stream prized by canoe paddlers and fishermen, a watershed saved from earth movers and cement mixers during a battle to build a huge dam in the 1970s. The riverbank was habitat of one of Maine's rare plants, the Furbish Lousewort. The river corridor had been nominated just the year before by Wommack and his staff as a project for the Conservancy's national capital campaign. The goal: protect a thousand-foot set-back for twenty to thirty miles along the river.

The ramifications of the Wagner overture were far-reaching. For the first time, the Conservancy had the ability to engage timber managers as partners in Conservancy goals. Moreover, the Conservancy had long wanted to bid alongside corporate giants as they bought and sold big blocks of Maine forest. So Wommack eagerly brought the Wagner proposal to the board. Wagner, in outline, proposed to bid for the entire acreage—valued between $35 million and $45 million—and then resell the riverfront later to the Conservancy, if and when the Conservancy could raise the money.

Wommack thought the deal bold and big. It would cost about $3 million, more than half the money brought in during the last capital campaign. But he was startled by the comment of one trustee, who asked why the Conservancy didn't buy the whole thing itself.

Wommack was taken aback. The Conservancy couldn't possibly do that, he answered. It would cost twice as much as anyone in the Conservancy has ever spent on a piece of land!

The Maine board agreed: Go through with the partnering deal. In the final package, a nonbinding handshake deal, the Conservancy agreed to pay $3 million to protect the river corridor and Wagner would put in $32 million for the timber. That was far short of the $18 million the Conservancy had spent on New Mexico's Gray Ranch in 1989, but the $3 million sum was still enormous, the best the Conservancy felt it could do. Wagner bid $35.1 million on behalf of itself and the Conservancy.

Wommack would have liked to bid for more land. Since the 1980s, the corporate titans of the Maine woods had been selling millions of acres of woodland. Each sale ignited a cycle of panic, as conservationists searched futilely for a way to buy a chunk of the land in play. In June 1998, South Africa Pulp and Paper, or Sappi, put 905,000 acres on the auction block. Then Bowater put up 1.6 million acres. Among the lands were the largest unbroken tract of frontage along giant Moosehead Lake, twenty miles of shoreline on Flagstaff Lake, and popular stretches of the Appalachian Trail. But no conservation group could make an offer to even begin to compete with the big companies. The sales frustrated conservationists no end.

By the time the St. John deal materialized, Wommack had rethought the money issue. In March 1998, he had hired fundraising firm Community Counseling Service to test a daring fundraising goal: $20 million. After interviewing about one hundred top donor prospects, CCS received gift "indications" of only $3 million to $4 million. CCS figured donors give about three times what they indicate, so Wommack was well shy of his target. Worse, CCS rated fundraising "leadership" as low. Interviews revealed that few major donors, even trustees, cared for the idea of leading a campaign.

Wommack pressed CCS to look again. In response, CCS reported that, in a stretch, Wommack could count on perhaps $20 million. But raising such a sum would demand finding new donors, strengthening leadership, running a disciplined campaign, and fine-tuning the fundraising approach. The toughest part: increasing giving by the trustees. The trustees had to think about much bigger gifts. They had to think about helping to lead the effort. In the hands of the trustees rested Wommack's ability to move Maine to reap much greater conservation victories.

Wommack was not to be deterred by CCS's assessment. He had talked with wealthy donors himself and knew some with a keen interest in the North Woods. With confidence in his resolve, the board approved the $20 million goal. In an unusual move, it also approved hiring CCS, in particular CCS's Tina Mattingly, to work with the Conservancy full time in its Brunswick headquarters. The price tag for CCS's services—nearly $300,000 per year.

Disappointing news hit just one week later, in mid-September. The Wagner bid on the St. John was the lowest of three. Wommack faced a familiar story. The corporate behemoths went home with all the marbles;

the conservationists departed with none. The Wagner/Conservancy bid wasn't even close. The winning bid, $41.5 million, was $6 million more.

Two months later, Wommack received a call from Wagner Woodlands, and the deal situation had turned upside down. The high bidder couldn't get funding. The second-highest bidder, offering $40 million, dropped out because it bought land elsewhere. But International Paper was willing to sell for $35.1 million, so long as it could close by December 31.

That was the good news. The bad news was that Wagner was out of the deal. It had spent its cash on other land. Wommack rushed into Mattingly's office. He wasn't sure this was bad news at all. What about a new $35 million goal to buy all of the St. John property? he asked her.

Mattingly was crestfallen. Wommack was sure that the scale of the project would motivate people to open their wallets, but she thought she'd never get out of Brunswick if she had to help him raise that kind of money. The dollars just didn't appear to be there. On the other hand, she knew that donors were itching to get in on saving the North Woods. During her earlier interviews, donors repeatedly pointed to the expanses of Maine forests and asked why, given the Sappi sales, the Conservancy wasn't buying some of the land itself.

Swept up by Wommack's daring proposal, Mattingly relented. But she warned Wommack that he had to run the campaign absolutely perfectly—ask for extraordinary gifts; hold the line and accept nothing less than the biggest gifts early on; ask people to raise their sights because the Conservancy needs more. She told him she would be right there with him, but he had to be aggressive. He had to ask for what he needed and expect it.

Mattingly knew this was not a fundraising approach Wommack or the Conservancy was used to, the assertiveness, the directness, and early on she had little confidence they could succeed. The whole notion was a big gamble—a gamble twice the size of the Gray Ranch, as a matter of fact.

Wommack talked the idea over with board members Wishcamper and Milliken. "How can we possibly do this?" Wommack and Milliken asked themselves at first.

And then they answered: "How can we not? We've got to try."

Wommack flew to Washington to talk with Conservancy president John Sawhill, who along with the national board would have to approve a loan to execute the deal by the end of the year. Sawhill was intrigued but cautious, given that the Gray Ranch, at half the price, had been hard to pay back. He asked Wommack how much capital Maine had raised in its last fundraising campaign.

"Five million dollars in five years," said Wommack.

Borrowing $35 million, Sawhill pointed out, would cost the Maine chapter $5 million in interest alone in two years.

Wommack persisted. He said that if Sawhill asked the board to give Maine the loan, Maine would have $10 million pledged to the project in six weeks.

Sawhill was sold. If you can do that, he told Wommack, I'll back it.

Wommack returned to Maine exhilarated and anxious. He had made the bet of a lifetime. When he brought the deal on November 18 to his executive committee, however, his enthusiasm was infectious. The trustees agreed and cleared it unanimously. When he brought it to the full board, in a November 24 conference call, they approved it unanimously. Of course, they had no fiduciary duty, but they knew the deal was right for Maine.

As Milliken later said of the board's decision: "It was as if we all held hands and jumped off the cliff together."

PLAYING TO THEIR HEARTS

Ten million dollars in six weeks. This was suddenly Wommack's and the board's joint challenge. Little did Wommack know that he had set in motion the winning move he had long pursued: the full engagement of the board. For the time being, though, he knew only that he had to come up with $10 million. He wasn't starting from scratch. By November 24, he had rounded up indications of $8 million from donors he talked to earlier. Now he had to actually secure the pledges, and to do that, he knew he had to follow Mattingly's advice: *Do everything perfectly. Run a "textbook" campaign!*

Mattingly had told him to get "leadership" gifts first—and only leadership gifts. So alone, he went to Leon and Lisa Gorman, the chairman of L.L. Bean and his wife. He asked for $1 million as the campaign's first pledge. They gave. He then asked Leon Gorman to go with him to see the Wishcampers. They asked the Wishcampers for $500,000. They gave. He asked Joe Wishcamper to go with him to see Roger and Margot Milliken. They asked for $500,000. And they gave.

Wommack toed Mattingly's line. His confidence grew. Still, he lay awake nights worrying. The conversations with donors were emotionally wrenching. These were people he knew well, friends, people he respected, and he was asking for sums that shocked the senses—ten times what these people had ever given in the past. The last thing he ever imagined was that hitting people up for so much money would be his much-sought-after means of engaging them. He was mostly worried about alienating them.

Wommack swallowed his anxiety and pressed ahead. Mattingly had warned him that he had to ask for and secure big sums if he was going to deliver $10 million. He invited to the office one donor who had given $1,000 per year for many years, and who had recently given $100,000. He didn't know the man's net worth, although he knew he had a soft spot for the North Woods. Wommack started to tell the story of the St. John project.

The prospect interrupted, saying he thought the project was great. "I'll give you $100,000," he said.

"That's so wonderful," Wommack replied, in effect. "We appreciate it so much. But let me finish describing the whole plan."

At the end of the pitch, the man allowed that the St. John plan was incredible. "I'm going to raise that pledge to $250,000."

Wommack thanked the man warmly and said that as soon as Maine entered the phase of the campaign in which it could take gifts of that level, he would come back and the man's gift would be the very first. With a sense of anguish, Wommack explained that he could only accept gifts of $500,000 or over if he was to raise the $10 million needed by December to secure a loan from the Conservancy's revolving loan fund.

Wommack left the meeting reeling. He had turned down a quarter-of-a-million-dollar gift, $50,000 more than the largest donation ever given by a living person in a previous campaign. Was he nuts?

Two days later, the man called the office and left a voice message: He wanted to pledge $500,000.

So Wommack learned he could hold the line in asking for extraordinary gifts. When people thought about it, when they looked at the list of other top donors, they raised their sights.

Still, doubt reverberated in his head. Mattingly, after reviewing one prospect, told Wommack he should ask for $1 million. Wommack's eyes widened, and he paused. He said what he would like to do is ask for a $1 million loan, a loan at no interest, maybe part would be a gift and part a loan with no interest, maybe down the road they could convert the loan to a gift.

Mattingly listened to him parry. She was unsure she should press him. She took the news back to her office and phoned her boss, William Hanrahan, CEO of CCS.

Absolutely not, Hanrahan told her. Wommack had to go out and ask for a cash gift of $1 million pledged to pay over five years. If Mattingly and Wommack gave in now to that kind of thinking, the campaign would be dead in the water.

Wommack, ever the good soldier, complied with the orders. And a funny thing happened over and over. Not only did people say yes, they thanked him, again and again. They thanked him for the opportunity to give, for the chance to be a part of something big. Brimming with gratitude, the trustees and donors awakened Wommack to what Mattingly had told him all along: *People give to be a part of something they care about in their hearts. They give big to realize their own visions of a better world.*

The vision of a protected St. John River, an icon of Maine heritage, took hold in the trustees' and donors' minds. They gave "sacrificial" gifts, as Mattingly called them, to be a part of that vision. And if the vision wasn't already big enough, one of the trustees enlarged it before Wommack even secured the $10 million. He shocked Wommack and the rest of the trustees by saying the Conservancy's goal should not stop at just 40 miles of river. It should expand to embrace the protection of the entire 120-mile river corridor.

This bigger thinking fit in well with a strategy Wommack, Milliken, and others had talked about for more than a year. Once they acquired pieces of ecologically unremarkable forest land, they could trade them. If we raise the entire $35.1 million, the trustees' thinking now went, we can keep all the land and trade unwanted parcels with other landowners to get additional pieces along the river.

With this buoyant thinking shaking the trustees from any timidity in their ambitions, Wommack rode his infectious confidence and optimism to hit his goal. He gained pledges of $10.2 million—just enough and just in time to make good on his promise to Sawhill. The national board then lent Maine an improbable $35 million.

Wommack crossed into 1999 learning one of the most important lessons of his business life. He had excited his board. He had inspired donors. He had earned press from not just state papers but from the *New York Times* and National Public Radio. He realized that engaging the board was a matter of asking them to join in fulfilling some of their deepest dreams. This was the message he could never have understood back in 1992, when a disaffected board said "you" instead of an engaged board saying "we."

IMPROBABLE VISION

Wommack would soon test the level of that engagement. In February, he sought to recruit the leadership for the rest of the campaign. He asked Carol Wishcamper to act as co-chair. She and Wommack then recruited Roger Milliken as the other co-chair. Both readily accepted. They were touched by the scale and spirit of the work. They realized this was a once-in-a-lifetime chance to make a contribution of huge significance. Wommack, a man who could unleash a deeper passion and will to action in others, then handed them the reins, and they ran the campaign.

This was an engaged board. In the first year, Wishcamper and Milliken asked Leon and Lisa Gorman to chair the drive for additional leadership gifts. By June 1999, the fund total rose to $20 million. In the next phase, they expanded work to accept gifts of $50,000 or more. Milliken tapped corporate donors, Wishcamper, individuals. By March 2000, they had raised $43 million.

In 2000, they publicly announced the "For Maine Forever" campaign, a $50 million fundraising drive—$35 million for the St. John and $15 million for the rest of Maine. With the help of events like a Bangor barn party—which raised $60,000—they guided the chapter to finish the campaign in early 2001. They had raised $57 million, ten times the money of the previous campaign in less than half the time.

As Wommack reminded the board, they had to make the project belong to everyone in Maine. And indeed they did. Donors came to include people who gave because they had broader and different visions: visions of self-determination—protecting Maine forests from global financial titans; of wilderness preservation—protecting a way of life for hunting, canoeing, and guiding; of healthy North Woods towns—saving timberlands from development to feed the mills that underpin jobs; and of outdoor recreation—protecting rivers for paddling, wild land for snowmobiling, woodlands for hunting, shores for public swimming.

The St. John project transformed Wommack's thinking. He could engage the board with a visionary challenge. And he could engage other constituencies with grander and broader visions aligned with the Conservancy's. Engagement was a matter of appealing to his constituencies' desire to fulfill their commitment to their nearest and dearest cares, and then giving them the ability to contribute. Everyone wants to leave a legacy.

To everyone's surprise, the lesson of engagement extended yet further. Wommack would learn just how much further soon after the close of the For Maine Forever campaign. For many years, environmental groups had coveted a tract of property encompassing the Debsconeag Lakes, a wild forest northwest of Millinocket, Maine. But these groups' efforts to talk with the owner, Great Northern Paper, had dragged on with no clear progress. The groups asked the Conservancy to give a try.

William Ginn, a Conservancy forestland dealmaker, learned in the spring of 2002 that the company couldn't sell even if it wanted to. The property was mortgaged to John Hancock Life Insurance Company for $50 million, and selling would trigger huge mortgage-prepayment penalties.

As it turned out, paper markets were in the pits, however, and Great Northern was unable to make payments on its note. Hancock was eager to get rid of the problem loan. So Ginn proposed the Conservancy buy the note from Hancock and thereby control the note provisions. The Conservancy could then swap a portion of the note for land and refinance the balance.

For the second time in five years, Wommack and his staff were poised to propose a precedent-setting deal—embracing the financial needs of a paper company, and helping that company's executives keep Great Northern's mills open and employees in jobs. Wommack's track record, and his leadership of the Maine chapter, opened the door to Great Northern's executive suite in June 2002. This was not an easy meeting. As the talks began, CEO Lambert Bédard of Great Northern folded his arms and declared: "So tell me, why should I trust you tree huggers?"

Wommack's heart sank.

But not for long. He discovered the chief financial officer had once worked with and admired his father at Mead Paper Company. That age-old relationship thawed the atmosphere considerably. Ginn then laid out the proposal. It essentially had three parts: John Hancock would sell the $50 million note to the Conservancy. The Conservancy would retire $14 million of the debt, and cut the 9 percent interest rate on the balance to 4 percent. Great Northern would cede the 40,000-acre Debsconeag Lakes wilderness tract to the Conservancy as well as put a conservation easement on a 200,000-acre woodland just south of Mt. Katahdin.

The deal, though appealing to the executives, wouldn't fly. Great Northern's most pressing need was for $4 million in cash right away to fight off a cash-flow squeeze. Ginn and Wommack huddled and then sweetened the deal: The Conservancy would arrange to advance Great Northern a $4 million option payment right away. The sweetened offer was a winner. On August 23, the company and the Conservancy signed the deal.

Two months later, Milliken talked to a crowd at the Conservancy's annual meeting in Minneapolis. He revealed the depth of the Maine board's engagement in the organization's affairs. "Our collective commitment to the organization's mission and to each other took a quantum leap" with the St. John, he said. "The joy was infectious"—for the board and for the people of Maine.

Now with this new deal, he added, the Conservancy would "address the relationship challenges" of working with paper mill managers and local people whose first instinct is not to trust conservationists. "But these are the new stakeholders who are part and parcel of [our] larger vision," he said.

In a turn of events nobody could have predicted, Wommack and the Maine chapter engaged a constituency long considered by other environmental groups as their nemesis. In a roundabout way, they empowered forest executives to contribute to the broader conservation vision for Maine. This was a crowning achievement in Wommack's tenure as state director in Maine. The power of engagement—of the staff, of the public, of the board, of even corporate executives—yielded unparalleled results. The thought of going it alone to conserve the best of Maine's biodiversity was now only a distant memory.

7

MORE THAN THE SUM OF ITS PARTS: Teaching the Organization to Work as One

WHEN JOHN SAWHILL TOOK OVER as president of the Nature Conservancy in 1990, he had much in mind an axiom often recited by management guru Peter Drucker: "Whom the gods would destroy, they first give forty years of success." The Conservancy, born when fifty people voted to adopt the name in September 1950, had chalked up numbers that rang the bell of success: 533,000 members, operations in forty-seven states and eleven countries, annual gifts of $110 million, land protected from destruction in the United States alone: 3.5 million acres.

But the Conservancy was in its fortieth year, and Sawhill saw that the gods had reason to be rubbing their hands with anticipation.

The preceding year, the blue-chip consulting firm McKinsey & Co. had issued a critical report based on interviews with fifty Conservancy staff members. The conclusions: Fundraising was bogged down, staff in state offices thirsted for guidance, administrative systems strained at capacity, and headquarters and regional offices were top-heavy, manned with roughly one person for every two in the field. When it came to vision, management style, fundraising, and accounting, the Conservancy—as rated by McKinsey with *Consumer Reports*-style icons—needed "major improvement."

Sawhill was the board's choice as fix-it man. His predecessor, Frank Boren, had run with his instinct to decentralize and force authority to the field. He had nurtured an egalitarian air and sense of "family." The Conservancy had grown rapidly, and many on the staff loved Boren for his style. But the family had gotten much bigger and more contentious. And the board worried that the organization was becoming fragmented. So the governors sought an outsider—and only an outsider—who could tighten administration and raise lots of money. Sawhill was the man tapped to rework support systems, build unity, and spur further growth.

To many board members, the problems Sawhill faced surfaced at home. In Oklahoma, Joseph Williams, chairman of Williams Companies and the volunteer leader behind efforts to save two ranches blanketed with tall-grass prairie, chafed at the poor service from headquarters. When the state office had a question about buried contaminants, it took six weeks to get an answer instead of days. When it wanted financial reports, it got them two to three months after the events, well after the numbers were needed for decision making.

McKinsey's interviews detailed the mess: "The financial and accounting systems are a nightmare because they are antiquated and backlogged," said one employee quoted by the consultants. "How can they expect us to plan and manage if we don't get timely reports?" asked another. "I had a check lost for two months. . . . It was sitting on someone's desk," complained a third. Conservancy headquarters should offer more leadership, pursue projects that cut across state borders, improve the field's effectiveness, and capture efficiencies, McKinsey maintained.

Sawhill, fresh from McKinsey himself, shocked the staff. Many could hardly believe the board had hired someone from Corporate America. Sawhill, a generation older than most Conservancy managers, had run McKinsey & Co.'s energy practice for ten years, where his patron saint was Marvin Bower, McKinsey's eighty-seven-year-old patriarch, often called the father of modern management consulting. Bower championed professional management, rigorous systems, and standardized practices.

He favored long-term thinking and eschewed "ad hoc management," that is, making things up one crisis at a time—as in growing organizations like the Conservancy.

Under Bower, McKinsey became known for settling for nothing but the best, challenging the client's opinion, finding the root problem by interviewing everyone, understanding the unique clockwork in each firm, and not leaving the office until the job was done—no matter what the hour. People claimed that more veterans of McKinsey went on to become CEOs than veterans from any other firm save General Electric.

At McKinsey, Sawhill kept a six-day-a-week schedule. His secretary, Ann Fouke, handed him a stack of mail, money, and a plane ticket each Saturday. She heard from him again, by phone, on Monday. He called before boarding the plane, after deplaning, and before and after his meeting. If she had phone messages, he would sometimes memorize two or three numbers, make the calls, and because he almost never had a pencil at hand, write the numbers down when he called again later. If she had urgent letters, she read them and he dictated an answer.

Sawhill allowed neither himself nor his people breathers. One McKinsey colleague, Les Silverman, often worked nights and weekends to prepare presentations. After a long day working with a client, the two would breathe a sigh of relief as they descended on the elevator. But by the time they got in a cab, Sawhill would invariably remark they were already behind for the next week's meeting. "Give me a break!" Silverman would think. But he came to respect Sawhill's habit, always thinking about the next hurdle, not patting himself or anyone else on the back.

Silverman marveled at how Sawhill seemed fearless in making commitments to win over clients. Talking with the chief of refining at one major oil company in the 1980s, Sawhill claimed that McKinsey had useful insights on refining. Sawhill himself had no idea what those insights might be, but he seemed to figure someone at McKinsey always knew something about anything. Once they left the office, he told Silverman to call a few people. "Give me something smart to say," he said, as he always did at such times. He was a quick study, and on the way to a client's office later on, he would read a report, digest the nuggets, and in minutes glibly deliver insights with a personalized flair.

Sawhill arrived at the Nature Conservancy at fifty-three, a trim man, a former wrestler at Princeton, with a swath of dark hair combed across his forehead. He always wore a suit and tie and dedicated every lunch to business. Nobody on the staff could tell if he cared about conservation—he had earlier taught economics at New York University, had bailed the university out of red ink as its president from 1975 to 1979, and served as deputy secretary of the Department of Energy under Jimmy Carter. But they knew he had a glittering track record in management. At McKinsey, he had boosted energy-unit revenues by 30 percent a year, year in and year out, and his success earned him a seven-figure salary.

At his first Conservancy board meeting, on March 3, 1990—three weeks before he began work—Sawhill was already hot on the Conservancy's case. Instead of general comments, he specified six priorities: "sharpen the Conservancy's mission; launch the capital campaign already on the drawing board; increase public awareness of the Conservancy; improve management systems; build the international program; and build strong links between state chapters and headquarters."

The governors liked what they heard so early on. Sawhill knew what it took to corral willy-nilly growth and restore order and unity to an organization. When it came time to discuss whether to amend the bylaws to name him, as president, to the board, the governors readily agreed—the first time in Conservancy history the professional president was made part of the Conservancy's governing body. The board viewed Sawhill as the epitome of the professional manager.

A TIGHT GRIP

Sawhill concluded the Conservancy amounted to less than the sum of its parts. State directors set priorities and ran their own fiefdoms. They raised money in, and for, their own states. The president mattered little—he ran a distant confederation. Only rarely did the states help each other, and their franchise-like autonomy, Sawhill believed, undercut the organization's strength. The Conservancy could do much more as an integrated organization, he felt, where everyone cared about the whole and worked to multiply, not just add together, the efforts of the parts.

Sawhill borrowed from Marvin Bower's playbook. Bower had built McKinsey on the concept of "one firm." Opening offices around the globe, he embedded a common set of principles and services everywhere. No matter where you went in McKinsey, everything from the stationery to the systems bore the McKinsey stamp. So at the Conservancy, Sawhill launched the "One Conservancy" concept. He even changed the name of the staff newsletter to *The One Conservancy* from *On the Land.*

When it came to fixing the organization, Sawhill took his cue from McKinsey's hallowed "7-S framework" of management, made famous in Tom Peters and Robert Waterman's 1982 book, *In Search of Excellence.* The framework, drawn in a hexagon with circles on each corner, featured six factors of success, one in each circle: strategy, structure, systems, style, staff, and skills. In the center of the hexagon was the seventh: shared values. Sawhill set out to address each factor.

As for systems, he hired a colleague from McKinsey, Niels Crone, and named him chief financial officer. Crone, the Conservancy's first CFO, found that state staff had plenty to complain about. As in Oklahoma, state staffs everywhere received budget reports too late to use variance data to correct mistakes. They endured repeated visits by creditors who showed up at their doors to dun them for bills—because headquarters hadn't paid. They put up with balky computer systems and erratic connections to headquarters. Given the poor service, state offices accorded the finance department zero credibility. Sawhill gave Crone a mandate to get the systems house back in order.

As for strategy, Sawhill brought in another colleague from McKinsey, Michael Coda, and named two scientists, one fundraiser, and one dealmaker to join Coda in drafting a strategic plan. Coda's team assembled advisory panels of state directors and chapter trustees to solicit advice. The team members interviewed seventy-five people, outsiders included, to come up with a consensus vision, mission, and set of initiatives. In September 1990, after sorting through hundreds of comments on a draft plan, they printed a final document with Sawhill's blessing. Among the top strategies: focus work on seventy-five bioreserves, or "functioning ecosystems," channel money to the most biologically diverse spots, and maintain the Heritage program while building science capability to serve bioreserve conservation.

As for staff, Sawhill reshuffled the management team, sidelining or firing some people, hiring others, promoting still others. He tangled early with veterans of former regimes, like David Morine, who'd been legendary as a dealmaker since the early 1970s. Morine loathed the McKinsey corporate style, and he clashed with Sawhill. When Morine argued to scuttle the deal to buy the 500-square-mile Gray Ranch in New Mexico, he crossed Sawhill for the last time. Morine considered Gray overpriced, not very significant biologically, and likely to be hard and costly to manage. He also resented that Sawhill would spend so much Conservancy money from the Land Preservation Fund that could be spent on more significant projects. Board chairman Clifford Messinger called Morine about the disagreement and advised him to resign if he differed, and Morine promptly quit.

Along with changes in staff, Sawhill started to remake the board. A shameless name-dropper, he recruited more celebrities and more corporate executives, figuring the latter controlled huge pots of money and tracts of land the Conservancy wanted. Onto the board came Samuel Johnson, chairman of S.C. Johnson & Son, and General Norman Schwarzkopf, newly retired and fresh from the fame of Operation Desert Storm in Iraq. Sawhill ended the long-standing practice of including two dozen or more staff at board meetings. (In one 1987 meeting in Snowbird, Utah, more staff than governors attended.) Sawhill now became the chief staff-board go-between.

Many staff and trustees didn't like the way Sawhill centralized control. Miffed by his unilateral decisions, they would react sharply to even hints of command-and-control incursions onto their turf. One chart in the new strategic plan showed, by region, the percentage of globally rare species left unprotected by bioreserve plans. In the East, the percentage was 58 percent; in the West, 91. Since the plan called for channeling cash to the most diverse spots, state offices assumed Sawhill would pour Eastern money into the West. This infuriated at least one eastern state director, who exhorted Coda never to publish such a chart again.

But the plan's logic was unassailable. "In fiscal year 1990," it read, "the Conservancy devoted 26 percent of acquisition funds to projects with less ecological significance." To direct money to saving the rarest plants and animals, it urged moving money from one state to another. "The President should review the current formulas for the allocation of dues and funds. . . . Wealthy programs should be encouraged to generate resources for other areas."

Sawhill defied the sovereignty of the Conservancy's state fiefdoms and expected levels of discipline, performance, and deference to the boss that people were unaccustomed to. Just weeks after taking over, he ordered John Cook, vice president of resources, to move to Gray Ranch to recover the capital outlay, secure adequate land protection, and assure the ranch stayed in private hands, a key concern of governor Williams. Cook, a nine-year veteran, had never been ordered around in that fashion before. Some people, Cook among them, adjusted; others didn't.

During the drafting of the mission for the new strategic plan, Robert Jenkins insisted "biodiversity" go in the wording. Jenkins argued the Conservancy should adopt the new catchphrase of the global movement, a movement the Conservancy had invented. Sawhill and other top managers wanted plainer language: "To preserve plants, animals, and natural communities that represent the diversity of life on Earth by protecting the lands and water they need to survive." A battle over the language ensued. Sawhill finally told the keeper of the mission for twenty years that the conversation was over. Jenkins stormed out.

Sawhill dressed down people with whom he differed. Gone was the laid-back, family style of Boren. Sawhill was appalled by the lack of professionalism of his staff. He felt they dressed sloppily and did sloppy work—and they left the office early. He wanted to hold people to high, if not McKinsey-like, standards of service, skill, and behavior. He held himself to the highest of all. He worked 8 A.M. to at least 6 P.M., often six days a week. He traveled constantly, in his first year visiting most state and country programs. He demanded phones be answered within two rings, and never by voice mail. He surprised staff by answering most memos in a day or two. When staff prepared talks for the board, he dissected them, allowing nothing amateurish, requiring endless iterations.

People would carp to Sawhill's assistant, Ann Fouke, who moved from McKinsey and ran his schedule and handled many personal details: "But Ann, he doesn't understand. This is how we've always done it!"

But Sawhill was out to change the way people had always done it. He had no plan to throw out the good with the bad, however. In 1992, he asked Bruce Runnels, a regional director from the Conservancy's Boston

office, to address another of the McKinsey S's, shared values. He asked
Runnels, who had practiced law for ten years in Indiana before coming
to the Conservancy, to lead a team to codify those values.

Many people thought the values work hokey. But Runnels was taken
with the idea and came up with a list everyone believed in: integrity beyond reproach, continuity of purpose, effective partnerships, innovation
and excellence, commitment to people, commitment to the future, and
One Conservancy. For the first time, the Conservancy had written down
one of the core elements of its culture. Sawhill believed strongly that a far-
flung organization needed a closely held set of values to bind it together.

As Sawhill worked on recasting the organization, he focused just as
much on what he believed was his top job in building the institution:
fundraising. The capital campaign on the drawing board was well conceived: a $310 million drive to save bioreserves. But the plan so far was
just on paper. He needed to launch it, and soon. Cash raised at the Conservancy had flattened or slid since 1988, hanging in at a bit over $80 mil-
lion. Headcount had meanwhile grown 33 percent.

Sawhill needed some big, flashy flagship projects to excite donors. The
Tall Grass Prairie project in Oklahoma and the Gray Ranch in New
Mexico, the first for $15 million, the second $19 million, fit the bill. Both
formed the core of bioreserves and the landscape-scale work championed
by Gregory Low. The combination gave Sawhill something he was very
much looking for: a big campaign concept (the bioreserve) and big flagship examples (Gray and Tall Grass). Together they formed a big idea that
would capture the imagination of staff, trustees, and donors.

The fundraising drive, called the Campaign for the Last Great Places,
appealed to Sawhill for another reason. It was a means to pull the Conservancy together. Neither the Oklahoma nor New Mexico state offices
could possibly pay for the Tall Grass or Gray projects on their own. They
needed "One Conservancy" to pitch in. Moreover, all state and country
offices had to submit bioreserve ideas and plans for approval—that is, they
had to run Low's gauntlet. Otherwise, they couldn't get funding under
the campaign.

Sawhill kicked off the "quiet phase" of the Last Great Places program
on May 14, 1991. Late in 1990, the board had approved 75 of 147 sites
proposed, including projects in North America, South America, and the

Pacific Rim. Under the Last Great Places banner came not only the Gray Ranch and Tall Grass Prairie, but the Delaware Bay Shore and Mississippi Flood Plain, the San Pedro River in Arizona, and the Yucatan Peninsula in Guatemala.

After the Conservancy raised more than $150 million, it announced the fundraising campaign publicly. The whole event showcased the new Conservancy under John Sawhill, reflecting big names, big projects, and big ambitions. Although the public mantle rested uneasily on Sawhill's shoulders—and he never relished the limelight like a celebrity CEO—on March 11, 1993, the Conservancy held a giant press event. Schwarzkopf acted as pitchman, just seventeen months after the end of the Gulf War. CBS, CNN, ABC, and TBS broadcast the talk. Schwarzkopf appeared on ABC's *Good Morning America* and *CBS This Morning.* The next day, Sawhill, chairman Williams, and campaign chairman Daniel Davison hosted lunch for big donors at the U.S. Capitol, where author Terry Tempest Williams read about Utah's Moab Slough. The event signaled the new strength of a new kind of professional organization.

Ironically, as Sawhill put the Conservancy on a footing where he broke bread with America's wealthiest people and attended meetings with President Bill Clinton and Environmental Protection Agency chief Carol Browner, disgruntled voices within the staff began to reach the board. Past board chairman Richard Weinstein and new chairman Williams fielded complaints about the brusque and controlling Sawhill.

"My god, this whole place is going to end up looking like a McKinsey company!" Williams would hear. "That's not what we're all about!"

Sawhill's changes had been extraordinary in scope: systems, strategy, style, structure, staff—he was reworking them all, moving from one to the next as fast as the organization could handle it. Many people at the Conservancy felt like they were being punched into shape by a corporate zealot, not guided along the path by a mission-driven environmental advocate. Sawhill acted as if he was making over the Conservancy into an industrial machine.

The truth was Sawhill put entrepreneurial managers on a short leash. He distanced top managers from staff by moving them to the 9th floor—dubbed "Cloud Nine." He shut down the male-dominated backslapping camaraderie of the past and showed hallowed veterans to the door. Jenkins, furious over differences with Sawhill on how to run the Heritage program, and whether to spin it off into a sister organization, fought his last battle with Sawhill. Riling his boss by telling him he didn't know a bit about science, Jenkins left in a rage—while stoking the story that Sawhill worked for the Conservancy only as a stepping stone to a presidential Cabinet post.

Through it all, Sawhill found himself crosswise with the two most powerful board members. In November 1993, Williams and Weinstein asked to talk with Sawhill alone for an entire day.

Williams told Sawhill that there was a common impression that he was centralizing the Conservancy the way McKinsey would if it helped a very loosely knit organization that had serious administrative problems. The easy solution, Williams said, was to tighten it up, get better control of the organization with stricter rules from on high. But the strength of the Conservancy, he stressed, had always been in the state organizations.

Weinstein and Williams wanted to bridle Sawhill—to restrain his drive for centralization. They also wanted him to rub shoulders more with people. The two governors recognized the good of Sawhill's work, the fruits of professional management, the benefits of centralizing units that were spinning out of control. But they felt he had gone too far. Sawhill, who didn't contest the board members' criticism, except to correct facts, was simply unaware that his manner and his methods were starting to hurt conservation.

In the same way Sawhill had been calling on the traditionalists to change, Williams and Weinstein wanted Sawhill to change. He had given the Conservancy strong medicine to great benefit, but the organization's effectiveness was starting to waver from side effects. Some trustees were angry. The two men wanted Sawhill to reformulate his approach to bring more balance to his hard-hitting, controlling manner.

BETTER BALANCE

The word got around to all the senior staff about Sawhill's meeting with Williams and Weinstein. Sawhill had been "taken to the woodshed," people said. The advocates of decentralization and the status quo felt redeemed. Overnight, three years after Sawhill had started, his mandate eroded. In effect, this was the end of his tenure as an outsider chief executive. He lost his authority for sweeping change, and would forever after work more as an insider instigating change at a more measured pace.

Williams and Weinstein respected Sawhill as much as ever. They simply believed he should recognize state directors as the principal conservationists, and better recognize state trustees as Conservancy ambassadors and fundraisers. Instead of sucking power and authority and prestige from the states, he should create a federal system, where the states took the lead in executing the mission.

Williams asked Sawhill, for example, to be sure at least half of the board came from the ranks of current or former state trustees. He also asked him to make sure at least 20 percent of the board consisted of distinguished scientists. The trustees knew what was going on in the field. The scientists assured that the Conservancy distinguished itself with science-based decision making.

For Sawhill, this was a midcourse correction. He was chastened. He recognized that the question was not whether he should centralize or decentralize, but rather when and where. When should the center exercise control, and when should the states? This question had arisen right from the start in 1990, and he was always trying to find the right balance. The board simply thought he was getting it wrong.

Many people wondered whether Sawhill could adjust. In some people's minds, he was too much of a micromanager. So particular was he that he would order the staff to change the color of napkins at board dinners. But already at the next board meeting, in December 1993, he reported to the governors about his quick work to strengthen trustee relationships. He had convened a task force to better define chapter trustee roles and responsibilities. He had scheduled a board and staff retreat for March 1994. And he had established a chapter relations office. Although he had often met with state trustees, he was now courting them as a valued constituency.

Sawhill similarly began to reach out to staff. At headquarters, where he was known for his humorlessness, scant praise, and dislike for chitchat, he kept his door open—but nobody dared walk in. So he began a ritual of "management by walking around," a practice much talked about in management circles at the time. Stephanie Meeks, director of development, was on the phone one day when Sawhill appeared in her doorway on an early MBWA stroll. She panicked—she had never had a meeting with Sawhill except at *his* office. "My god," she thought, "what have I done that's so bad that he's come up here to see me?"

But as Sawhill began talking, she realized he just wanted to chat. The encounter was painful. Although Sawhill was a gifted networker—he kept a 3,000-name Rolodex file—he was not good at small talk, at least with subordinates. One awkward moment followed another in what Meeks knew was a response to Sawhill's talk with the board. She resolved, in the future, to always have something to talk about—a book, a movie—as a conversation starter with her boss.

Sawhill meanwhile started cutting the red tape states had bemoaned. In January 1994, he told the staff his New Year's resolution was to relieve the administrative burden and encourage entrepreneurship throughout the Conservancy. He charged William Weeks, his chief operating officer, to lead a task force titled "Excellence, Agility, and Growth." "I will be taking a look at some companies that have managed to grow and yet stay very decentralized and very entrepreneurial," Weeks told a reporter. And he would seek tips on operating philosophy and structure.

By spring 1994, the board was pleased with Sawhill's rapid work to get through what Williams was calling a "mine field." At Sawhill's annual performance review, Williams commended Sawhill and conveyed the board's total support. "It has not been easy for you, John," Williams said. "It has not been easy for many of the people who have had to abandon their old ways of doing things."

Behind the scenes, the board felt Sawhill's strength still needed a counterbalance. It voted a waiver on the two-year limit on board chairmanship so that Williams—the only board member to whom Sawhill clearly deferred—remained chairman for another two years.

Sawhill kept up with his efforts to change, although practices that didn't fit him, like MBWA, gradually died. He invited his management team to a retreat at his home on Blue Mountain Lake in the Adirondack Mountains of New York in the summer of 1994. He still hadn't secured the full trust of his staff. He was still dogged by speculation that his post at the Conservancy was a stepping stone. He asked an old friend, corporate psychologist David Goodrich, to help him out.

Although Sawhill and Goodrich saw eye to eye—Marvin Bower was an icon for both—Goodrich had a more congenial, almost fatherly demeanor. Sawhill asked Goodrich to help bring about a consensus on the meaning of "One Conservancy." Goodrich got the group talking, and recorded thoughts from each senior manager. California state director Steven McCormick said it meant maintaining "unity of purpose and application of techniques to pursue efficiency." Michael Dennis, general counsel, said "our belief in our central mission and each other and the free exchange of ideas" was crucial. William Weeks said the Conservancy was not a "confederation" but "one organization with an agreed-upon agenda."

Goodrich summarized. Everyone believed in partnership, innovation, and the scientific method to do their work. "Our belief in our central mission?" he asked. "Yes, everyone seemed to agree on that. In each other? That's not so clear. There's a fair amount of skepticism if not outright cynicism."

Sawhill had more work to solidify his credibility and strike the right balance between headquarters control and field-office freedom. One manager told Goodrich that the "One Conservancy" concept meant "we are to do whatever headquarters tells us." Goodrich raised the question of whether people believed in a free exchange of ideas. "There is some uneasiness about whether that was really so," he reported.

When Weeks later issued the report of the Excellence, Agility, and Growth task force, Sawhill adopted its recommendations for a new management philosophy. In an August 1 staff meeting, Sawhill said that staff at all levels should be guided by values and commitment to the Conservancy as a whole, rather than by administrative policies that stifle creativity. Empowerment, trust, and accountability, he explained, should be key elements of the managerial process. To signal how big a change this was, he reorganized top management.

He disbanded his management committee of department heads. He created two new committees, one for conservation, one for operations. Whereas the old group was a horizontal slice through the top of the hierarchy, the two new ones were vertical slices drawn from the top of the hierarchy to the bottom. In addition to these committees, Sawhill created a third, the management council, which comprised roughly 150 managers from all parts of the organization, which would meet once a year to review the work done by the other two.

Niels Crone, named to head the operations committee, drew a diagram he felt captured the way Sawhill was running the organization to balance centralized control and decentralized entrepreneurship. It was simply a box. On the top was mission. On one side was values. On the other side was policy. Crone said Conservancy managers were free to run things as they liked, so long as they worked within the bounds of a unified view of values, mission, and policy. Managers could freely exercise creativity and entrepreneurship in the space *inside* the box—which then produced strategy. Sawhill and other managers embraced the diagram, and used it over and over to give people latitude for action without bringing unnecessary risk to the organization.

SPURRING RENEWAL

With the balance of management better in hand, Sawhill moved to another issue. He and the board were bothered by not having a good understanding of the end game. If the Conservancy fulfilled its mission, Sawhill wanted to know, what would that achievement look like? How big would the job be? What would "One Conservancy" accomplish? Sawhill wanted to place before everyone's eyes a picture of ultimate success.

As if in a test of his organization, he handed this question to the Conservation Committee. He gave the group free rein to air and test new ideas. Starting in late 1994, they wrestled over this next frontier of Conservancy ambitions. In a memo giving the group its charge, Sawhill simply outlined the team's responsibilities—to develop objectives, test new approaches, establish new priorities, and develop new systems to measure performance. Sawhill then stood back and let the team do its work.

What the team started to come up with was both more—and less—than Sawhill anticipated. It was less because it didn't offer a numeric target for conservation. No acreage figure. No dollar figure. No figure at all that would define the ultimate goal of conservation. Up to that time, the Conservancy routinely relied on "bucks and acres"—dollars raised and acres acquired—to measure success. These traditional measures were a poor gauge of efficiently protecting species and natural communities. Despite working for two and a half decades with science as its guide, the Conservancy didn't use science to measure success.

But while the team failed to give him numerical goals, it offered much more than he anticipated in another respect. It described a brand new approach to painting the picture of success he wanted—mapping the United States by "ecoregion," each ecoregion to be defined by similar plants and animals, and then choosing within each a "portfolio" of sites representing the region's biological diversity. With the maps and list of sites, the Conservancy would have a vivid picture of the end game. The ecoregions would be zones like the Mid-Atlantic Coastal Plain or the flatlands neighboring and influenced by the Great Lakes.

After months of work, the team's "conservation agenda" outlining this new approach took shape in mid-1995. The emerging agenda opened some old wounds. Some people called it a stealth attack on the autonomy of state programs, as many ecoregions spanned states. Others didn't like change, period. And yet others resisted change because they disliked people on the team—this in spite of the committee having involved more than half of Conservancy staff in its work.

But the plan alleviated much anxiety, too. People in Maine, North Dakota, and other northern states had worried they would get short shrift. If the committee, in looking for diversity "hot spots," left out colder, less-diverse states, the northerners would lose money. But the verdict was otherwise. Led by scientist Kent Redford, the team adopted "representativeness" as a guiding principle. It decided the Conservancy should preserve all representative forms of life in each ecoregion. All states thus got representation, so nobody was left out. The concept was both biologically and politically ingenious.

Sawhill embraced the agenda. He liked the biological conclusions, to be sure. But what he liked even more was that ecoregions crossed state boundaries. If the organization was to conserve them, state directors would have to work together. The Great Lakes Ecoregion spanned eight states and one Canadian province. The new agenda would force the states to cooperate. It was a tool for both better conservation and for loosening the rigid, state-based autonomy that hindered the integration needed to establish "One Conservancy."

By the end of 1995, Sawhill had reason to feel good. He had two huge new achievements to his name. First, he presided over the development of a new scheme, formulated with the help of more than 50 percent of the Conservancy's staff, to deliver a picture of future Conservation success. This was not a crib of past work but a visionary design for the future.

Meantime, he closed the largest and most successful capital campaign ever. The final tally for the $300 million Last Great Places campaign soared to $315.4 million.

Everyone who knew Sawhill was sure of one thing: He could rally the institution to raise funds like never before. Sawhill had honed those skills years earlier at New York University, and now he secured the future of the Conservancy with the same. He believed that a nonprofit group should always be in the middle of a capital campaign, and he made sure to act on this belief, even though some of his staff couldn't believe he kept raising the bar.

No sooner had the Last Great Places campaign wound down, in the fall of 1995, than he asked Meeks to start planning the next one. He was always asking for money. He won many major gifts from corporations, where he worked a rich set of connections. One executive at the time called him "the most adept individual at picking the pockets of Corporate America."

In one gambit, Sawhill traveled to Williamsburg, Virginia, in March 1996 to give a speech before a group of utility-industry executives. In view of worry over global warming, he told the group of executives, they should spend $75 million on tropical forest protection by the end of the century to earn carbon credits. As utilities, their companies emitted huge amounts of greenhouse gases that contribute to global warming. They could mitigate those emissions by preserving rainforests and thus preventing carbon dioxide emissions that stem from destruction of these forests. They could also assure future growth in those forests to absorb atmospheric carbon dioxide. By taking this approach, he pointed out, the executives would also meet the central mission of the Conservancy—protecting biodiversity.

Dale Heydlauff, vice president of American Electric Power (AEP), a utility based in Columbus, Ohio, followed Sawhill out of the room. He wanted to shrink this environmental leader's expectations.

Heydlauff told Sawhill that the utility industry had already done a lot to address this issue.

But Sawhill was not dissuaded and said he wanted to meet at AEP headquarters in Columbus, Ohio, with Heydlauff and his CEO, E. Linn Draper. There they could discuss a future collaboration on carbon sequestration.

Draper would have none of it. So much had Sawhill's reputation grown that Draper told Heydlauff they would not trouble Sawhill to meet them in Columbus. In late 1995, Sawhill had earned one of the most coveted forms of recognition in the world of management: The *Harvard Business Review* featured him in a one-on-one interview. So Draper and Heydlauff traveled to Arlington instead. Arriving with AEP's chief forester, they came to the meeting with a reservoir of respect for Sawhill and a willingness to listen to Sawhill's pitch.

Sawhill saw the chance for deal making. He asked Draper to make AEP a member of the Conservancy's International Leadership Council, at a cost of $25,000. The council, just set up the previous year, was a sort of corporate-giving club. It helped fund Conservancy work while it offered forums for business executives to discuss environmental issues.

Draper agreed.

Sawhill then pulled out two forest carbon-sequestration projects, one in the Bolivian rain forest, another in Panama. Sawhill urged Draper to invest in one of the two. AEP would then get credit for paying to protect forests that, as they grew, would capture millions of tons of carbon each year, mitigating emissions from AEP's coal-fired power plants.

Draper was interested. After talking with Heydlauff and AEP's chief forester, he chose the Bolivia project.

Though Heydlauff counseled Draper against investing—he felt that AEP would never earn the promised "carbon credits" in untested world commodities markets—Draper went ahead anyway. As for Heydlauff's objections, on account of financial risk, Draper told him that AEP, an advocate of carbon sequestration, should put its money where its mouth was. AEP thus committed $5.25 million over five years. Draper believed that even if AEP could never sell the carbon credits it earned—bought at a bargain $0.25 per ton of carbon dioxide—the investment was the right thing to do. After all, AEP was the biggest emitter of carbon dioxide in America—and a huge target of environmentalists.

It was with this kind of deal making that Sawhill raked in the fuel the Conservancy needed to grow. The new plans would take millions more to execute than the Conservancy had already raised. Sawhill, ever worried about financial stability, would make sure the Conservancy had it.

WHAT SUCCESS LOOKS LIKE

The Conservancy published its new agenda for conservation, dubbed "Conservation by Design," in January 1996. A great achievement or not, the agenda didn't fulfill all of Sawhill's desires. He still didn't have good numeric objectives. He still didn't have any means to measure progress. The big goal he asked for in late 1994 from the Conservation Committee still eluded him. "One Conservancy" had to have one goal—and one way to measure progress toward it. This was a crucial part of his work to professionalize the organization and turn it into an integrated whole.

Several ticklish problems arose, however. One was that coming up with measures continued to defy a workable solution. Sawhill charged a new team to tackle the problem, and it came up with the idea of having a small family of three kinds of measures—for biological impact, conservation work, and organizational capacity. That equated to measures of, for example, biodiversity health, projects launched, and money raised. The following July, top managers endorsed this scheme, giving the green light for further development. But ultimately, staff shelved the work, and the puzzle of how to best measure conservation success would remain a conundrum as it had for many years.

The other problem was that the picture of success provided for by the new ecoregional planning approach would take years to produce. That's because ecoregional maps took so long to prepare, as the staff had to invent a way to gather, interpret, and compile data, and then map all of it. Until that job was done—which the staff felt would take five or more years—the Conservancy would not have properly plotted priorities for conservation. There would be no "blueprint" for conservation, as Sawhill called it, until the mapping job was done.

In the meantime, Conservation by Design triggered a burst of experimentation—in education, health care, public policy, and the like—all responding to the Conservancy's push to move beyond its traditional land-buying business to deliver conservation results. One manager called this the "let a thousand flowers bloom" period. Sawhill suddenly began to worry about mission drift, about losing the focus he so relentlessly sought. This was just when Low was working to instill the discipline of his 5S planning process, to keep people from addressing the wrong threats and mitigating them in the wrong way.

In late 1997, Conservancy managers actually put a moratorium on Conservancy-wide initiatives. Sawhill chartered two new task forces, one to narrow the work of too many creative conservationists, another to offer an organizational design to guide their work. "What areas should the Conservancy focus on," he asked the first group, "and perhaps more important, what activities should we stop doing?"

The first task force concluded that the Conservancy should focus on three things: applied science, expansion of community-based conservation programs, and applying the community-based conservation lessons on much bigger landscapes by influencing the practices of government and corporations. But it said the Conservancy "needs to be more disciplined in employing a community-based approach only at those places where it is the most appropriate strategy . . . lest we squander this opportunity by spreading ourselves too thin . . . or by investing resources in activities that do not directly conserve biodiversity." In other words, part of what the team concluded was what Low was learning at the Virginia Coast Reserve and other bioreserves. The Conservancy couldn't go too far afield, and it had to work harder to come up with crisp Monday-morning strategies.

At the urging of his second task force, Sawhill launched a sea change in structure. He disbanded the conservation and operations committees, closed regional offices, moved administrative work to headquarters or states, merged science with operations, and required state directors to spend 20 percent of their time on "One Conservancy" work. "Form follows function," Sawhill wrote in adopting the structure. He positioned the Conservancy to support the ecoregional vision of success. His conclusion, now at odds with his initial years at the Conservancy, was that the organization needed more decentralization.

It was at this juncture that Sawhill turned over executive management to Weeks, named for a second tour as executive vice president, and Low, named head of U.S. conservation. The core of the new management team comprised a dozen new division managers, each of whom, unencumbered by administrative duties, would work full time conserving landscapes in the emerging ecoregions.

Of course this still left a clear conservation goal up in the air. The picture emerging from the ecoregional maps would be the end-game portrait of success. But what was the Conservancy's numerical goal? What number could Sawhill set in front of people to inspire them to success? In January 1998, the board had approved an easy-to-grasp dollar target for the next capital campaign. The Conservancy would raise $750 million, more than double the preceding campaign. But the answer to what amount of conservation product that would buy was not clear.

In late August 1998, Sawhill convened his top managers—among them Low and the ten vice presidents of his new divisions—for a retreat at the resort-like Airlie House conference center in Warrenton, Virginia, forty-five miles southwest of Arlington. On three of the hottest days in August, with temperatures in the nineties, he put this hottest item at the top of the agenda: the drafting of ten-year conservation goals to fulfill the Conservancy's commitment to community-based conservation and to the ecoregional planning of Conservation by Design.

Sawhill didn't come to this meeting to poll his lieutenants for their opinions. As in so much of his work, he preferred that people hash out a consensus behind the scenes, so that during a public outing he could show a united front, all votes in favor. He had been floating various ideas among his managers, and they floated ideas in return. In January he told the board he wanted the current roster of one hundred bioreserves to grow to three hundred or four hundred by 2010. Low later floated even bigger numbers.

Now, at the meeting, Low and his vice presidents backed the goal Sawhill had signed on to: a breathtaking ten-year target of five hundred landscape-scale projects and two thousand conventional conservation sites. They recommended a goal of a hundred more projects outside the United States.

Five years earlier, during the 1993 Last Great Places campaign, Sawhill had written: "I believe that the challenges of this initiative will rejuvenate the Nature Conservancy. We will emerge a more effective and efficient organization, having simultaneously advanced our cause and ourselves." That campaign was the largest of its kind in conservation history. It indeed advanced the enterprise, the people, and the cause. With this second conservation initiative, Sawhill appeared to want the same response.

"I think you have to keep putting new challenges in front of the organization," Sawhill told a reporter in January 1999. "It's very easy to become complacent when you've been growing at 20 percent a year, like we have. But it isn't going to continue on into the future unless we're constantly renewing ourselves."

Sawhill didn't always succeed in setting goals that spurred renewal. In 1992, he sought to expand membership to 3 million by 1998. The staff wouldn't embrace the goal; some even laughed at it. In 1995, he tried again with a campaign called the "Million-Member March" to expand membership to 1 million by 1997. He fell short on that, too, by two years.

Still, he—like Noonan years before—knew goals could stir passion and aspirations for the cause. As he liked to quote from Robert Browning: "Ah, but a man's reach should exceed his grasp. Or what's a heaven for?" The ultimate way to integrate, to create One Conservancy, was to unite everyone behind one audacious goal. That was what Sawhill set out to do.

ASPIRE AND WIN

Sawhill took news of his new reach to the annual meeting in Keystone, Colorado, a resort in the heart of the Rockies. He announced the "big hairy audacious goal" that Low had advocated: launching five hundred landscape-scale projects, preserving two thousand conventional sites, and opening a new office every eight days for ten years to do it.

The attendees—staff and 180 trustees hailing from most of the fifty states—were veterans of the Conservancy cause. They knew what the Conservancy's map of ecoregions would look like—sixty-three colored sectors blanketing the center of North America. Sawhill painted a vivid picture of a huge new challenge. The Conservancy trustees knew that the organization had given birth to about ten projects per year for ten years. Now it would quadruple that pace.

Sawhill told the audience that the staff and the board had already jump-started the effort. In the "quiet" phase of the Campaign for Conservation, starting in July 1998, $124 million had been raised. This was paced by the $10 million gift by Daniel and Lori Efroymson, as well as a grant of $10 million from Robert Wilson of New York. The Conservancy was well on its way with huge grants to support the new vision.

In October, the *Washington Post* let Sawhill further trumpet his goal. "What does success look like?" he asked in an op-ed piece. No other environmental group was answering that question, he said. But once the Conservancy finished ecoregional planning, it would define mission success. He could tack on his wall a blueprint colored in all shades of green—a map marked with 2,500 high-priority sites.

The organization took the approach to heart. A year later, Sawhill reported that the Conservancy had opened twenty-five new project offices—from the Serpentine Barrens of southern Pennsylvania to the Laguna Madre of coastal Texas—and made plans to open forty more in the next year. It raised its fundraising take to $300 million, almost as much as in the entire previous five-year capital campaign. Among the gifts: thirty-seven donations of $1 million or more, more than five times as many such mega-gifts received as in the entire preceding campaign.

In February 2000, Sawhill raised aspirations again. The Conservancy had raised $370 million in the latest campaign's first sixteen months. He told the board the Packard Foundation had just given $15 million, donor Robert Berry $10 million, the Kresge Foundation $1.5 million, donor Ward Woods $1 million. Sawhill, ready to announce the campaign publicly on March 16, recommended to the board a new goal: $1 billion.

"Why raise the bar?" Sawhill wrote in a March 9 letter to the 1,500 state-chapter trustees. "In part, the answer is because raising the bar—in terms of conservation achievement, fundraising, and organizational excellence—is what the Conservancy is all about. The minute our organization becomes complacent about the urgency and importance of our mission is the minute we will cease being a great institution." One-third of the nation's plants and animals are at risk of extinction, he noted, citing new data from Conservancy scientists, and more than five hundred species known to have inhabited North America were already extinct.

The board approved the $1 billion goal—but Sawhill would never see the outcome. He died of complications from diabetes on May 18, 2000, after falling into a coma in his hotel room.

After all his accomplishments, some people still felt this professional manager had never cared about the mission. And it was true that he talked about management all the time—in particular the balance he had finally mastered to unify the organization. "The secret to our rapid institutional growth, I believe, lies in our success at being both big and small at the same time," he wrote in one of his last letters to members. "When it comes to getting lasting conservation results, small is beautiful—but so is big."

But to those who continued to feel he cared only for managerial glory, Sawhill left one parting shot. The Monday after he died, his assistant Fouke got a call from the office of a corporation on whose board of directors Sawhill sat. The caller, to Fouke's surprise, said Sawhill had named the Conservancy as beneficiary of his life-insurance policy. The caller wanted to know who would handle the paperwork.

Fouke gave the caller the names of Conservancy people to contact, and then she asked, almost as an afterthought, how much the policy was for.

"$1 million," the caller replied.

Sawhill had indeed left a legacy to the cause of conservation. Still, even many of the idealists, underachievers, and entrepreneurs he emasculated over the years conceded his contributions as a manager amounted to his most important legacy of all. He left a template for using professional management to create a single, integrated organization that balanced centralization and decentralization.

As if signaling his legacy was largely complete, Sawhill had, before he died, set several of his top managers to redrafting the outline for Conservation by Design. It contained six parts: mission, vision, goals, measures, values, and a strategy for setting priorities. Dubbed "Sawhill's greatest hits" by his staff, this document was the essence of the "One Conservancy" concept, a McKinsey-like map of Sawhill's brand of management. It was the map he used for salvaging the best of a disjointed organization and knitting it together into a powerful whole.

8

MANAGE THYSELF:
Leadership in a
Shared-Power World

WHEN THREE FRIENDS FROM the U.S. Fish and Wildlife Service heard Katherine Skinner had landed a job at the Nature Conservancy, they took her to dinner to celebrate. Skinner, a Vanderbilt MBA and thirty-something aide to North Carolina Congressman Walter Jones, had for five years bird-dogged House appropriations bills. When her boss, the chairman of the Merchant Marine and Fisheries Committee, wanted the lowdown on where money flowed for conservation, he asked Skinner. When the Conservancy's Gregory Low wanted $3.4 million to fund the Currituck Wildlife Refuge on the Outer Banks of North Carolina in 1984, Skinner took the call.

At dinner with her friends in 1986, Skinner enjoyed the good-natured teasing of her well-wishers: "Well, Katherine, you're going to be managing people now."

Skinner was nonchalant: "But how hard can it be managing six people?"

She would soon eat those words. Learning to manage six people would take an apprenticeship of more than two years, and learning to manage a growing staff in a growing organization would take a career. In the U.S. House of Representatives, she set her schedule and agenda by the twists and turns of legislation. As a manager, she would have to set them by herself—with other people depending on her. She would have to become a role model of management.

Over more than eighteen years, Skinner would show what it takes for a talented professional to make the jump to talented manager. Many successful professionals assume the transition will come naturally. But as Skinner discovered, it doesn't. Success as a manager depends on a willingness to remake oneself, to learn about managing others, to overcome one's personal blind spots, and to defer to mentors who step forward to bridge the trouble spots. As she would learn, the education of a manager proceeds one stage at a time, each deeper and more nuanced than the one before.

At her new Conservancy office in Chapel Hill, North Carolina, Skinner did not, at first, occupy herself with the job of management. She jumped to the main task the board hired her for—getting dedicated state funding to buy conservation land. Her trustees had a $31 million shopping list, and they wanted her to bankroll land acquisitions largely with North Carolina and federal funds. Thus primed for stepping into the political fray, she got off on the wrong foot at the office.

"You know, we don't really lobby," ventured one of her staff not long after she started in the fall of 1986.

"I never want to hear you say that again," retorted Skinner. "I am a registered lobbyist in the state of North Carolina."

None of the staff had ever seen the likes of Skinner before. They had just spent two years raising $2 million in private donations, where gentility counted most. They were accustomed to the reserved, cerebral demeanor of her predecessor. They didn't cotton to a woman who reveled in the tactics, intrigue, and horse-trading of politics.

That Skinner had no experience as a supervisor didn't stop her from acting like one. Blonde and brassy, she came on strong. Her speech surged and swooned in the rhythms of eastern North Carolina. Strangers would sometimes dismiss her as a dizzy dilettante, only to be brought up short by her quick mind. As Low would say, she was one of the few people in his Conservancy career who beat him at poker.

The trustees recognized her chutzpah as a golden touch for lobbying, but they were boggled by her so-called command presence, the kind the men on the board remembered from the Armed Forces. Nobody would ever accuse her of the timidity of a retiring Southern lady. She announced herself in exclamations heard around the office. One trustee remarked that she could act like General Patton on the top of a tank. Indeed, when she arrived in Chapel Hill, that's just what her staff thought.

Skinner didn't mince words. She bluntly informed her staff she was hired to go after public money. And off she went to wheel and deal.

Within weeks, the board heard complaints about her management. Some staffers didn't think they could work with such a brash female. The trustees, six months into her tenure, wondered whether they had made a mistake.

Skinner was an enigma to a staff ignorant of politics. She spent 80 percent of her time lobbying, and many didn't know what she was doing. The fundraisers shrank at the thought of taking her on calls, where she might let fly her boisterous political tone in the presence of a refined Southern philanthropist. As she would say herself, "For me to be low key, I've got to be sick."

Amid falling morale in the spring of 1987, T. D. "Bud" Hunter, an auto franchiser from Hendersonville, North Carolina, took over as board chairman. Hunter got an earful from a contingent of his board that didn't find Skinner's behavior becoming. They didn't see Skinner as a manager fitting into Conservancy culture. Hunter went to the staff, talked with most of them, and asked the question he thought most pertinent: Where do you think Katherine's heart is—is it back with Congressman Jones?

The staff, though buffaloed by Skinner's management, told him that nobody was more dedicated to the Conservancy than Skinner. They knew she loved the work.

Hunter and like-minded board members could see Skinner's devotion to land protection. She was inspired by some of her formative years. She might have gotten a D in seventh-grade biology, but she spent all of her summers as a teen and college student working at Camp Green Cove and

Mondamin. As a camper, based in the mountains of western North Carolina, she canoed every white-water river in the region. She counted her summer camp pals as lifelong friends and runs down rivers like the Chattooga and Little Tennessee among her fondest memories.

Hunter decided that if Skinner's heart was in the work, he would protect her job. She was a work in progress, true, but she would get better with time. Hunter was sure of it. He and other board members argued to keep her on the job.

Skinner's standing improved markedly when she started delivering big-time money. In 1987, she secured $4 million from the federal Land and Water Conservation Fund to buy an inholding in the Alligator River National Wildlife Refuge, a 118,000-acre swamp in eastern North Carolina, home of the northernmost alligators in the United States. She then shepherded legislation through the North Carolina General Assembly to create the Recreation and Natural Heritage Trust Fund, a pot of state money, $275,000 to start, for buying conservation land.

When the board sat down for Skinner's first job review in September 1987, the trustees couldn't dispute her success. Starting cold, she had brought in millions in cash. With the first slug of money, the staff became more accommodating. Nobody could figure out how she could succeed so, but they loved the flood of funding. The board debated: Should we give her a full raise and a top performance rating? Or should we ding her in some way to show our displeasure over her management?

Some argued for the raise but not the top rating. Others argued for avoiding the mixed signal of misaligning her performance rating and pay. She had delivered results, after all. The decision ended up mixed: The trustees gave her a full raise and docked the rating.

Skinner appreciated the financial endorsement. But she took heed of the accompanying message: If you don't fix the management problem, you're gone. She had succeeded in what she knew best—politicking. But she had floundered in her task of management. In effect, she had parachuted onto the turf of a manager, and the landing had knocked her off kilter. Now she would have to learn how to handle the new terrain. Like many novice managers, she had no choice. Until she proved her mettle, she didn't have the unanimous backing of her board.

APPRENTICESHIP

Thus began a period of uncertainty for Skinner. She took tips from Hunter and others, and she tried to improve her management. But given the board's thirst for money, she still spent most of her time on politics. This put her at a grave disadvantage in making headway in learning the skills of management. What's more, it led some on the board to believe she might not want to stay on. Some figured, given her success, she would go back to politics full time.

And the success was striking. Not long after her performance review, in early 1988, she lined up $6.1 million from the Land and Water Conservation Fund to buy Panthertown Valley. The valley was a broad 6,550-acre flat parcel in the Appalachian Mountains, flanked by steep, rocky 300-foot cliffs, embracing the headwaters of the East Fork of the Tuckasegee River and including twenty miles of native trout stream. The new money added to her reputation as having a golden touch.

In spite of the money, insiders still grumbled. In April 1988, one trustee and a former North Carolina staffer went to her new boss, Charles Bassett, and asked him to fire her. Fortunately for Skinner, Bassett had taken over just the week before. As the supervisor of thirteen state directors in the Conservancy's southeast region, he was not to be rushed to judgment. Besides, Skinner was far from his biggest problem.

"Well, thank you for your advice and input," Bassett basically told the men, "but let me tell you how I work with every one of my direct reports."

Bassett explained how he built a year-long relationship to get to know each of his people. He then set goals, and then those goals served as benchmarks to evaluate performance the next year. He told his visitors he worked the same way with all thirteen of his state directors and five regional office staff. As for firing Skinner, he had no intention of doing so. He was not one to make rash decisions. In fact, he worked so systematically that he kept a diary of his every management move.

Bassett didn't make his visitors happy, but he did meet with Skinner. This meeting would mark the first turning point in her career as a manager, and Bassett would become her first critical management mentor. Bassett told Skinner that she could have a career at the Conservancy if she wanted to, but she would have to learn to manage, both herself and her staff. As an alternative, he told her, she could have just a job at the Conservancy, stay around for a time, and leave when either she got tired of the organization or the organization got tired of her. Bassett gave her that stark choice.

Skinner wanted to stay. She listened as Bassett outlined what amounted to a program for her apprenticeship as a manager. To master the basics of management, she would have to spend months working on the ABCs: how to set good performance objectives, how to give good feedback, how to encourage people without being sappy, how to handle conflicts, how to manage her own behavior.

One of Bassett's most crucial moves was to give her time and room to practice. To provide cover for her apprenticeship, he shut down the grapevine through which complaints had traveled from the staff to both the board and upper Conservancy management. He told Skinner that they would solve these problems in the North Carolina office. They were not going to have people passing rumors and sniping. Meanwhile, he advised her not to overreact to her adversaries.

North Carolina board chairman Hunter backed Bassett. The two veterans' patience gave Skinner breathing room. With Bassett as a sounding board, Skinner saw how her style clashed with the staff's. She could be quick to pull the trigger—shoot from the hip, shoot so fast other people didn't get a chance to air their views. She could also bowl people over with her energy, closing off criticism and shutting people down. In most cases, she wasn't even aware of it.

Bassett kept reminding Skinner that she had to work at being a manager. He told her it takes someone who looks the part, acts the part, and works on a schedule other people can count on. It takes thought, perspiration, and gut-wrenching courage to tell people bad news. It takes the patience of Job to let people prattle on about something when there are a lot of other things to do. It takes restraint not to lose control or chew someone out in front of others. He told her that people looked to her, the boss, as a benchmark of performance, and she had to fulfill that role.

Skinner worked hard on what Bassett called his four managerial rules of thumb: Setting good performance objectives, giving people the tools they need, giving them feedback regularly, and getting the hell out of their way. Skinner rehearsed that sequence over and over, especially on giving feedback to direct reports.

Bassett made a compact with her: In meetings with peers, once she spoke, she had to allow three other people to talk before she could speak again. "God gave you an advantage, two ears and one mouth—take advantage of it," he said.

Skinner held her tongue, or at least tried to. Some of her staff still didn't like her style, and several left. Skinner thought her staff would simply "get over" her political habits and tone, but many didn't. Her fundraising people still feared taking her on donor calls. Skinner, who found it just about impossible not to talk, might say the wrong thing about conservation, or she might come on too fast and strong.

Skinner's staff felt it had good reason to believe she could go off on a flyer. In 1989, she was working to pass a bill to raise vanity license plate fees by $10. The new revenue, expected to be $1.5 million yearly, would fund the Recreation and Natural Heritage Trust Fund. Skinner had strong support in the state Senate. But a member of the House had attached to the bill a pet piece of his own legislation—to ban topless dancing on Topsail Beach, a coastal resort. The legislator figured his bill could get a hearing by piggybacking on the popularity of the vanity-plate bill. The problem was that the vanity-plate measure, adulterated by the rider, got stuck in house committee.

Skinner began to fight the topless-ban provision, worried her bill was on the way to becoming dead on arrival. Her staff was dumbfounded.

"Katherine, what does topless dancing have to do with conservation?" the staff would ask.

Skinner explained that a good bill could get through a legislator's door because of goodwill. But that was only the start. Other members might not care about it, or have something else they care about, or may object to it. So the legislators do a lot of trading over what moves forward. The reality was plain, she said: "Our bill is stuck, and I have to get it unstuck."

Her staff members—scientists, fundraisers, real estate dealmakers— were bewildered by this talk. While she loved the arm-twisting of politics, her staff couldn't believe all this happened in the name of the Nature Conservancy. They wondered what she was doing, and just how political the Conservancy had become.

Skinner enjoyed the politicking on this and other measures. She finally went to the leader of the Senate and asked him to help her out. The senator, though himself amazed, promised to give the topless-ban bill a hearing to assuage its sponsor. Just one day before legislative recess, he did so. The vanity-plate bill was thus set free—in time for passage on August 12, 1989.

Solving the political crisis of the moment kept bringing in cash, and everybody appreciated the ongoing flow of funds for projects. Skinner's tallies steadily mounted. On top of the vanity-plate funds, she pushed the final Panthertown appropriation from $6.1 million to $8 million.

As Skinner exercised her political acumen, she began to combine it with her improved management skills, to further conservation. She worked especially well with Frederick Annand, then the assistant director and a seasoned hand who'd been with the Conservancy since 1980. She knew nothing about protection, and especially not about real estate deals, so from the start she gave Annand free rein to handle them.

In 1987, Annand began to put together a deal with the U.S. Fish and Wildlife Service that would lead to years of long-term conservation. The plan was to protect the Lower Roanoke River, its waters and swamps and woodlands, including the most extensive stands of bottomland hardwoods in the Mid-Atlantic region. With Annand running point on dealmaking, and Skinner managing politics and money, North Carolina Governor James Martin agreed in 1989 to a plan creating the 33,000-acre Roanoke River National Wildlife Refuge.

The deal was divisive. County officials in Martin and Washington counties worried about the erosion of their tax base, preclusion of development, and condemnation of land. A number of hunting clubs railed over losing their exclusive, long-term hunting leases. But with the Conservancy as negotiator, the governor found a compromise he could support: splitting the project and properties between the U.S. Fish and Wildlife Service and the North Carolina Wildlife Commission. Many hunters fumed. Skinner, from nearby Williamston, knew many people who wouldn't talk to her on the street anymore. But the conservation project, and Skinner's lobbying of county officials and Congressman Jones, was a landmark for North Carolina.

Through such deals, Skinner began to see that good management and good conservation went hand in hand, and by the end of 1989, Bassett figured she had emerged from her apprenticeship. He ceased thinking of himself as a mentor. If Skinner called, he would dissect management challenges with her as a co-investigator. Skinner was no longer a novice. She was ready for prime time.

MANAGE THYSELF

When Bassett was asked where in the South the national board should hold its spring 1990 meeting, he had no trouble choosing. Skinner was ready for the shot in the arm a board meeting could give. He recommended the governors meet in North Carolina. The meeting was held in March in the seaside resort of Sanderling, on the Outer Banks. It was at this meeting that Skinner became acquainted with a man obsessed with better management: John Sawhill.

Sawhill, fresh from ten years at McKinsey, talked about professional management all the time. Management was a cycle to Sawhill: act, retool, re-act. He was committed to continually improving the organization's ability to deliver results, whether at headquarters in Arlington or in the state office in North Carolina. Skinner and her board saw at Sanderling how North Carolina trustees fell short of the professionalism of the national board.

In some ways, Sanderling marked the start of another stage in Skinner's education as a manager. In the spirit of Sawhill's commitment to constant improvement, she spent the next several years upgrading her skills. Sawhill stressed planning as a starting point in management. "If everything's a priority, nothing's a priority," he would say. Strategic goals and objectives should lead to operating goals and objectives should lead to individual goals and objectives.

So Skinner started working on planning. Through the middle of 1990, a team at headquarters—including Annand—worked on a new national strategic plan. No sooner had Annand returned than Skinner rallied her staff to develop a plan for North Carolina. The planning process itself improved the way she managed. Ironing out contention among staff was agonizing, but it gave everyone common cause, a valuable exercise she would remember.

The plan then revealed the scale of the management challenge ahead. During the planning process, the North Carolina staff pinpointed fifty-nine sites of utmost biological significance. It figured the tally for protecting the targeted 300,000 acres would come to $112 million in public funds and $40 million in private funds. The task would demand that the North Carolina office expand its ranks from a dozen to twenty-seven people in five years, raise the operating budget 20 percent every year, and launch a $10.5 million capital campaign—five times bigger than the preceding one.

Skinner had her work cut out for her. As for the management challenge, one of the principal gaps in her knowledge was how to raise private money. This time around, she had to focus not just on government funding but on private donations. It would take both to succeed. To get started, she kept raising money from state and federal sources. In a 1991 coup, she lobbied to earmark fifteen cents of the deed stamp tax for the Recreation and Natural Heritage Trust Fund. This single piece of legislation would yield more than $1.7 million per year for conservation.

But she had to embark on a new education in the art of private fundraising. Her first move, in 1991, was to hire Jeanne Phillips, a North Carolina public-radio fundraiser. As it turned out, Phillips would become Skinner's closest mentor in learning the part of the job she had yet to master and where so many people had once doubted her potential. The two often went on fundraising calls together—just the situation earlier fundraising chiefs had so feared.

At first, Skinner let some of her impatience show through. She wanted to measure success by whether she walked out the door with a donor's money. Phillips taught her to slow down, to express appreciation in fresh ways, to think about engaging the donors in the organization and not just collecting pledges. After each fundraising call, the two talked over what went right and wrong. Skinner took great satisfaction in building the fundraising muscle she felt she had let languish.

Meanwhile, she advanced her skills in other ways. Whereas Bassett had taught her the basic formula for management, now she learned how to tailor her approach for greater effectiveness. She realized she needed to handle people individually. The free rein that worked for Annand didn't work for everyone. When she hired Phillips, the seasoned fundraiser was concerned about Skinner's style, and asked her how she managed. Skinner made it clear she relied on feedback from others on how to best tap everyone's skills.

"Well, I tell the folks what to do and they do it," Skinner said. "And they tell me what to do and I do it. We play to each other's strengths."

That satisfied Phillips, who was about to become Skinner's third fundraiser in five years. By this time, Skinner felt she had learned enough about management not to drive a talented person away. Phillips played to two of what she considered Skinner's innate strengths: Skinner was always willing to go out and meet people, and she loved to ask for money.

Skinner's staff came to admire—and appreciate—how she was always making an effort to learn better management. As part of her self-improvement effort, she took courses at the Center for Creative Leadership in Greensboro, North Carolina. A week-long course in 1993 touched her deeply. In one exercise, each person was given a list of action items to rank in order of priority, acting as a boss who had to decide what to do first. Everyone was then grouped in teams of five. Each team was then videotaped while developing a consensus list—while center staff posted individual answer sheets for all to see.

Skinner was staggered by the video of her performance. In one segment, a quiet woman offered her opinion only to have everyone else pay her but passing heed. The more dominant players, Skinner among them, seemed to ignore an opinion offered just a single time. The video revealed the error of their dominant behavior. The team missed a perfect score by three because it had not genuinely considered the quiet woman's input. When the answers revealed the quiet woman as having the best individual score, Skinner swung to her and blurted, "How did you do that?"

The woman replied that she didn't know. She just felt it was logical.

"How'd you do that?!" Skinner blurted again, unable to contain her astonishment.

Skinner knew all along that she talked a lot more than she listened, but these video images showed it. It was one thing to be told about your demonstrative behavior; it was another to have it paraded on a screen before a group of peers.

When she returned to the office, Skinner didn't contain herself. "They told me I was forceful!" she declared.

No kidding! everyone thought.

Before going to the Center for Creative Leadership, Skinner believed that people who didn't talk didn't have anything to say. That some people would choose not to talk had not dawned on her. She grew up in a family where people talked and listened at the same time. Sometimes they would have two or three conversations at once. It wasn't until college that she learned that not everyone used mouth and ears simultaneously.

"What I have to say and how I say it are both important," she realized. "I've got to give people who aren't as demonstrative as I am a chance to talk."

Skinner became ever more convinced that good management—managing people and managing herself—produced good conservation results. Every time she took steps to upgrade her management skills, she felt she delivered improved performance. So convinced was she that she urged other senior staff to work on their management skills as well. She even obtained scholarships for people to take courses at the Center for Creative Leadership, one of the most powerful experiences in her education as a manager during the 1990s.

DREAMING BIG

Skinner sought to make the most out of what she had learned. As she moved through the 1990s, her guiding management principle followed from Bassett's "get the hell out of the way" dictum: Dream big, urge the staff to dream big, throw a lot of support behind the innovations that emerge, and stand aside. She invested her full confidence in her talented staff—her "intellectual capital," as she called them—and she let them run with their smart ideas.

As for her political work, she helped to pass a bill in 1994 to create a Parks and Recreation Trust Fund that funneled half of the state's real estate transfer tax to acquisition of park and conservation land. In 1995, her work helped reallocate 100 percent of the second dollar of the deed stamp tax to conservation. In 1996, she helped pass a Clean Water Management

Trust Fund, which set aside at least $30 million yearly for cleaning water-ways and protecting watersheds.

As for private fundraising, Phillips and her people brought in $9.7 million by October 1993. By March 1996, the chapter hit its goal of $15 million, the largest state fundraising goal in the Conservancy at the time. With Phillips and Skinner working in concert with campaign volunteers, Skinner showed she could excel in the art of working with private donors.

As for conservation, in 1994, Annand engaged Georgia-Pacific in unprecedented talks about the company's vast real estate holdings in the river's floodplain. The Conservancy became the company's partner in managing land and timber and sensitive ecosystems on 21,068 acres of Georgia-Pacific's land. Through the donation of a conservation easement, Georgia-Pacific banned logging entirely on 6,500 acres and severely restricted timber management on another 14,500 acres. The deal protected rare plants and animals including the Cerulean warbler, while providing Conservancy expertise to Georgia-Pacific for forest regeneration and managing timber for minimal impact on wetlands.

In another pioneering effort, Annand held talks with the U.S. Army at Fort Bragg. In 1996, he orchestrated a landmark agreement to work with the Army to help protect five federally listed endangered species including the red-cockaded woodpecker on and next to the Army installation, a site in the Sandhills region amid the longleaf pine forests of south-central North Carolina. The Army pledged $7 million to the effort with a Conservancy match so long as soldiers retained limited access to the land for low-impact training. Although the agreement was controversial within the higher echelons of the Army—including at the Pentagon—the Conservancy, officials at Fort Bragg, and the Army Environmental Center considered it a necessary experiment to balance Army readiness and conservation.

This arrangement led several years later to negotiations for the purchase of 2,500 acres next to Fort Bragg. The Department of Transportation would ultimately buy the land for $5.3 million for future highway-construction mitigation, transfer it to the Conservancy, and endow it with $600,000 to be restored and managed for the endangered woodpecker. The Army supported this and other land deals as an effective way to create buffer lands between themselves and homeowners complaining of noise and smoke.

In April 1998, Merrill Lynch, another of Skinner's dealmakers, closed the largest real estate transaction of the time, to buy 17,829 acres of the isolated South Mountains for $13.4 million. The state reimbursed the Conservancy for the parcel with $4.2 million from the Clean Water Management Trust Fund, $2 million from the Natural Heritage Trust Fund, $1.15 million from the Wildlife Resources Commission endowment, $1.45 million in donations, and $5 million from a special appropriation from the North Carolina General Assembly.

Skinner and Annand then brokered a compromise to protect the Jocassee Gorges, a string of ravines sliced in the Blue Ridge escarpment next to South Carolina. Hunters fought the deal, which aimed to create the first state park west of Asheville, but Skinner and Annand, working with state representatives, came up with a workable compromise. In the end, the state got 9,750 acres of conservation land, some for park use, some for hunting. The Conservancy thus saved a unique pocket of the southern Appalachians, dotted with waterfalls, which received eighty inches of rain a year. The purchase price was $8.5 million, backed by a $5 million special appropriation by the North Carolina General Assembly.

The successes consummated under Skinner's management began to pile up to an impressive degree. In some ways, however, they culminated in a project of perhaps the greatest long-term significance: protecting riverside habitat along the Roanoke River. After years of studying water flows and digesting data that showed dam-regulated flows harmed downriver plant and animal diversity, in the early 1990s the staff became convinced it had to control dam releases. Sam Pearsall, a Ph.D. in geography and head of science, persuaded Skinner that buying land would not protect river habitat. Even if the Conservancy could buy all the land available, it couldn't control the ecosystem's health if it couldn't protect the river itself.

Data showed that the pattern of water releases prolonged bottomland flooding during the growing season. The late-season wetness disrupted ecosystem functioning, including hardwood-tree regeneration. In one case of nature getting knocked out of whack, tent caterpillars proliferated in Tupelo trees because the parasites that would have slowed them down died in wet soils. The Tupelo canopy thinned, and as bees tapped a declining

Tupelo nectar supply, Tupelo honey producers' yields fell. The extra-heavy droppings from the caterpillars, meanwhile, polluted the water.

In the mid-1990s, Pearsall floated the idea of "adaptive management" to address these problems. The notion was to get dam operator Dominion Power to schedule flows to mimic natural patterns as closely as possible, check for helpful signs of diversity recovery, and then fine-tune flows to balance economics and biological health. With experimentation, Pearsall figured, the operators could run profitably while helping Mother Nature regenerate and maintain a more diverse ecosystem—bringing back favorable conditions not just for the Tupelos and honeybees but for butterflies, moths, wild turkeys, amphibians, and more.

There was only one catch: To make this happen with Dominion Power, the Conservancy would have to "intervene" in the company's bid to renew its license with the Federal Energy Regulatory Commission (FERC). The license-renewal process lets anyone with a complaint intervene and comment on dam operations. By law, Dominion was obliged to listen to state, federal, and private comments. But the Conservancy was by policy and culture nonconfrontational. It just couldn't pick a fight with a company in a federal licensing process.

Pearsall warmed everyone to an innovative alternative: Gain agreement by all parties, including Dominion, on an adaptive management plan *before* renewal. The Conservancy, state and federal agencies, and others could then intervene *on behalf* of the renewal application. The intervention would then be nonconfrontational. Pearsall proposed they "optimize" future flows for ecosystem health, power generation, wildlife habitat, and community welfare. By 1998, after several years of work, he presented a full-blown plan.

The North Carolina board of trustees was reluctant to take such a step. That the Conservancy would intervene in a license renewal, or that it would meddle with the commercial operations of a utility company, or that it would advocate for a change in the water-flow policy—that was nonsense. But Skinner backed Pearsall. The Conservancy had helped protect 51,000 acres downstream from Dominion's Roanoke Rapids dam since 1982, spending over $12 million. Pearsall had proposed the only possible way to protect that investment and start the revitalization of the riverside ecosystem.

Skinner finally persuaded her trustees. She knew that was just her first stop, though. She had to also talk to the national board of governors. In September 2000, she walked into a room in Arlington to meet the Conservation Committee. The governors on the committee, normally chatty, interrogated her. They knew that FERC interventions could get nasty and by their nature were adversarial. A line from a Jimmy Buffet song ran through her head, "Wish I was somewhere other than here."

But in the end, although the FERC proposal was the most controversial item on the agenda, the governors gave her the go-ahead based on confidence in her track record, asking only that she show them the papers before signing anything.

This put the Conservancy, in effect, in the business of developing policy for federally licensed power production. The intervention led to unprecedented change along the Roanoke, driven by a process undertaken by the Conservancy in league with homeowners, the U.S. Fish and Wildlife Service, and state agencies. Dominion accepted a reduction of 2 percent to 4 percent in electricity generation. That allowed boaters to enjoy stabilized lake levels and the Conservancy to assure more favorable flows, allowing riverside habitat to recover. In return, Pearsall urged FERC to give Dominion a valuable forty-year renewal term, rather than the normal thirty years.

For Skinner, the intervention was a triumph many failed to appreciate. Pearsall was putting the chapter squarely into the new business of the Conservancy—the business of community-based conservation for landscape-scale protection championed by Gregory Low and John Sawhill. Of hidden significance, she was also realizing the fruits of her drive to deliver great conservation through the application of professional management. As a capstone on a decade of huge conservation wins, the intervention was awe-inspiring. And as the decade closed, Skinner and her people's work were becoming legendary in the Conservancy.

Of course, Skinner's inimitable style, aside from conservation wins, gave people plenty to weave a legend out of. In the fall of 2001, a story about cooking a pumpkin pie started circulating. It seems that a generous donor, living in Indiana, had been promised a pumpkin pie by Skinner in 1986. Skinner hadn't seen the donor in years, although the donor had given in the states of Indiana, Florida, Kentucky, and North Carolina. The last time the Indiana staff had seen the donor, the pumpkin pie promise came up in conversation—as it had every time the donor met Conservancy staff elsewhere.

The staff from Indiana called Skinner and asked he what they were going to do about the pie.

"Just go bake her a pie!" Skinner exclaimed. "I'll give you the recipe."

The recipe wasn't going to be enough, though. Skinner discovered, to her dismay, that the Indianan conservationists didn't know the difference between an orange jack-o-lantern pumpkin and a yellow one for cooking. What's more, they were talking about using canned pumpkin of all things.

"Okay," Skinner said, "I'll come make that pie myself." She figured that was the least she could do for a donor who had done so much for the Conservancy over the years.

So she shipped two cooking pumpkins to Indiana by overnight mail on a Friday. She then flew to Indiana, where she cooked first the pumpkin and then the pies using her father's own recipe. On Monday, she personally delivered the pies in a surprise visit—to an astonished donor.

Conservancy staff still tell the story. This was the kind of behavior that demonstrated the swagger of a successful state director in any era of the Conservancy. For Skinner, after fifteen years on the job, it was part and parcel of a sense of mastery in management that everyone had come to respect.

ONE STEP BACKWARD

Skinner's sense of mastery was to fade with the end of the decade. At first she thought this had to do with several events she had little control over. The stock market skidded nearly 10 percent in 2001, just as the chapter was ramping up a new $25 million capital campaign. Conservancy top management changed the formula for allocating donations, cutting North Carolina's take by $1.2 million. Then on September 11, the terrorist attacks in New York and Washington froze people with fear.

Meanwhile, Steven McCormick, the new president, launched a change program to reposition the Conservancy as a global organization. He asked people to rededicate themselves to one organization and embrace conservation in Chile and China as much as in Maine and North Carolina. He replaced top managers, reconfigured reporting lines, and required a self-appraisal of every chapter—of conservation, fundraising, government relations, and operations. He told his state directors they had to rectify inefficiencies or explain why not.

The new pressures to perform in more harrowing circumstances took their toll. Employees, asked to tackle tasks they didn't fully understand, became disoriented. In North Carolina, Skinner asked a Conservancy senior manager from outside North Carolina to guide a meeting of her staff in early 2002 to help sort out the confusion. This was when Skinner would get the first hint that she faced yet a new stage in her management education.

The manager listened attentively to a description of the portfolio of projects, and the creative work of her staff. Everything done in the 1990s and everything the chapter continued to pursue were testimony to the talent Skinner had hired and cultivated. But her senior management colleague caught her off guard when he asked, "How do you set priorities?"

"Priorities? Why we set priorities . . . "

The question triggered a realization by Skinner: She had slipped into letting the chapter pursue opportunities, not priorities. It wasn't that her intellectual capital wasn't putting top-notch conservation on the ground. It's that she had let her people decide, empowered them to decide, and they had gone in more than a few directions, each running with a piece of the conservation mission, each in a different part of the state.

At a time of tight money, the question that moved to front and center was, Are we making the best choices on how to spend our next dollar to most meaningfully do landscape-scale conservation?

Over fifteen years, Skinner had worked hard on management. She felt pride in the professionalism of herself and her staff. But she understood that her most basic job as a manager was being called into question: deciding what to do first. Sorting out priorities was much harder than it had once been, given the agenda for community-based conservation and working at a more global scale. How could she compare the priority of buying an Appalachian forest with lobbying for a change in dam releases? Or how could she compare working with the Army at Fort Bragg with helping fund conservation planning in the South Pacific?

Some answers to the priority question were easy. One was cutting back operations at places like Nags Head Woods, North Carolina's flagship project from the 1970s and 1980s. The maritime forest was not a landscape project, as critical as it was in setting the standard for land protection. Particularly troublesome were its education programs for kids, which were clearly outside the Conservancy's current core mission. Skinner told the local preserve board: We don't want to abandon you, but we need to divert money from education back into our core conservation priorities.

Other activities were harder to assess for their priority. Perhaps the most confusing were lobbying for policy change and figuring out how to involve the chapter in the global mission. In any case, the staff was confused about its new role, so at its suggestion, Skinner held a full staff retreat in November 2002. She wanted to help people see how they fit into the picture of a changing Conservancy.

But the retreat didn't resolve the angst and confusion. People echoed the kinds of comments Skinner had been hearing for over a year: "We don't understand how decisions are being made. We think communication is erratic. We don't really know what's going on."

The uncertainty and ambiguity were threatening. The pinch on funding, the change of CEO, the shift to landscape-scale work—all of this sent people into a tizzy. Skinner wasn't sure how to get her people back on track, but she knew she had to do something. The unhappiness of staff was greater than she had ever seen. So in January 2003, she took her staff's advice and called in two consultants, Cam Danielson and Douglas Austrom, management experts who had earlier given the chapter advice.

The challenge of management had grown beyond boundaries she and her top managers recognized. Although Skinner didn't realize it at the time, she was about to deepen her management skills yet further. For the next stage in management, she needed to go beyond her previous training. Skinner was in effect hiring her next mentor.

To the consultants, Skinner said she had a straightforward job. She needed their help to get agreement on priorities. The two consultants, however, dug deeply from the start into the nature of Skinner's management. They interviewed Skinner and nearly thirty of her staff in January

and February 2003. They wanted to know how the chapter worked, what
the complaints were, and what people were trying to accomplish.

When Danielson and Austrom issued their report in March, they laid
out a much broader analysis than one just on priorities. In fact, Danielson
called her concern about priorities just a growing pain. The bigger issue
was that the work had grown, the staff had grown, the demands from
headquarters had grown—but Skinner was managing in the same way she
had when her chapter was smaller.

Skinner's practice of delegating and stimulating bootstrap growth had
spawned conflict. She was the powerful patroness who sent her talented
explorers out to make good on the promise of conservation. Their voy-
ages of discovery had ignited fabulous advances in conservation—on the
Roanoke, in the Sandhills, in the Appalachians. But she had relinquished
coordination of the group as a whole, and now the explorers were collid-
ing as they pursued conflicting visions of conservation.

"'Heroic' action and leadership is much more the norm rather than
cross-functional, bipartisan negotiation and collaboration," the consultants observed in their report. "Your highly opportunistic, entrepreneurial
operating style was entirely appropriate when you were much smaller,"
they added. "It is also characteristic of most start-up organizations."

The consultants quoted staff: "There is confusion about where/how
decisions are made." "People get blind-sided by decisions that seem to
come out of the blue." "[We] need to balance opportunity with priority
setting." "Katherine doesn't draw us together as a team."

"Conversation by walking around" is how Danielson termed Skinner's
communication style. She had no methodical way to keep everyone up-
to-date. This worked in a small organization, where all the news fit to
know circulated quickly, but not in a larger one.

Skinner had earlier lamented to Danielson, executive director of the
executive program at Indiana University's Kelley School of Business, how
her top managers only tenuously grasped priorities in the state as a whole,
and how they stayed focused on their turf, budgets, and their own conservation priorities. Danielson surprised Skinner by saying the cause lay not
with her people but with herself: She was enabling this behavior. She managed her state staff as the Conservancy managed its fifty state directors, giv-

ing each so much autonomy few had the skill or knowledge to rise above it for the sake of the whole. In some ways, she had over-empowered her people.

When it came to the issue of priorities, the consultants found there was no agreed-on understanding of what constituted a priority in the first place. Among things people called "priorities," there were real priorities, stated priorities that weren't treated as such, unstated priorities that actually were treated as priorities, and nonpriorities that were priorities for some people. People were failing to communicate partly because of this confusion, and they weren't listening closely enough to each other to realize it. The room for disagreement was as big and wide as North Carolina.

Danielson and Austrom counseled Skinner to relinquish the heroic model and adopt a shared one—shared responsibility for leadership, management, and communication. The two consultants recommended a permanent team manage the North Carolina operation together. If the complexity was beyond one person's grasp, they argued, Skinner could let the team sort it out.

Skinner's job as manager had changed again. In the 1980s, she supervised most of the staff directly, and she had final say. In the early 1990s, as the staff grew to a dozen, she added a management layer and delegated authority and responsibility. She let her intellectual capital run. Now she had to shift once more.

Danielson and Austrom advised Skinner to name a management team. Working on the team would require a change for everyone. Top managers had to accept the idea that the buck might stop on Skinner's desk, but they were part of a team of eight people around that desk taking responsibility. Whereas people used to think, "If things don't go right, it's Katherine's problem," now the management team, together, would be on the hook.

This was simply the evolution of management in a growing organization. In the 2000s, Danielson told Skinner, you have to share leadership. No more heroic feats of management. Danielson galvanized Skinner for embarking on a new stage in her development, seventeen years after she first came to the Conservancy and donned the management mantle.

BEYOND HEROISM

In April, Skinner gathered her direct reports at the state headquarters in Durham, where the team would work together to shape a new concept of management. The first task the team had to undertake, with the help of Danielson and Austrom, was drafting a charter. That meant talking over purpose, values, roles, responsibilities—starting from scratch to clarify what they did, how they did it, who took charge, and what protocols to follow so the team worked best together. The charter would be a playbook for team management.

That playbook grew to thirty pages. It detailed everything from how to put items on the agenda to which style each person preferred for dealing with information. In one exercise, Skinner learned her first preference when getting information was to react right away, with little detail, to get quick results. Or if that was inappropriate, she would take time to methodically go through the detail, undeterred by the challenge, and then act. She shared this pattern with no one on her team. Most of the others preferred one of two other thinking styles first—indulging in analysis to develop the best possible solution or starting by generating ideas that integrate new concepts into the decision.

Two critical elements in the charter included the "working agreement"—how everyone's behavior had to change so they could work as a team—and a table listing decision-making responsibilities by person. Monitoring overall chapter performance was no longer Skinner's province alone. She shared it with the team—as well as sharing a host of other executive decisions, such as managing staff morale, communicating, setting priorities, resolving feuds between departments, and managing the budget.

The agreement detailed a new model of management—a team model. Skinner was once go-to person in crisis; now the team would ask, "How can *we* help?" Skinner once made a lot of decisions quickly, sharing her deliberations with just one or two people; now she would lead a "Delta Force" that consciously coordinated management.

The creation of the team in 2003 capped for Skinner a period of turmoil that she found even more trying than her first months in the job back in 1986. The question, of course, was: Will this work?

In mid-2003, Skinner got her answer. Just a few months after the team took shape, she attended a board meeting where the trustees expressed deep concern over funding. The stock market was still on its face after the dot-com crash. Money wasn't flowing in as in the past. One trustee pressed the board to rethink spending.

"It's not just a budget shortfall this year that's worrisome; it is a multi-year problem," he said. "Our budget consumption rate is too high."

The trustee called for slower spending. Worrying him most were investment returns. The chapter was spending too much of its endowment—5 percent a year. In some endowment accounts, the principal had fallen below its original value. The $600,000 given by the Department of Transportation for the tract next to Fort Bragg, a part of a highway-construction mitigation agreement, had shriveled to $521,000.

The trustee insisted that they needed to cut the endowment spending by at least $200,000.

Adding to the sense of financial duress, fundraiser James McDuffie gave the capital campaign report. The weak economy, depressed philanthropy, and an unfunded request for a $4 million grant had brought the chapter up short. The team of trustees and senior staff hadn't been able to secure the "top of the pyramid" gift hoped for—$5 million.

By the end of the meeting, with money so tight, everybody was wondering what they were going to do.

When it came to conservation, work raced ahead. The year before, the chapter had closed its biggest financial deal ever: It bought 38,320 acres from International Paper on North Carolina's coastal plain. Soon thereafter it arranged to buy 4,400 acres along the Little Tennessee River—one of Skinner's childhood canoeing streams—for $19.1 million.

But the budget crunch cast a pall over everything. It led the finance committee, for the first time, to refuse to approve the chapter's annual budget. It instructed Skinner and her team to prepare three different budget-cutting scenarios. If North Carolina revenues dropped through the floor, what was Skinner and her team going to do?

And so the management team was handed a challenge on which to cut its teeth. Skinner scheduled a day-long team meeting in Durham with her eight direct reports, including Annand, Pearsall, McDuffie, and others.

The board had specified three scenarios, one entailing a small budget cut, two others, big cuts. The board instructed the staff to report back with contingency plans for all three, including dates for cutbacks based on the specific revenue triggers.

This was new territory for the team members. They were used to managing growth. Now they had to prepare cuts in people and programs. When everyone turned out at 10:30 A.M., they weren't mentally ready. One of the team declared the recession over; hence they didn't have to do anything. Another reworked equations in the budget to try to make shortfalls vanish. The team tried mightily to reason its way out of dealing with the cuts. It was in denial.

The board believed that if it didn't keep insisting, the staff wouldn't make any contingency plans at all, and it was probably right. But with Danielson's prodding, the team came to accept that the contingency budgets, stretched across a lot of programs, had to undergo serious paring down. He reminded people the whole mission was in jeopardy if they chose to do too many things and didn't do them well. He had seen groups struggle before like the North Carolina team. He knew that to the staff of a nonprofit, to give up on anything seemed like giving up on the mission.

The whole meeting turned into an agony for everyone—agony because of decisions about cutting colleagues and friends and decisions about cutting urgent work. With Danielson's guidance, the team finally produced the plans. Skinner and the team successfully negotiated one of their first big challenges in shared leadership. Unlike the past, this was not Skinner, alone, beset by unsavory decisions. It was the team. And in what became known as "the infamous budget meeting," the staff moved beyond simply advocating for individual functions or projects to looking out for the best for the chapter. They looked at trade-offs together. Do we freeze jobs? Cut a program? Take a little bit from all programs?

As a result of the meeting, the finance committee finally got a report it wanted. It knew what the scenarios were, it understood the triggers, and it felt prepared if the worst happened. The contingency plan was a significant milestone, and it remained so even though the chapter, buoyed by a rebounding economy and donor contributions, never had to execute it. The process bonded people like never before. By rallying managers around a tough task requiring team management, Skinner had positioned herself as a manager relevant to the Nature Conservancy in the twenty-first century.

Skinner was no longer Patton on a tank calling the shots. "Every person on the North Carolina staff creates and contributes to vision and leadership in his or her own way," she said of her management style by the mid-1990s. "It's not my vision or leadership; it's ours." Now, in 2004, by listening to her staff and outside advisers, by recognizing new challenges and issues, she took this emphasis one step farther. Her top managers were on board with her, each trying to listen as much as talk, one playing to another's strengths, all buying into team action. This was the essence of shared leadership.

9

GLOBAL DYNAMO: Taking the Organization International

A S A CHILD, KELVIN TAKETA NEVER KNEW MUCH about the biota of Hawaii. He grew up on a ranch on the north side of Oahu, where he raised 4-H steers, rode horses, and tended three hundred head of cattle. He surfed and fished and camped. Despite his time in the outdoors, however, he couldn't pick out a native Hawaiian plant from an imported one. He didn't know the 'ōhi'a lehua, a common tree, was native, the strawberry guava introduced. Nor did schooling help. He learned biology from a text from the continental United States—and all the pictures showed trees that lost their leaves in winter.

But by his mid-thirties, as director of the Nature Conservancy in Hawaii, the incurious boy had turned into a veritable naturalist. Outspoken and well-schooled, he could wax philosophic about saving native Hawaiian flora and fauna, from the 'i'iwi honeycreeper to the Kamehameha butterfly. So strongly did he feel about his passion for conservation that he frequently shared his musings with his staff, often at the local watering hole.

179

One day in 1986, he was talking with his new staff attorney, Timothy Johns. Taketa told Johns there were three things worth working on for the future of life on earth: zero population, world peace, and conservation. Taketa, speaking for himself, said he couldn't do much about the first two, but he could make a tangible difference, a big difference, in the conservation of biodiversity.

Taketa could discomfit subordinates when he started in with such talk. Pontificating in this way, on the part of a short, mustachioed young man who would walk barefoot around the office, could come off as patronizing. Nonetheless, Taketa, who could out-argue just about everybody, and if not, charm them over a drink, persuaded not just his staff but some of the most conservative people he met of the urgency of conservation.

By the late 1980s, Taketa was talking about much more than Hawaii. He was talking about the loss of biodiversity across the entire tropical Pacific. In September 1989, at thirty-five, he was named director of Hawaii and the Pacific. Up to this time, the Conservancy had simply not applied its expertise in the Asia Pacific region. But as in many growing organizations, people like Taketa felt the opportunity for making a difference abroad rivaled or exceeded the potential at home.

Though well known for his successes in Hawaii, Taketa would ultimately leave his most indelible impression on the Conservancy for his work in the Pacific and Asia. And his work would offer a view of the difficulties of creating a strategy for expanding globally. Over the course of nearly a decade, he would show that an organization can employ its domestic strategy to get started in a new global theater of operations, but it soon finds local political, economic, and socio-cultural conditions call for a change of approach. At first, they require some tailoring of the strategy, but in the end, they require a revolution.

In 1989, the Pacific was, ironically, new ground for Taketa. He knew by heart only the story of conservation in Hawaii. When he started in Hawaii in 1980, 98 percent of Hawaii's bird species, 93 percent of its plants, and almost all of its invertebrates lived nowhere else on earth. Marooned in the Pacific 2,500 miles from the nearest continent, they provided a showcase for the fabulous and unique variations produced by evolution: ambushing carnivorous caterpillars, flightless flies, the tufted spear of Maui's silversword.

But by the late 1980s, human damage ravaged the biota on the islands of Kauai, Oahu, Molokai, Maui, and the Big Island. Hawaii had sustained 70 percent of all plant and animal extinctions in the past two hundred years of U.S. history. It suffered from having a frightening 27 percent of all current rare and endangered plants in the United States. It risked losing, scientists said, 88 of its 150 natural community types within twenty years. In short, the state faced an extinction crisis.

If you knew Taketa, you knew the story of the crisis. If you watched one of his slide shows, you saw people cry under the spell of his tale. A magnetic Japanese American with degrees in English from Colorado College and law from the University of California, he described species like the ʻoʻo, a once-common forest bird, down to two individuals by the 1980s and fast on the way to extinction. Staff like Johns, charged with expeditiously closing deals to save land, sometimes had trouble sleeping at night because Taketa would go on so about the risk of another bird going extinct if a deal wasn't done the next day.

Now Taketa was adapting his knowledge of the island-biodiversity crisis to the rest of the Pacific. At first, he knew little about other islands. Hawaii was eight hours by plane from Guam, eleven hours from Palau, thirteen hours from Manila. But he was soon to learn much more. By luck, Chuck Cook, a former Tennessee state director who had worked to protect huge wetlands in the Mississippi River Delta and Matagorda and Mad Islands in Texas, came through Hawaii at the start of a seven-month Pacific sabbatical. Foremost on Cook's mind was fishing the Pacific for the likes of coral trout, giant trevally, and tuna. But Taketa saw in Cook a seasoned scout for the Conservancy's expedition to the conservation frontier.

Taketa grabbed his chance to get some advance intelligence on the Pacific. He suggested that Cook base himself out of Hawaii and spend a couple of extra days in each island country to talk with conservationists. Cook, tall, blond, congenial, and crazy about fishing, bought the idea. He visited sixteen island nations, from Tonga, Fiji, and Palau to Guam, American Samoa, and Papua New Guinea. He returned with certain news: The Pacific offered plenty of conservation opportunity—and the saltwater fishing was fabulous.

Thus began the Conservancy's westward jump to the Pacific and Asia. Taketa's main question, both in the beginning and later, would be one of strategy. How could he accomplish the most long-term good by applying Conservancy expertise abroad? He would push himself as he always pushed his people, not just to think about the next step in conservation, but about the next level. In meetings, Taketa was known to lean back, look at the ceiling, and say, "Isn't the problem really . . . ?" And he would reframe the discussion. In the Pacific and Asia, he would reframe the Conservancy's discussion about expanding globally—and challenge his crack team of conservationists to fashion creative new approaches to conservation success.

NATIVE LEARNING

In working out a strategy for a program reaching into the Pacific, Taketa had in mind the precedent of Conservancy operations in Latin America, where the organization had operated since 1980. But he decided from the start that he would have to diverge from that precedent. The human setting in the Pacific was different: The people of each archipelago had their own cultural and political systems. The management situation was also different: Taketa was starting with a blank slate in a much bigger organization. And the geography was different as well: These were small islands for the most part.

Taketa fell back first on what he knew best—the lessons of ten years of experience in protecting the island geography he called home. He'd started in Hawaii in August 1980. His kickoff assignment, hardly a dream job, was cleaning up a real estate dispute in Kipahulu Valley, a remote mountain ravine plunging into the Pacific on the southeastern shore of Maui. The initial valley property came to the Conservancy in 1969 through Huey Johnson's efforts at the start of Patrick Noonan's tenure. The dispute later erupted when the Conservancy tried to transfer about a thousand acres of additional Kipahulu land to the National Park Service some years later.

The entire set of Kipahulu parcels were an irresistible addition to Haleakala National Park. The holdings ran from the subalpine shrubs near the 7,000-foot rim of the park's volcanic crater to the wave-pounded Pacific shore. There was one prickly problem that remained after the Conservancy sorted through the various holdings. The title to seven parcels in the lower valley wasn't clear, and the Park Service wouldn't accept the parcels that way. In a handshake deal, the Conservancy and Park Service hatched a plan to clear title: condemn the parcels.

But condemnation—in which the Conservancy and earlier owners claimed to perfect the title by having owned the land for decades without anyone contesting it—triggered an explosion of pent-up anger. A firestorm of newspaper articles and picketing erupted. The story ran statewide: The park service, said reporters, was ripping off claims of native Hawaiians, and the Conservancy was in cahoots.

Neither the Park Service nor the Conservancy had such ill intentions. The title was clouded because native land rights, from distributions by the Hawaiian monarchy in the 1800s, and Western land rights, from a century of land transfers thereafter, overlapped. Clarifying the title was, in some places, impossible. The Hawaiian community, nonetheless, called the condemnation a land grab by the feds, because although native Hawaiians left the land years before, they hadn't abandoned their claims.

Enter Taketa, who took a chastising from locals—not only from native Hawaiians but from moneyed residents of the neighboring town of Hana who suspected the Park Service of planning to ruin their unspoiled tropical haven. The Park Service withdrew its plan to condemn, but Taketa was left to turn the tide of opinion back in the Conservancy's favor. This was when he learned the biggest lesson of success he would transfer to his Pacific expansion: to work effectively, put people on the ground locally.

In Hawaii, as across the Pacific and Asia, good relationships carry more weight than good business skills. Taketa, savvy to the feelings of fellow islanders, flew to Hana from Honolulu, rented a car, bought a twelve-pack of beer, and visited his critics in Hana and nearby Kipahulu. His primary mission: "talk story." In Hawaii, talking story means talking about fishing, or kids, or going swimming, or hanging out, or even about business. By talking story, he made friends of his fellow Hawaiians one by one.

Taketa, meanwhile, recruited an advisory panel to write a plan for the title-contested lands. This was his key strategy for turning hostile Hawaiians into Conservancy boosters. Among the panelists: John Hanchett, manager of the Hana Ranch, Mike Minn, bank manager and community activist, Bill Chang, a young community activist and artist, John Lind, a community organizer who represented local landowners, and Teve Kahalewai, a native Hawaiian who spoke for his own. The panel agreed on a common goal: to protect the local land and endangered species, protect local rights to farm and hunt, and protect the way of life.

Taketa's main gesture of good will was to let the panelists decide what to put in the plan. Of course, he wanted the group to embrace the land transfer to the Park Service. And he wanted it to bless the sale to conservation buyers of biologically unimportant parcels. The Hawaii chapter badly wanted to sell the unimportant land, albeit with development restrictions, to pay down a $1 million debt on the project that had accumulated owing to legal and other costs.

But Taketa wanted more than anything else to have people believe the Park Service and Conservancy were good stewards who looked out for local people. He never felt the locals cared that much about the plan itself. They were worried about the character of the Conservancy: Is the Conservancy going to cut the local people out? Is the Park Service going to then overdevelop the property? Is the Conservancy going to shut down hunting and gathering rights? After the condemnation tactic, nobody trusted the Conservancy.

Taketa's strategy worked. In late 1981, the panel produced a plan that earmarked part of the disputed land for the Park Service, part for farming. It provided as well for the Park Service to build a visitor center and help the community with kiosks. In the process, Taketa believed that local people came to feel the Conservancy was a good thing, not a bad one. In turn, Taketa was on the way to becoming the trusted face of the Nature Conservancy in Hawaii, and easing people into thinking of the Conservancy as a local organization more than a national one.

All that talking, all that planning, all that work locally on the ground— the effort of that first year drove home to Taketa an enduring point. Good plans, good intentions—they don't count if you fly in from San Francisco, run a meeting, and fly home. You have to put in face time as if you're a local. Taketa counted as his most crucial gesture during this whole period a promise to dissident members of the Hawaiian community: "If you're upset about something, you call me and within twenty-four hours I'll be here." Taketa burned up many hours flying to and from Hana.

As Taketa got the Kipahulu dispute under control, including settling most lawsuits for land or money, he learned to pursue a classic Conservancy approach to conservation: Find big chunks of land, get people excited about them, raise the needed funds, and transact deals, one by one, with willing owners. Starting in 1980, he worked with state representative Hardy Spoehr and Conservancy veteran Henry Little to find several chunks. By the time Taketa took over as director in 1983, the threesome had lined up the 2,774-acre Kamakou project on Molokai and the 5,230-acre Waikamoi project on Maui. He and Little then launched a $3 million capital campaign to fund the deals.

In the next five years, Taketa continued to use the traditional buy-and-protect strategy. He took the fledgling Hawaiian operation launched by Little and turned it into the pride of Hawaiian environmental groups. As a measure of success, in the late 1980s he launched—and later finished—a $10-million capital campaign to fund his slate of land-protection projects. It was one of the largest-ever capital campaigns in Hawaiian history, second only to the $12 million campaign of Taketa's alma mater, the 140-year-old Punahou School in Honolulu.

Taketa was by then looking for other ways to expand the Conservancy's effectiveness. That's when he came to learn a second lesson he would take to the Pacific: Avoid going it alone when you can engage others to leverage your effectiveness. At the time, the extinction crisis continued—the 'o'o bird dropped to one individual, a male, found by scientists only by playing a recorded call and listening for him to call back. Taketa saw clearly the limitations of the traditional strategy to make a substantial impact on the diversity of life in Hawaii. Like other Conservancy managers, he came to understand that he could only do so much by buying and controlling land.

As it happened, Hawaii had a 108,000-acre Natural Area Reserves System (NARS), established in 1970. With scarcely any funding or staffing, however, the system was a network of "paper reserves" that had deteriorated badly. Taketa and his team decided on a strategy of working with the state to protect the reserve lands. Attorney Johns thus spearheaded an effort that led to the legislature approving, in 1987, $250,000 for state-land management, and in 1989, another $4 million, paid from hotel room tax revenues to support not only management of state land but private land of similar biological value.

Though this was heady money, Taketa saw that no amount of cash would enable the Conservancy, alone, to save biodiversity in Hawaii.

That's when he reexamined his conservation strategy and established a principle he would use during his global expansion. On October 1, 1989, as the chapter drafted a new strategic plan, he met with his board and told them the chapter needed to try new ways of doing business. "We need to institutionalize conservation, not the Conservancy," he told the board. He wanted the Hawaii chapter to become more than an owner and builder of preserves. He wanted it to play the role of architect.

At a board meeting a couple of months later, he was more explicit: "We will work cooperatively with other organizations even more than we have in the past," he said. "Our aim is to position the Nature Conservancy of Hawaii as a coordinator."

A third lesson he would take to the Pacific emerged at the same time. The Moomomi ocean-front project on the island of Molokai brought the lesson sharply into relief. Moomomi, on Molokai's north shore, featured desert-like coastal dunes sprouting morning glories, beach grass, and five unique endangered plants. In many places, the sands had lithified, or petrified, trapping traditional Hawaiian artifacts like adze blanks and fossils of extinct Hawaiian birds. It was a rare remaining example of a beach habitat once common in the islands but since lost to development or sand mining.

The whole parcel cost several million dollars, but the Conservancy only had the money to buy half, for $1.25 million. In 1987, Taketa chose the strategy he always had, to buy the more precious piece, based on its greater biodiversity. But while walking on the Moomomi beach one day in 1989, he rethought the deal. He had been certain at the time they had bought the right piece—the beach. But it dawned on him: He had bought the wrong one.

The right piece would have been the bay. Though not rare habitat, its purchase would have eliminated the real estate development value of both parcels, and left the beach still available to acquire later. Taketa had caused no harm. Neither piece had deteriorated. But he rued his lack of long-term strategic thinking. In the Pacific, he would try not to make the same mistake. In the game of global conservation, buying the best pearl in the necklace was not necessarily going to lead to protecting the most valuable parts of the necklace as a whole.

At Kipahulu, at Moomomi, and on the Natural Area Reserves System, Taketa learned three key principles that would stick with him as he tackled a global expansion: establish a local presence, work strategically on bigger landscapes, and spread the ownership by working with others. These principles would be the springboard for his strategy in conserving the diversity of life on other islands in the Pacific.

PLANTING FLAGS

On December 2, 1989, the national board of governors authorized Taketa to create a pilot program for the Pacific. In mapping out a strategy, he sat down with his fundraiser, Carol Fox, and board member David Cole, an entrepreneur, venture capitalist, and philanthropist who had worked for and founded several high-tech firms. Cole was Taketa's strategic alter ego, and pressed Taketa and his team to break free of traditional thinking.

Cole and his wife, Maggie, preferred "venture philanthropy," investing in high-risk, high-return charitable projects. In Taketa, Cole saw a conservation entrepreneur. Taketa had a track record of taking risks and Cole, who grew up in Hawaii like Taketa, trusted him—and funded him—to explore the conservation frontier across the Pacific.

Cole, Taketa, Fox, and soon scientist Audrey Newman and others worked as a team to hash out next steps. Cole himself ran a brainstorming session to decide where they would launch the first projects. The first principle they followed was pragmatism. They wouldn't go anywhere they hadn't been invited. In regional conferences, many conservationists from other island nations had asked them to help out. They would explore some of these invitations.

Next, they would choose sites where they could accomplish the most, the quickest. The debate raged as they ranked options according to half a dozen criteria: the need to stop imminent threats to natural diversity, the ability to assure long-term viability of the targeted site, the receptivity and strength of local people and groups, the safety and sophistication of working conditions, the level of cultural and legal support for conservation, and the potential for creating great examples of conservation to show off and duplicate elsewhere.

The vetting was agonizing. Some of the neediest countries ranked low. The Philippines and its marine reefs and tropical forests teemed with unique plant and animal life threatened with extinction. But the jewels of biodiversity had deteriorated badly, and the country's regulatory regime and working conditions were unfavorable. In the end, the team settled on a slate of five start-up sites: Indonesia, Pohnpei (in the Federated States of Micronesia), Palau, Papua New Guinea, and the Solomon Islands.

The first test of the expansion strategy fell to Cook, who by now knew the region better than anyone else. Taketa took Cook's advice and assigned him to Palau, a sovereign nation of three hundred islands 500 miles east of the Philippines and 4,500 miles southwest of Hawaii. Cook, who had earlier gotten a warm reception in the country, packed four suitcases and an ice chest containing a fax machine and flew to the capital city, Koror, to find a home and office. Though it took him two years to get a phone, he had moved to a Pacific paradise. Nearby were Ngeremeduu Bay, Micronesia's largest and most pristine mangrove estuary, and the Rock Islands, a group of forested gumdrops dotting an aquamarine sea interspersed with fifteen world-class diving sites.

Cook launched a classic Conservancy start-up. He began with initiating an ecological inventory to identify critical land and marine sites that would make the best parks and protected areas. The inventory turned up 1,300 species of reef fish, 400 species of hard coral, and animals ranging from the saltwater crocodile to the dugong to the hawksbill turtle. With the help of fishing chum Noah Idechong, the chief of the Division of Marine Resources, he arranged a memorandum of understanding to conduct the inventory, mapping, and talks with landowners to give up or change land and water uses.

The next year, Taketa dispatched Marty Fujita to Indonesia, the second test site for the expansion strategy. As international conservation officer at the Smithsonian, Fujita had pestered Taketa to start work in the home country of 40 percent of Asia's remaining biologically important rain forests, second in size only to Brazil's. Fujita, who spoke Bahasa Indonesia (the lingua franca of Indonesia) from earlier work in Kalimantan, was keen on conservation in the more politically stable Sulawesi, the island east of Borneo and south of the Philippines. Taketa told her to write a paper about the island's needs, and when he read it, he hired her.

Fujita, in daring bootstrap form, flew to Jakarta in June 1991 with two suitcases. She worked to secure a memorandum of understanding with the Indonesian Ministry of Forestry to allow the Conservancy an official presence in the country. In a pattern set by the Conservancy in Latin America, she proposed beefing up protection in preserves already designated by the country, rather than creating new ones. She set her sights on Sulawesi's Lore Lindu National Park and Morowali Nature Reserve, forested wildlands inhabited by animals like the Sulawesi black macaque, maleo fowl, Red-knobbed hornbill, and Sulawesi civet, all species found nowhere else in the world.

Fujita wanted to test the idea of melding conservation and economic development. In fact, she had no choice. In the developing world, people and nature intertwine everywhere. In Lore Lindu, she faced a trade in coffee, chocolate, and rattan. At the northern end of the park, villagers planted coffee and chocolate on park lands. In the south, they harvested rattan, the climbing palm used for cane furniture. Villagers often retrieved the rattan by felling huge canopy trees. Instead of an ecological inventory, Fujita started with a land use and socioeconomic survey, beginning with the 566,000-acre Lore Lindu Park. She then proposed small-scale, community-based economic development projects in the buffer zones around the park. The idea was to give economic incentives to people to adopt livelihoods that didn't harm park lands.

The next year, Taketa and his team opened the third expansion program in Pohnpei, Micronesia, and in 1993, a fourth in the Solomon Islands. In Pohnpei, a former Jesuit agricultural volunteer, Bill Raynor, worked to protect the small island's watershed. He was plagued by villagers who cut trees to provide sunlight for plantings to make sakau, an intoxicating drink made by pounding and processing a pepper root. Raynor faced an uphill battle convincing villagers that forest clearing eroded upland soils, which in turn smothered aquatic organisms inland and reef life offshore. He began a two-year tour to visit two hundred villages, every one on the island, to spread the word to a skeptical audience.

As Taketa and his team opened each new project, he tried to keep in mind the strategy. But as they set to work, the local conditions in the developing world demanded some rethinking. First off, the team realized it had not appropriately identified the highest-priority targets for protection. Some of the most fantastic biodiversity, they discovered, appeared not on land but on ocean reefs. Soon after Fujita started work in Sulawesi, Cook scouted nearby reefs, and saw the riches of biodiversity firsthand.

In 1994, he would zero in on Indonesia's Komodo National Park. Komodo, revered by tourists for its giant lizard-like Komodo Dragons, also encompassed reefs at the center of the bull's-eye of marine biodiversity. Komodo had more than 900 fish species, 250 reef corals, and 70 species of sponges. The riches in the sea demanded Taketa and his team shift their focus to cover both the land and the ocean.

Second, the team couldn't look upon supporting local jobs and economies as an adjunct to conservation. As at Lore Lindu, it was a prerequisite. At the white board, Taketa had foreseen jobs as important. But on the ground, the team saw them as paramount. This became one of the biggest lessons of working in the Asia Pacific region. Community- and development-based conservation was not just a new business, as Gregory Low had described for the United States. It was the only business.

In Lore Lindu Park, the demand for rattan defeated conservation altogether. In Pohnpei, the production of sakau did. In Komodo National Park, dynamite and cyanide—blasting or poisoning reefs to harvest fish—overwhelmed conservation efforts. The team couldn't just save pristine preserves. It had to conserve working landscapes where people made—and would continue to make—a living.

MCKINSEY VETTING

Taketa and his team sought to rework their strategies accordingly. Taketa never expected their approach to survive unchanged. The early work was experimental by nature. Nobody yet knew what the correct strategy was. They would just keep trying new things and adjusting as they went.

Of course, not everyone agreed with the Asia Pacific strategy in the first place. How to conduct business abroad was under constant debate at the top echelons of the Conservancy. Geoffrey Barnard, Taketa's rival as chief of the much larger and older international unit in Latin America, crafted another approach altogether, the "Parks in Peril" program. Barnard's people specialized in finding local conservation groups, offering them expertise and funding, and guiding them in protecting existing designated parks. Barnard did not build a local presence, as did Taketa, but his formula worked wonders. Starting in 1990, he set a goal of creating two hundred Parks in Peril projects. By 1993, he already assisted forty partner organizations in launching sixty-one programs in twenty-two countries.

Precisely because of their differences, the two international chiefs attracted the attention of John Sawhill, who as a new president in 1990 promised to make the Conservancy an international organization. Sawhill saw his global programs going in two directions, and he wanted a unified strategy, all the easier to manage and explain to donors. Taketa resisted the notion of a one-size-fits-all strategy, and instead lobbied fiercely for his approach, which was tailored to island nations, small but diverse ecosystems, weak regional institutions, and countries influenced by developed nations varying from France and Australia to Japan and the United States. He and Sawhill sparred often. The question that hung in the air could not be avoided: Was Taketa's global-expansion strategy sound?

Sawhill was serious about applying professional management to find the answer. He wanted to put the Conservancy on track for the most effective possible international program. So he invited McKinsey & Co. in September 1992 to study the Conservancy's entire international effort. Taketa took this as a bad sign. The study was concocted, he believed, to bless the Latin American approach and delegitimize his own. After all, the Latin American program was bigger and better established. Worried about the study, he and some of his team even talked about starting their own organization if their program was shot down by McKinsey. As far as Taketa was concerned, he was fighting for the life of the Asia Pacific expansion.

The McKinsey findings started trickling in, and the study did start to call the Conservancy's work into question—but not just Taketa's. Around the world, McKinsey found the Conservancy had planted lots of flags, and many sweetheart stories about Conservancy successes had appeared in the press. But many projects, McKinsey said, amounted to no more than pins on a map—"green measles," some people called them. On the ground, the projects often failed at permanently conserving anything. Many parks, for example, enjoyed little protection from damage driven by economic and social forces like those at Lore Lindu. The land simply hadn't been saved.

When McKinsey issued its preliminary reports in June 1993, nobody won plaudits as a hero. McKinsey considered the Conservancy's global strategies in delivering biodiversity protection as inefficient. In an attack on one hallowed Conservancy precept, it said that protecting many small sites gobbled up too much cash in land and salary costs. A bunch of isolated sites with tenuous protection hardly dented the extinction crisis globally. The Conservancy was spread way too thin.

McKinsey faulted both programs. The approach Taketa favored—saving sites—cost a lot, took a lot of time, yielded paltry benefits globally, and risked creating ungainly and unsustainable programs in nations without mature conservation laws, regulations, and regulators. The approach Barnard favored—building up local nongovernmental organizations—risked crushing small NGOs and relying on the wrong ones. In any case, both were "insufficient to protect biodiversity," concluded McKinsey. Both missed the mark and needed work.

While McKinsey came to these conclusions, Taketa and others were coming to similar ones of their own. Results on the ground bore them out. By the summer of 1993, Cook had worked for three years in Palau to win help from officials to back his agenda, but because the Palauan administration at the time ignored conservation, he hit a dead end. Despairing over government stonewalling, he called Palau a failed experiment, and considered packing his bags and flying home. To be sure, he had a biological inventory and had talked to communities, but he had no land or marine protection to show for it.

Instead of heading home, he headed out to fish with Palau Marine Resources chief Idechong, who echoed a theme Taketa and his team began to recognize: a global strategy springboarding directly from the U.S. experience was unworkable. Idechong then brought Cook around to this kind of thinking as they hand-lined for wahoo and Spanish mackerel and spincasted for grouper, bluefin trevally, coral trout, and Bohar snapper. In Palau, Cook realized, he was trying to be the driver, acting like the U.S. state director he once was. He had to instead let local people run the program. He had to sit in the back of the bus, not the front.

McKinsey recommended changes for a broader agenda. The firm concluded that international conservation required six strategic parts: a system of recognized conservation sites, local conservation capability, policies to support conservation, scientific research to inform actions, integration of people using the sites and conservationists trying to protect them, and long-term funding. Taketa's team called McKinsey's model the "six bubbles." All six had to be in place to assure lasting success.

McKinsey also said the Conservancy had to rein in global expansion. "Go deep, not broad," it said. Don't just protect valuable sites for their sake alone; create "demonstration" sites others can learn from. By limiting expansion, McKinsey argued, the Conservancy could leverage its scarce funds to greater benefit. It had to at least turn each of its small-patch preserves into a model, or "learning bed," that could influence or inspire similar conservation elsewhere.

In some ways, the McKinsey work didn't change life much for Taketa. It cited a "promising start in the Pacific," lauding in-country personnel, a tailored conservation approach, local-level action, community involvement, and a budding focus on policy as pluses. On the other hand, it cooled his ambitions. Taketa had been speedily planting flags to build a network of protected sites and was eager to plant more, eyeing everything from Vanuatu to Vietnam. For his expansionist tendencies, one board member dubbed him "Genghis Kelvin." In no time, people joked, he would be coming over the horizon from the east. Taketa had a practical reason to favor breadth rather than depth: It helped attract funding from foundations and agencies that favored organizations with broad global presence. But he had to acquiesce to a slowdown. And he instead had to lay down more robust programs in each place. Cook, for starters, needed to build local capability.

The lessons flowing in from the field, along with the McKinsey report, cast a new light on how to shape a strategy for global expansion. Taketa and the team had originally chosen targets of opportunity. The sites were proving grounds for new techniques, prototypes for an approach they could use elsewhere. They helped the team come to grips with new politics, new regulatory regimes, new cultures, and new economies. The Conservancy was now working with communities, working with in-country partners, and melding conservation and jobs. But through it all, the projects were site-based. They were small-patch experiments.

Now the assessments pouring in sent a message: You have to spend your time and money to reap far greater impact. McKinsey posed a question in its report: "How committed is the Nature Conservancy really? [Is it] willing to move away from site-based conservation and deal with issues of global importance?" More simply, accumulating experience forced Taketa and others to answer the question: What is the Conservancy going to do to make a difference on a global scale?

DEMONSTRATION SITES

Taketa and his team rewrote the Asia Pacific strategic plan in late 1993. The plan was a new and broader template for conservation, more fully formed, more ambitious, yet more focused on six to ten demonstration sites in five countries. The work on the ground began to reflect both the McKinsey analysis and the growing experience of Taketa and his team.

In Indonesia, Fujita narrowed her work to Lore Lindu Park and opened an office in nearby Palu, Sulawesi, to integrate economics and conservation. She took a carrot-and-stick approach. As for the stick, she equipped foresters with boots, backpacks, binoculars, and other equipment to help stop people from cutting rattan and planting coffee. As for the carrot, she sought to create jobs in microenterprises—in wild honey harvesting, rafting the Class 5 rapids of the Lariang River, and butterfly farming, where she laid plans to teach butterfly-farmers-to-be how to care for larval food plants, plan production, and market for export to a growing trade destined to stock tropical butterfly houses worldwide. Meanwhile, she launched a number of community outreach and conservation awareness programs.

On Palau, Cook redoubled his efforts. Working with Idechong and other Palauans, he launched a local group, the Palau Conservation Society, to lead the work. The society's first big project was a one-year public awareness campaign on the biib, Palau's endemic fruit dove. Using puppet shows, posters, billboards, and music videos, the campaign opened the eyes of schoolchildren, local communities, and political decision makers to the wonder of the biib and the lands and waters it depended on.

The society grew quickly when Idechong accepted the executive directorship. In one effort, he convinced the chiefs of Palau to reinstate the traditional closure of ocean fishing at six individual spawning and aggregation sites from April to July. The closure let stocks of grouper mate undisturbed and replenish the species. Idechong then went on to rack up a string of conservation successes and win the coveted $50,000 Goldman Prize and a $150,000 Pew Fellowship for protecting the environment.

Demonstration sites like those in Palau and Lore Lindu could indeed inspire conservation work elsewhere. They also responded to the one- and five-year goals Taketa and his team hammered out in September 1994, reflecting the group's broader thinking. The first set of goals extended beyond conservation to "conservation and compatible development." The second extended beyond organizational development to "institutional development"—of strong outside institutions that could lead conservation over the long term. A third called for more than partnerships to create protected sites: partnerships to change conservation policy.

A chance to act on this more sophisticated strategic thinking came at a meeting in 1994, when neither Taketa nor anyone on his team was quite expecting it. The meeting, like others when the team gathered for two-and-a-half-day retreats in Hawaii, was the crucible for breakthrough strategic thinking. Taketa set an example of disciplined analysis, openness to new ideas, and the willingness to challenge—indeed, to strip down and rebuild—any idea on the table. They were all sitting in a conference room in Honolulu, considering how to protect the rainforests of Papua New Guinea. Because of a booming economy in Asia, the Papua New Guinea Forest Authority was eager to sell timber concessions to Asian clear-cutters, and trees were falling fast.

With a map of Papua New Guinea on the wall, the team talked over the emerging possibility of creating "wildlife management areas." Papua New Guinea had passed legislation years before to create such protected sites, and the Conservancy could probably stimulate action to save land under the old law. The lands were certainly valuable, and the threat urgent.

A visiting William Weeks, the Conservancy's chief operating officer, listened to the brainstorming. After about thirty minutes, he interrupted in an interchange that went something like this:

"I have a question. What's the killer threat to forests in Papua New Guinea?"

"Logging," said the team, in a chorus of agreement.

"What do wildlife management areas have to do with logging?" asked Weeks.

"Nothing," said the team, again in a chorus of agreement.

A pregnant pause followed.

Weeks's comment brought immediate order to everyone's thinking. Taketa and his team saw how their focus was missing the target. If they went after wildlife preserves, they would be going down a path that might keep them busy with site-based conservation while the biggest threat to biodiversity persisted. What kind of model program would that be? How would that serve the team's new goals?

The team bemoaned the threat of logging. The archenemies, the Malaysian and Korean timber barons, took logs out of the forests for a song, paying a fraction of the timber's market value. Local villagers, eager to earn royalties on their timber, gave national officials the authority to market concessions in their area. Provincial committees vetted proposals and chose the best one, but national officials often awarded concessions to barons who were pulling strings in Port Moresby, the capital. In the end, the barons reaped a windfall, while Papua New Guinea forests were plunged into a biodiversity death spiral.

Weeks interrupted. He asked the question: If the loggers can take wood out for, say, less than 10 cents on the dollar, why couldn't the Conservancy beat them at their own game? Why couldn't the Conservancy take logs out for 50 cents on the dollar and do it responsibly?

Weeks had no idea if the question was fair. He piped up because he was impatient with the circling discussion. But his comment triggered a powerful moment of reflection by the team.

Everyone began to ask each other: Why couldn't we do better? Why couldn't we figure out how to log in a way that conservation and timber harvesting worked together?

The Asia Pacific team had tried small-scale economic development—butterfly farming, sport fishing, and so on. But dealing with hundreds of thousands of acres in a logging concession was a whole different matter. Taketa was intrigued. On that day, the team didn't emerge with a plan. They simply tossed around ideas of how to work with or compete against the big barons. Within a couple of months, however, they had decided: the Conservancy would apply for a Papua New Guinea forestry concession and show the government that a company could log sustainably and make a profit. This would be model project of a new scale: an industrial enterprise created to do conservation while delivering better returns to landowners. This would indeed be a demonstration site dealing with an issue of global importance.

REFRAMING STRATEGY

A year later, Taketa gathered his team for another retreat, this time at a beach house on the north shore of Oahu. Taketa had a special purpose in mind. This was one of those times when he planned to press the team to look at not just the next step but the next level. He wanted to reframe their strategy entirely. He didn't know what that meant exactly, but he wanted to elicit from the team the creative ideas that would move them well beyond any of their previous thinking.

As the meeting started, he first asked everyone to assess progress since the changes sparked by their early work and the McKinsey report. How had they done? Clearly, they had established some solid demonstration projects, built credibility, learned some lessons. They had met their objectives. Now Taketa wanted everyone to assess the outlook. What were they going to do to make a difference on a global scale?

If we back up, zoom out, what should we be doing next? Taketa challenged.

Taketa worked a flip chart, playing his typical role as driver and catalyst, challenging his tough-minded conservation entrepreneurs. The Papua New Guinea logging deal was on the drawing board, now managed by team member and New Zealander Peter Thomas, a veteran of many South Pacific conservation projects, and William Ginn, a businessman and forestry expert (who subsequently worked with Kent Wommack in Maine). It would be a big project, but Taketa sought a strategy to affect many more places at the same time. As he teased out ideas and wrote them down, the discussion migrated to the notion of killer threats again.

All along, the group believed that among the challenges they faced was the need to tackle ever bigger threats. They had tackled local ones, site threats. They had established many beachheads. The Papua New Guinea deal promised one of their biggest yet. But what about much bigger threats, killer threats that spread across the entire region? Could the Asia Pacific team have an impact on a systemic killer threat?

The notion of addressing a systemic threat focused the discussion. Owing to the timing of the meeting, it also brought front and center one of the threats on everybody's mind at that time: the trade in live reef fish. The capture of fish from among the region's thousands of miles of reefs was causing massive damage. Some fish sales went to people to stock aquariums worldwide. Others went to stock restaurant larders. In both cases, the trade was vigorous and posed a terrifying risk to biodiversity.

Cook had first learned about the trade and its most damaging aspects in the Philippines several years before. Responding to global demand for tropical aquarium fish, divers plunged to the fringes of the country's magnificent coral reefs, squirted sodium cyanide solution into nooks to stun prized specimens, and then scooped up and revived the most marketable fish to sell. Many fish died in the process, but even if they didn't, the cyanide killed the coral. The aquarium trade left a trail of devastation requiring decades to recover.

Cook soon learned that cyanide was popular among commercial fishermen, too. At Komodo National Park, many reefs died after divers stunned and captured cyanide-dazed wrasse and groupers, many weighing a hundred pounds or more. The ships dumped the fish into holding pens, revived them, and hauled them to Asian markets. Chinese diners prized the live fish for their flavor and texture, cooked immediately after killing, untainted by rigor mortis. Every Chinese gourmet could taste the difference, and wealthy diners paid dearly for live fish when they feted others during business or celebratory feasts.

Cook remained unaware of how enormous the trade in live reef fish was until one day in 1992, when the Palauan attorney general's office called. Come down to the pier and help us look at this, the caller said.

The marine police, patrolling Palau's Helen Atoll, 350 miles south of the capital, ran across an Indonesia-based vessel fishing for the Chinese market. Capable of carrying fifteen tons of live reef fish, its tanks teemed with two to three hundred gorgeous specimens, the kind Cook knew well—greenish-blue Napoleon wrasse, blotchy brown and white groupers, speckled green, blue, and gold-colored coral trout. The ship had been poaching with cyanide, and the police had impounded the vessel. Cook was awed. Some of the fish, the treasures of Pacific reefs, weighed up to two hundred pounds.

The fish were also the treasures of Chinese restaurants across Asia. Live Humphead wrasse fetched $82 per pound in the market. In a restaurant, the lips of the Humphead wrasse, a delicacy, brought $225 a plate.

The incident appalled Cook—all the more so because the fish in this case neither reached the market nor got back to the reefs. They were caught in a legal wrangle and all died in the ship's tanks. But the incident put Cook and Taketa's team on notice. The live reef fish trade—and the killing of reefs with cyanide—was not just a local problem. All nations near Chinese markets, especially Indonesia and the Philippines, were at risk. So were nations farther east in the Pacific, like Micronesia and Melanesia.

As the reports of coral-reef destruction mounted, Cook hired Australian marine ecologist Robert Johannes and fisheries economist Michael Riepen in early 1995 to document the trade. The collaborators tracked vessel movement and sales and began to accumulate evidence that shocked the team into action. The two confirmed that many ships were coming to Indonesia, filling their boats with wrasse, groupers, and coral trout, and taking them to Hong Kong, Taiwan, and elsewhere to stock the tanks of pricy restaurants. Half the fish died en route.

In March 1995 Cook presented preliminary information to the board of governors. Commercial fishermen ran a hit-and-run operation, he explained. They would bamboozle local villagers into giving permission to fish, destroy the reefs, and never come back—paying little to locals for the catch. The massacre of fish and coral was devastating. Sixty percent of Komodo's coral reefs were damaged. And with the trade so lucrative, Cook expected soon to see ships in Papua New Guinea, the Solomon Islands, and elsewhere in the Pacific.

At the retreat on Oahu, the threat posed by the live reef fish trade played right into the discussion on strategy led by Taketa. The problem was so large it cast doubt on the notion that demonstration sites could have a global impact. What if cyanide fishing stopped at Komodo, and Palau, and Papua New Guinea—but not fifty or a hundred other places in Southeast Asia and the Pacific? How much damage would there be in twenty years? How much good would they have done if they protected only a handful of demonstration sites?

The group together realized it couldn't solve this problem one site at a time. China was supplying divers and cyanide. Hong Kong was supplying ships, capital, and a market. And Indonesia and other countries were supplying reefs and the fish. The issue cut across the region. The team members realized they had been working from the bottom up. If they were going to save the biodiversity of the marine ecosystem, they would have to work from the top down, too. The next step, the next level, meant dealing with issues like this regionally.

Taketa was delighted. Here, through the typically intense heat of discussion, the team emerged with a breakthrough in their thinking. They would reframe their strategy to embrace a program that extended beyond local sites. If they didn't act at a regional level, the threat could rout their conservation efforts at every marine site in the Pacific. The group decided it would attack the threat in an entirely new way for the Conservancy—by influencing regional policy. After five years on the job, Taketa had learned a lesson he would bank on for the remainder of his work at the Conservancy.

In October 1995, Johannes finished his report. The live reef fish trade was bigger than they thought. Tracking vessel movements and fish marketing throughout Asia, Johannes estimated that, in the next year, 20,000 to 25,000 metric tons of live reef fish, caught by hundreds of fishing boats, would be shipped to Hong Kong, Taiwan, Singapore, and China. Fishing companies would pump hundreds of tons of cyanide per year into coral reef communities. Since coral and small fish die at cyanide concentrations far lower than that used by divers for large fish, the cyanide was catastrophic—killing not just the fish but their habitat. Full recovery of some coral reefs would take centuries.

MAXIMUM LEVERAGE

The conservation challenge suddenly looked different to Taketa and the team. They had started with the strategy launched in Hawaii, to build a network of sites to save the most biologically diverse places. They had moved to building demonstration sites, documenting what they learned to move their works to new sites. And now they were looking at building a program for maximum leverage. They were getting into a new field of operations, making a difference by addressing policy regionally. This was a new, high-leverage part of their global expansion strategy.

This new mindset forced into the limelight two projects, the live reef fish trade and the Papua New Guinea logging plan. To tackle the Papua New Guinea project, Taketa had hired forestry expert Ginn. Working with team member Thomas in Auckland, New Zealand, Ginn put together a plan in the last half of 1995 to start a profit-making company, win a logging concession from the Forest Authority of Papua New Guinea, and find a strong for-profit logging company as an operating partner.

To propose that the Conservancy start a logging company struck some in the Conservancy as heresy. But to Conservancy pragmatists, it made its own kind of sense. There was no way the Conservancy could intercede to stop Papua New Guinean logging. The Papua New Guinea government was hungry for revenue, Asian markets were hungry for wood, and forests were going to fall to the chain saw. But the team was eager to show that the Conservancy could come up with an environmentally sensible, sustainable, and commercially viable alternative to putting the concessions into the hands of clear-cutters who would raze forests and destroy watersheds. The officials could instead sell to a company that would generate a profit over the long term while producing timber products using environmentally friendly standards certified by the Forest Stewardship Council.

The idea wasn't to say, "Stop logging." The idea was, "Log forever." Taketa's team wanted more than to save a piece of forest. It wanted to prove something much harder: the possibility of putting together a business plan for sustainable logging.

In late 1996, the Conservancy's forestry company, Sustainable Forest Resources of Papua New Guinea, submitted its proposal for the 250,000-acre Josephstaal forestry concession in Madang Province. A bold plan appeared on track. Alas, although the Conservancy won the concession, events later derailed the project. Surveys showed the merchantable timber volume amounted to considerably less than thought—too little to support a mill, a key to reaching long-term profitability. Thomas and Ginn sought to reconfigure the deal to make it economically viable by enlarging the concession. But then the Asian economic crisis of the late 1990s slammed timber markets, and the price of logs and lumber plunged. The business plan no longer showed a profit. To complicate matters, government officials said that if the Conservancy couldn't restore its original plan, it would withdraw the Conservancy's status as an approved concessionaire.

The deal collapsed by late 1998, under the weight of slumping markets, red tape, and the Conservancy's inability to bring a well-capitalized commercial forestry company into the partnership. The chance to create a model of a sustainable forestry enterprise was lost.

Still, the Conservancy did influence the thinking of provincial and local officials and landowners—while teaching the team more than a few lessons about influencing bureaucrats in a developing country. And the Conservancy's four years of work saved the site from the saw. Ed Mayer and Susan Brown, a husband-and-wife team hired by the Conservancy, worked with local villagers during the intervening years to build support for land protection. Their work eventually led to locals petitioning the court to withdraw their lands from the concession area, removing the heart of the merchantable timber. In hindsight, this was the biggest achievement—buying time to work with the communities to change local thinking about logging. Forty thousand acres in the heart of the concession were saved from logging in perpetuity.

The program to protect live reef fish ramped up during the same period. Andrew Smith, an expert in coastal resource management, took the lead on Pacific policy. Cook and Fox took the lead on international awareness. The board of governors nixed a Conservancy-fronted lobbying drive. Delving firsthand into regional policymaking was still too risky for most governors. But the board did approve an effort fronted by Johannes as spokesman.

Fox and Johannes then took their case to Hong Kong. They came with two blockbuster lobbying aids. One was Johannes's report. Another was a twenty-minute film acquired by Cook of divers dousing coral with cyanide, banging and breaking coral fronds, and yanking stunned Napoleon wrasse and grouper with tongs from pockets in the reef. Any viewer with half a heart for the health of reefs and half a mind for an ample fish supply recoiled at the pictures of the poisoned corals and the litter of dead fish left behind.

At first, Fox and Johannes approached the Hong Kong government and got a disappointing hearing. Fox's contacts from earlier fundraising work basically told her, "This isn't Hong Kong's problem. It's Indonesia's." But Fox felt otherwise. She wangled a series of radio and television interviews for Johannes, and a showing of the video to Hong Kong legislators. Stories ran locally and in the *New York Times, Time,* and the *International Herald Tribune.*

The breakthrough for Fox came when CNN ran a report featuring Johannes and running clips from the distressing cyanide-fishing video. Fox then showed the heart-rending CNN segment repeatedly to policy-makers and donors. Along with Johannes's research results, the video shocked viewers. It became a key tool for Fox to raise awareness and raise money to stop the trade.

Fox attacked both the supply and demand sides of the trade. On the demand side, one of her biggest efforts came in 1997, when she dared Chinese gourmets to prove wild fish had superior flavor. A lot of people told her wealthy Chinese would never eat grouper from fish farms. They liked wild-caught everything. Fox challenged them by holding fancy din-ner parties in Hong Kong, Taipei, and Shanghai. At each she invited thirty top gourmets, who were offered four selections: pond-raised grouper, sea-cage-raised grouper, wild grouper, and coral trout.

Fox was simply playing an age-old game: running a taste test. Could the gourmets tell the difference? The results were the same each time: The gourmets preferred the coral trout first, the sea-cage-raised grouper sec-ond, the wild grouper third. They all ranked the pond-raised grouper last. The gourmets could indeed tell the difference between each of the fish. But Fox made her point: grouper farmed in cages could replace grouper caught wild in the cyanide trade.

Along with Cook, Fox pursued the supply side as well. They worked hardest at building a case for mariculture. Their message was not to tell people not to eat fish, but to eat fish raised sustainably. They could tell mer-chants the fish tasted good even to gourmets. Moreover, with mariculture, the fish suppliers could control fish size and the supply channel. The concept appeared so promising that by 1997 consultants hired by the Conservancy examined and approved a sea-cage mariculture operation in Komodo National Park in Indonesia.

Armed with the results, Fox, Cook, Johannes, and others promoted a change in policy. In May 1997, the Asia Pacific Economic Cooperation (APEC), the only regional organization that includes China and "Chinese

Taipei," passed a resolution on destructive fishing practices, urging a stop of cyanide fishing and supporting the retraining of people to work in mariculture.

In the end, in Palau, Papua New Guinea, and the Solomon Islands, where the trade had not gained a firm foothold, Andrew Smith's education and policy advocacy stopped the live fish trade. In Southeast Asia, especially in Indonesian and Philippine waters closer to Chinese markets, cyanide fishing persisted. Indeed the war was not won, but an important battle went to the conservationists. The Conservancy initiated a rethinking of fisheries policy across Asia. Eventually, Smith helped transfer this work to the policymakers themselves, the South Pacific Commission, a regional organization responsible for fisheries, later renamed the Secretariat of the Pacific Community.

Taketa's team was now playing on a much more visible stage, with more sophisticated strategies for global conservation. They were helping the Conservancy come around to a notion McKinsey broached in its 1994 report: "playing the pyramid." At the base level, McKinsey said, the Conservancy should address national conservation policy, at the middle, regional policy, and at the top, global policy. At each level, the Conservancy enjoyed greater leverage, and greater conservation impact.

This expanding scope of the Asia Pacific team's work readied Taketa and his players for the crowning step of the 1990s. A Bangkok developer, Vikrom Kromadit, had bought a concession to develop a ski area on Jade Dragon Snow Mountain in the lofty peaks of Yunnan, China, northeast of Burma. He didn't get very far with his plans. When he hired a ski consultant from Colorado, the consultant came back with bad news—Jade Dragon was too high and got too little snow. The consultant suggested instead a national park and called in the Conservancy to float the idea.

Taketa, hungry for Chinese support for conservation across Asia, let an eager Carol Fox investigate the notion. Fox, fluent in Chinese from years as an expatriate, led the way. Her strategy reflected the experience of the Asia Pacific team. The way to win the business of the Chinese was to talk not about conservation but about regional development policy. With the help of McKinsey & Co. in Hong Kong, she raised Chinese sights above the notion of mass tourism, which degraded the environment and paid poorly. She sold the concept of developing high-grade tourism— protecting the most precious lands in a sort of Chinese Yellowstone Park.

Fox hired Rose Niu, a native Naxi from the project area in northwest Yunnan, to run the program. Niu eventually cut a deal for creating the Yunnan Great Rivers project: The Chinese pledged $3 million and the Conservancy $2 million. Niu and Fox arranged for Sawhill to sign the pact in June 1998 in China, sealing a deal for the Conservancy to develop conservation plans for a 67,000-square-kilometer project area, about the size of West Virginia.

The Yunnan project was the start of a huge effort by the Conservancy in China. It climaxed in February 2002, when Conservancy board member and Goldman Sachs chairman Henry Paulson, project adviser Ed Norton, Fox, and Niu met with Chinese president Jiang Zemin. In a milestone for conservation, Jiang said to an assembly of officials that he liked the Yunnan model and he wanted the Conservancy's systematic conservation methodology, Conservation by Design, to become a model for China. The Conservancy's approach and Taketa's global expansion strategy, won approval of the biggest nation in Asia. This imprimatur marked the strategy's ongoing success.

As for Taketa, recruited to run Hawaii's largest charitable foundation, he resigned at the top of his form, as the China program was launched by Sawhill. As for finding the right strategy, he still wasn't at all sure he had succeeded. In the blur of expansion, his work was often more tactical and less coherent than the results suggested. He did know he had come a long way, from a network of experimental site-based projects to well-honed demonstration sites to influencing regional development policy. Through it all, he had taken the Asia Pacific operation through a strategic revolution.

But there was one caveat: As he resigned, he cautioned Sawhill that he would find no obvious proof of success in any single approach to international conservation. The Conservancy would never be able to say, "*That's* the strategy." "Ultimately the game is all about leverage," he later said. "You can't do this work incrementally." That meant the Conservancy would always have to put its faith in far-flung on-the-ground entrepreneurs. It would have to challenge them to tear apart and rebuild their assumptions and operations. And it would have to exhort them to move their thinking not just ahead one step, but up one level.

10

THE SENATE IS CALLING: Accountability and Governance in the Face of Crisis

WHEN THE *WASHINGTON POST* PRINTED the three-part series on the Nature Conservancy in 2003, Steven McCormick was pictured on page 1. The photograph of the fifty-two-year-old president appeared above the fold in a story headlined, "Nonprofit Land Bank Amasses Billions." For all the world, the handsome, fine-featured lawyer, caught in a half-frowning, mug-shot-sized image, looked like the latest in the lineup of corporate miscreants. Newspaper readers, attuned to executive looting from the 2000–2002 dot-com bust, were familiar with this kind of story: Big cheese with big salary squanders money and snookers public.

McCormick bought the early edition of the Sunday paper on the evening of Saturday, May 4. Invited with his wife to dinner with two other couples, he brought the paper because his host once worked for the Conservancy. Though generally quick to laugh, McCormick, the man running what the *Post* called a "corporate juggernaut," was humiliated. He didn't know the other couples—one of the wives turned out to be an editor for another section of *Post*.

The dark portrayal of the Conservancy pained McCormick no end. The Conservancy was his life's work and passion. He had started with the organization twenty-six years before, was proud of his accomplishments, and felt he had continued to guide the Conservancy on a trajectory of significant achievement. In just the two years since the *Post* started reporting, the Conservancy had protected more than 2 million acres of land. In light of the record, the portrayal by the *Post* seemed flat out unfair.

Unfair or not, McCormick had a crisis on his hands. He didn't fully recognize the nature of that crisis on that Saturday evening, although the lean, six-foot five-inch chief executive did feel like he had been punched in the solar plexus. But over the next twelve months, he would come to understand that the *Post* series, recounting how the Conservancy logged forests, drilled for natural gas, sold its logo for profit, and resold land for a bargain to insiders, raised fundamental questions: How accountably had he and the board run the organization? And how responsibly had they governed to assure the organization ran at the highest level of performance?

McCormick would answer these questions under great duress—under the scrutiny of one of the world's most powerful newspapers in one of the most unforgiving cities in America. He would explore first one and then another means to respond, but in the end conclude the Conservancy had to examine every process and procedure of organizational oversight. He would then have to revamp internal oversight and guide the board in restructuring governance. An overhaul of management at the highest levels was the only way to quell the crisis and get back on the road to focusing on conservation.

What McCormick did recognize on that Saturday evening was that the deals unearthed by the *Post* put him horribly on the defensive. As he boarded a plane for San Francisco the next morning, shuffling down the aisle with dozens of people carrying the same paper, he ached with the thought of how badly he had been personally portrayed. The main article repeated a decades-old beef he was used to—corporate relationships tainted the Conservancy's work. He knew how to answer that one. But an inside story took him to task over his pay.

At a time when executive salaries were drawing ridicule from the public and censure from lawmakers, the Conservancy had not disclosed all aspects of his compensation, which included a $275,000 base salary, a $75,000 signing bonus, a $75,000 housing allowance, and a $1.55 million home loan. Although he considered the lapse inadvertent, when reporters questioned McCormick directly, his answer was inconsistent with the earlier information, eroding his and the Conservancy's credibility. If he could have built trust during the reporting process to induce favorable coverage, he had blown his chance.

The unfavorable nature of the reporting became clearer the next day, Monday, when the second part of the series ran. It was an exposé of the Conservancy's two worst bloopers. In one article, the *Post* suggested the Conservancy put the well-being of the near-extinct Attwater's prairie chicken second to the pumping of natural gas—some of which the Conservancy sold without paying the rightful owners. The Conservancy denied endangering the birds, located on a Texas City, Texas, preserve, but settled the charges of gas theft in 2002 for $10 million.

In a second article on Monday, the *Post* reviewed the failing for-profit venture launched at the Virginia Coast Reserve, the enterprise championed by Gregory Low in the 1990s. "The troubles demonstrate the difficulty of the Conservancy's strategy of blending for-profit businesses with community-based conservation," wrote the *Post*. Neither these troubles nor the multimillion-dollar spill of red ink were news to Conservancy insiders, but they certainly were to outsiders. The deal described in the newspaper, no matter how much value it had as a learning experience, looked like a gross waste of time and money.

The biggest blow in the series came on Tuesday, the third day. The *Post* published an exposé of "conservation buyer" deals—where people buy land from the Conservancy at a discount from the original price, in compensation for the Conservancy's encumbering the deed with development restrictions. In the cases cited, Conservancy insiders bought land for a bargain, built on the property the homes they wanted anyway, and then wrote a check for a donation to make the Conservancy whole. They then took tax deductions. The reporters maintained the Conservancy lost millions of dollars on the deals, which in any case smacked of handouts to rich celebrities like David Letterman.

With the appearance of the third story, McCormick was devastated—as were many staff and board members. The story was much more powerful than expected. It pictured opulent homes, money-laundering-like flow charts, and a headline to incite disdain: "Nonprofit Sells Scenic Acreage to Allies at a Loss: Buyers Gain Tax Breaks with Few Curbs on Land Use." Although the deals were legal and preserved land, they used the tax code to, in essence, transfer cash from the pockets of taxpayers to the trust accounts of the rich. McCormick canceled his West Coast plans and flew back to Arlington.

McCormick had never handled such a crisis before. Before moving to Washington as Conservancy chief in 2001, the farthest east he had lived was Berkeley. Brought up next to a dairy farm in Tiburon, across the bay from San Francisco, he dedicated himself to preserving his native state. As a child, one of his dreams was to be a forest ranger. As a teenager, he was able to name every tree he came across. His hobby was taking field trips to identify and photograph plants. In law school, he imagined he would go into the public sector, working for the attorney general's office in California, suing bad people in the public good.

At the Conservancy in California, McCormick started his land-saving efforts by buying 5- to 10-acre parcels in subdivisions to protect desert tortoises from dune-buggy traffic. Later, in his most lauded work, he sought to protect the endangered fringe-toed lizard, which "swims" through sand dunes. Conflict arose when the lizard's presence in California's Coachella Valley blocked the construction of housing, hotels, and golf courses near Palm Springs. Developers were up in arms. McCormick hammered out agreements to save critical lizard habitat and allow developers to build on remaining lands.

John Sawhill tapped McCormick in the mid-1990s as a rising star. He asked McCormick to help manage the creation of the Conservancy's new agenda for conserving biodiversity in large ecoregions. He later recruited him as a successor for president, but the California son swore he would never leave California. Instead, after sixteen years as state director of Conservancy operations in California, McCormick left to start a law firm. He was courted back to the Conservancy months later, after Sawhill's death in 2000, only by a persistent search team from the board.

"I love having a cause," he said of his comeback. "I love organizing things around a purpose." He added that he didn't realize how much he liked doing that until separated from the Conservancy.

A devotee of the Conservancy's mission, McCormick came from a point of view far different from that of a pair of skeptical investigative reporters. He believed the *Post* articles distorted the Conservancy's record, misconstrued facts, and failed to give a representative picture of the Conservancy's accomplishments. By spotlighting isolated missteps and conflicts of interest, the *Post,* he felt, led readers to believe mismanagement was the rule, not the exception. *To whom are journalists accountable for such reporting?* McCormick wondered.

David Ottaway, first on the story for the *Post,* had a similar question in mind. The issue of accountability had come up in previous reporting he had done on the work of nonprofits opposing an oil pipeline project in Chad. At that time, he had been struck by how a small band of decision makers called all the shots in global nonprofits. *To whom are these decision makers accountable?* he wondered. He and later partner Joe Stephens wondered even more as they unearthed questionable deals by the Conservancy in Texas, Virginia, and elsewhere.

By raising the issue of accountability, the *Post* series left a durable impression: The Nature Conservancy, like the Enron and WorldCom corporations, was no longer a poster child for goodness and excellence. It was an enterprise under investigation.

In an online chat with reporter Joe Stephens on Tuesday, May 6, one chatter's comments suggested the way in which the Conservancy's image had taken a hit: "Who has been in charge at TNC that needs to go?" wrote the chatter. "It sounds like there are too many lawyers, accountants and fundraisers at TNC, and not enough morally upright men and women doing oversight on the board and on staff."

Readers of any of the *Post's* ten stories in the first three days were anxious for an explanation. McCormick simply had to act. His response, both immediately and in the following months, would determine the freedom of the organization to operate on the basis of trust established with members, donors, and other constituencies. His response would also, in the process, provide a lesson for top managers of organizations everywhere of how to—and not to—react to a crisis in accountability.

SEEING THROUGH OUTRAGE

McCormick's first impulse after the *Post* series was to strike back. "Repeatedly I—and others—were quoted incompletely and out of context," he e-mailed the staff on Monday, May 5, just as the second story in the series appeared. A response team, he promised, would deliver "a more accurate and complete portrayal" of the Conservancy in the coming days. Sharing a sense of outrage was Anthony Grassi, chairman of the board. In frequent phone calls, he and McCormick resolved to tell the other side of the story.

The first item on the docket was correcting mistakes. Chief financial officer Steve Howell checked all the numbers. He was on alert, since the Conservancy's accountants told him the *Post* stories would prompt an IRS audit. But he couldn't find any errors in the financial figures in the stories—even though people kept complaining about a bunch of bald-faced lies. Media chief James Petterson, urged by angry colleagues to demand the *Post* recant errors, similarly checked the narrative. But he couldn't find any outright errors either. All he found were mild inaccuracies and, like Howell, what the Conservancy called a pattern of mischaracterizations, omissions, and missing context.

The *Post*'s worst transgressions, Petterson decided, were scarcely worthy of a published correction. The *Post* said the Conservancy was best known for "buying wilderness"—while its mission is actually protecting biodiversity. It said conservation buyers built houses on "pristine beach and grasslands" on Martha's Vineyard—while they actually built on former pasture. Petterson's conclusion was that the *Post* reporters' facts were largely unassailable.

McCormick and Grassi, however, sought to offer a different view of the Conservancy's work, because they felt the sequence of facts, quotes, and anecdotes in the stories allowed readers to draw inferences misconstruing the bulk of the Conservancy's work. Petterson thus posted the Conservancy's side of the story on its Web site. The board of governors took a collection to pay for three full-page ads in the *Post,* printed on May 9, 11, and 12, proclaiming the Conservancy's good works. McCormick, Grassi, and Petterson met with the *Post*'s editorial writers to plead for balance. McCormick even appeared on C-SPAN.

The C-SPAN appearance captured McCormick on the defensive. Perched on the front half of his seat, he championed the Conservancy's achievements, but he was visibly agitated as he recited the Conservancy's mission and defended its approach. He labeled the *Post* reporting misleading. He explained the Conservancy does *not* lose money on conservation buyer deals. He even graciously handled a caller suggesting the Conservancy was Marxist. But nowhere did he allow that the *Post* series might have merit.

Was the *Post* series "fair?" he was asked by the C-SPAN host. "No," he replied.

McCormick's defense, however skilled, was no match for a powerful newspaper. On Wednesday, *Post* columnist Steven Pearlstein wrote "Nonprofits: Not So Transparent," calling for the Conservancy to disclose bad news as well as good. On Thursday, cartoonist Tom Toles drew a shrinking McCormick at the head of a boardroom table surrounded by cigar-puffing corporate tycoons. "So," said the McCormick caricature, "Why this perception that our mission has been compromised? Ideas?"

The Conservancy was outgunned in the court of public opinion—in spite of the competence of what the *Post* called the "whirring marketing machine" at the Conservancy. In fighting the allegations of a big paper, McCormick felt powerless. He and his team were worried the worst could happen: the *Post* would ignite interest by reporters and broadcasters across the United States. The *Post* could blacken the Conservancy's reputation nationwide.

One board member McCormick spoke to regularly by phone was A. D. "Pete" Correll, CEO of Georgia-Pacific. Correll invoked over and over the old maxim: Never argue with someone who buys ink by the barrel. If the Conservancy's record included some ugly facts, Correll argued, so be it. That was true of all big organizations. The gist of Correll's advice: "If the baby is ugly, let's call it ugly and move on to tell people we're good parents and fixing things."

McCormick got similar counsel from his staff. The team he assigned to devise and deliver a response included Petterson and top managers Michael Coda and chief administrative officer Stephanie Meeks. Coda called outsiders with experience in similar crises. From nonprofit colleagues at the Red Cross and U.S. Olympic Committee he heard the same thing: You have no hope of arguing with the *Post*. A defensive strategy is futile.

McCormick and Grassi quickly came around to this thinking. Although early on they debated which *Post* allegations to fight, they migrated to asking, What are legitimate criticisms we should correct? McCormick and the team had to admit: some of their practices in oversight and documentation were sloppy. Indeed, the baby did have some ugly aspects and the parents had been oblivious to them.

The team hesitated. It felt that any step to address *Post* allegations would validate the reporters' portrayal. Still, not taking action was not an option. They had to do something to show *Post* reporters, to show the public, to show *Post*-reading politicians, the Conservancy was paying attention and not aloof to criticism.

All during this period, people at all levels would ask Petterson, "What are you doing to discredit the *Post?*" Petterson was incredulous. Discrediting the paper was not a tenable strategy. The Conservancy, if only because it was perceived to be on the wrong track, had to remain deferential.

McCormick and Grassi took their first public act on Friday of the first week. They huddled with staff and decided to suspend four practices singled out by the *Post*—resource extraction on nature preserves (like gas drilling in Texas); employee loans (like McCormick's house loan); conservation buyer deals (like that on Martha's Vineyard); and cause-related marketing (like selling the logo).

None of the practices suspended were core to the Conservancy's mission. Coda had called a dozen state directors to ask if the suspensions would cripple their work. The answer was no. In fact, the suspensions applied to only a handful of the thousands of deals in progress. But they were symbolic, and they sent a loud message: The Conservancy was tightening up.

In announcing the suspensions on Friday afternoon, McCormick acknowledged, via e-mail to all employees, "In markets where the series has run, I think it is safe to say that our reputation has been dealt a serious blow." Newspapers in Albuquerque, Seattle, Denver, and a handful of other cities had picked up at least some pieces of the story. The crisis was spreading beyond Washington.

No sooner had McCormick and Grassi issued their decision than the klieg lights of Washington scrutiny intensified. Senator Chuck Grassley, chairman of the U.S. Senate's Finance Committee, issued a memo to the

Washington Post: "The *Post* shed light on questionable practices by this charity that many have viewed as a pillar. . . . I'm committed to holding the Nature Conservancy accountable, just as I did with United Way and Red Cross. . . . I'll be overseeing the charity's actions, asking tough questions and following through until satisfactory answers are given."

McCormick and the Conservancy were now on notice by the Senate. This was the same Senate that, the year before, passed the accounting-oversight and corporate-governance bill called the Sarbanes-Oxley Act. It was the same Senate that decried the greed of CEO Kenneth Lay at Enron, Bernard Ebbers at WorldCom, and Martha Stewart. This was the Senate that saw fit to rattle the executive suites of Corporate America with an abundance of reforms in auditing, executive loans, whistleblower protections, accounting disclosures, and much more.

Striking back was a bankrupt strategy. The question for McCormick now: What is the successful strategy for handling the crisis? The most powerful body in Washington was abuzz with the desire to make an example out of somebody over a lack of accountability. It could easily choose to skewer the Conservancy more deeply than the *Post* already had. It could handpick McCormick as the executive-du-jour to roast. The time for figuring out the right response was short.

GOING PUBLIC

Some people had the impression McCormick was not taking the crisis seriously—or worse, that he was acting indifferently or arrogantly in the face of an inquisitive Senate. Indeed, the morning after the suspensions, the *Post* reported that Grassley and the Senate Finance Committee's ranking Democrat, Max Baucus, were drafting a letter to the Conservancy seeking answers to questions raised by the *Post.* "Senate Finance Committee members have grown concerned by the appearance that Conservancy officials have dismissed the controversy," reported the *Post,* "without issuing any public statement that the nonprofit plans a self examination."

McCormick, however, was concerning himself more than anything with the reaction of his most precious constituencies, Conservancy staff and donors. As he and chief administrative officer Meeks created a plan for communicating with Conservancy insiders, he placed call after call

216

and met person after person to maintain morale and reassure staff and outsiders of the Conservancy's performance. He asked his constituents, "What troubles you? What advice do you have?"

When he reached by phone long-time funder Jonathan Fanton, president of the John D. and Catherine T. MacArthur Foundation, Fanton offered encouragement. He told McCormick to keep the crisis in perspective, care for his staff's morale, and keep up the good conservation work. But he warned that the *Post* raised real issues that demanded a fresh look—perhaps a look from someone outside the organization.

Other donors, both big and small, gave less support than did Fanton. They told McCormick the Conservancy had gotten too full of itself. Even if it was right, its work was not above criticism. Now that the organization had been called into question, McCormick had to show he took the *Post*'s allegations seriously and planned a response.

McCormick had tried to respond the first week, but only postings on the organization's Web site appeared for public consumption. He, Grassi, and Petterson had asked the *Post*'s editorial board on the first Friday for space to respond. But although they were able to put an editorial writer in touch with an expert to explain Conservancy tax dealings, they were too late to preempt yet another article. On Monday, May 12, the newspaper weighed in with an editorial citing a number of Conservancy practices as "disturbing."

The first highly visible response from McCormick came only ten days after the first newspaper story. "We have already taken vigorous measures to respond," he wrote in a *Post* column on Wednesday of the second week. "We are committed to changing any of our practices that do not live up to our mission and values. . . . The Conservancy's Board of Governors will therefore dedicate its entire June meeting to a frank discussion of our practices, policies and procedures."

One difficulty for McCormick and his team in deciding what to do next was that the messages pouring in conflicted so. McCormick met during the week of May 12 with a couple of dozen members of Congress. In one office, the staff reassured him that the controversy wasn't so grave— their boss understood the caprice of the newspaper business. But when he sat down with the lawmaker, the first thing he heard was, "You've betrayed me." McCormick was astonished.

He met also with Senator Baucus, a long-time supporter. Baucus, whose mother was once on the Conservancy's state board in Montana, had even appeared at a Conservancy dinner in January. But McCormick felt the senator was visibly disappointed. Baucus told him the Senate took the *Post*'s allegations seriously, and so should McCormick. Baucus's staff then told McCormick there would be not only a letter but probably an investigation.

The ire of the public and Conservancy members spread. The Conservancy received more than five thousand letters and e-mail messages filled with scolding remarks. When McCormick and his team held five open houses to field member questions in the Capital area, McCormick stood for hours as outraged members vented what galled them: his $1.55 million house loan, insider deals, gas drilling near endangered birds, cozy relations with business.

"I've come here to ask for your resignation," said one woman.

A few people defended him. But most felt the Conservancy had run amok, especially with self-dealing conservation-buyer transactions. Only painstakingly did McCormick, who was not even president when most of the reported mistakes occurred, quiet the emotions of a series of hopping-mad audiences. Even then, his audiences, most of whom trusted the *Post*'s version of the facts far more than the Conservancy's, left the meetings with what seemed to be an indelible impression: the Conservancy, and McCormick, had done wrong.

McCormick's every move now raised suspicion. He hired Donald Moorehead, once chief counsel to the Republican side of the Senate Finance Committee, to advise the Conservancy on how to work with the Senate. He hired Leslie Dach, vice chairman of public relations firm Edelman Worldwide, to advise the Conservancy on how to preserve the organization's image. In response, the *Post* ran a story headlined "Charity Hiring Lawyers to Prevent Probe." Just beneath the surface lurked the proverbial Washington question: Was the Conservancy mounting a cover-up?

From the open houses, from the press, and from the Senate, McCormick got the same message that executives like him in similar public brouhahas had gotten before him: *You have to be humble: You've made some mistakes, and you have to improve.* Of course, McCormick and his team didn't know what the improvements would entail. They were trying to sort that out day by day.

SALVATION IN OPPORTUNITY

McCormick had taken the first step to show he had not dismissed the controversy. He promised self-examination and change. The question now was what to propose to the board in June, and the question became urgent. He had to be sure the governors' action responded overwhelmingly to the *Post*'s allegations and Senate's concerns. To regain the trust of the public, the Conservancy would have to *overreact*. McCormick and the staff cast about for the right next step.

MacArthur Foundation chief Fanton and others had floated the notion of an outside group to examine the Conservancy. That was an appealing idea to McCormick, to show the Conservancy was open and had nothing to hide. Fanton even suggested McCormick look at the turmoil as an opportunity. McCormick could use the crisis not just to look at the issues raised by the *Post,* but to push through other reforms.

But the notion of bringing in an outside group in response to outside criticism provoked protests by Grassi, Correll, and others, veterans of the corporate world. That's what Arthur Andersen did after its alleged complicity in the Enron accounting scams. Only bad guys and guilty parties hired outside examiners, the men argued. But a related notion did pass their muster: recruiting an outside group restricted to advising the Conservancy on a direction for the future, a group constrained from looking into allegations of the past.

As key board members and staff warmed up to the idea of an outside panel, the staff turned to the next question: What territory would the panel cover? That question was critical. If the Conservancy was to retain some kind of control over the agenda for change, it had to first of all narrow the debate to the appropriate subjects.

In conversations with others, McCormick became convinced that all the problems boiled down to oversight lapses. Getting at the root problem meant getting at institutional governance. That of course was what corporations had been doing for several years. Audit Committee chairman Correll had even asked the January before for CFO Howell to look into which parts of the Sarbanes-Oxley Act applied to nonprofits. If governance needed revamping in Corporate America, perhaps some of the change would help nonprofits, too.

Governance was much on the minds of Conservancy observers, governors, and staff. In fact, McCormick had to admit that the *Post* even pointed him in that direction. The hurtful Toles cartoon, picturing a boardroom conclave, suggested the need for governance reform graphically. *Post* editorialists had opined more explicitly: "The more troubling issues . . . concern questions of corporate governance similar to those that have faced for-profit corporations."

McCormick and the team gradually coalesced around a two-part solution to propose to the board in June: First, tighten up policies and procedures, including all that the *Post* singled out; second, recruit an outside, pro bono panel to advise the Conservancy how to govern. The Conservancy would not wage a point-by-point fight with the *Post*—a fight the Conservancy could never win. It would broaden its response to embrace changes in its entire system and structure with the aim of running a more accountable organization.

McCormick's next challenge was to sell the proposed solution. If the board, at its June 13 meeting, rejected the plan, he didn't know what he would do next. The panel was the centerpiece of his team's solution. It was their overwhelming response to the *Post* and the Senate. He had to work with his team to put together a winning presentation to sell that response at the board dinner on June 12, the night before the critical board meeting.

As McCormick floated the solution before the meeting, many board members protested. They lived in cities where nobody read the *Post*. They thought the crisis nonsense and Conservancy operating procedures perfectly fine. They recommended the Conservancy fight the charges and not legitimize them by responding as a guilty party. They argued the whole to-do would flame out inside the Beltway.

McCormick, certain the outside panel was the right response, had a challenge on his hands. On June 12, projecting plain, black-and-white slides, he, Coda, and Meeks explained how the *Post* story had run in forty-seven cities in the United States and in six international newspapers. It had aired on several locally produced National Public Radio programs and C-SPAN. It had elicited innumerable complaints in e-mail, at open houses, and in letters. It had prompted corporations, foundations, and state and federal agencies to ask questions and distance themselves from decades-old

relationships with the Conservancy. Most worrisome of all: It had triggered more than a hundred calls from big donors—and some were taking
the Conservancy out of their wills.

Truth be known, McCormick explained in his presentation, the Conservancy had done nothing wrong. But it had consummated transactions
and used procedures that *looked* wrong. Deals with trustees, gas drilling,
and executive loans had provoked outrage. They had shattered the Conservancy's halo as a ne'er-do-wrong. The health of Conservancy relationships in both government and the private sector were on the line.

The next day, McCormick saw that the presentation had worked—
but not without stirring passions of many governors. Emotions at the
meeting ran high. Many governors still objected to the panel vehemently:
Is this even a board-governance issue—and not a media or recordkeeping
issue? they asked. Doesn't this suggest we're at fault? Doesn't this suggest
that the board couldn't fix its governance problems itself and is asleep at
the wheel? The board was split. To suggest there was an element of sanity
in what the *Post* said seemed crazy to some.

In the end, the board did vote to tighten or ban five practices treated
as scandals by the *Post*. But it couldn't reach a consensus on the panel,
even in the face of pleas by McCormick, Grassi, and outspoken board
members like Henry Paulson, chairman of New York investment bank
Goldman Sachs. They took a vote, and a handful of governors refused to
go along with the majority. In his two years as CEO, this was the first time
McCormick had ever seen board members vote against anything.

McCormick was relieved, however. With an affirmative vote from the
board, he had in hand a plan to defuse the crisis and turn it into an opportunity for healthy change. That evening, he and Grassi worked with his
team to draft an announcement. "The board will enlist independent, outside advisors to assist it in achieving its aspiration of making the Conservancy a recognized leader in governance and oversight," it said.

As for the mission of the panel, they settled on three buzzwords aired
by the *Post,* donors, members, and others: *governance, accountability,* and
transparency. Improving all three would be McCormick's central thrust in
focusing upcoming change. They were the guiding principles for the
"right" response to the crisis in accountability, moving the debate from a

case-by-case defense of past errors to system-wide reform to preclude need-less mistakes in the future.

BIG LEAGUE GOVERNANCE

As the board took a stand, the fears of the minority voters were borne out. The next day, the *Post* did appear to portray the board's discussions as an admission of guilt. "Conservancy Abandons Disputed Practices," read the front-page headline. Media chief Petterson called the actions "significant and concrete," but there was no indication that, as McCormick hoped, the panel's creation would be received as a signal of the Conservancy's ded-ication to openness.

On the contrary, in their story, the reporters didn't even highlight the decision about the panel. They did note it, but only in a sentence buried in the text. The *Post* reporters chose instead to detail the vote on sus-pended practices, although the Conservancy board actually abandoned only two of the practices suspended earlier. It voted to continue two oth-ers with tightened oversight. The two earlier items now banned were employee loans and oil-and-gas drilling.

The board voted to ban a third practice it had not earlier suspended— buying from or selling land to trustees (who had advisory influence, although no governance authority). Many governors hated to take this step. It was, after all, a critical tactic in conservation rainmaking. This would mean the loss of land transfers from the 1,500 trustees of boards in each of the fifty states, even if the trustees wanted to sell land to the Conservancy at a reduced price. Since many state directors recruited trustees precisely for their deal-making capacity, the ban would actually torpedo many worthy deals.

Although the ban affected a very small percentage of deals, even some outsiders felt it was a step backward for conservation. They felt it would have been better to tighten conflict-of-interest provisions, preventing abuses while preserving benefits. Still, the board as a whole felt the Conservancy had to prohibit the practice to get on the right side of the Senate, the *Post,* and the public. It was, they believed, a big step forward for the perception of clean dealing. And in this new climate, cleaner-than-clean dealing was a new exigency, even if it meant new hurdles in the task of conservation.

In spite of getting scant recognition for creating the panel, McCormick felt the outside group was his only avenue for retaking control of the Conservancy's future. Directing the panel along a constructive path now became McCormick's main task. If the panel was the right response to the crisis, he now had to form the right panel with the right agenda.

McCormick's team, led by Coda, set out to draft a charter to make that happen. For starters, they fleshed out the three key words of governance, accountability, and transparency. *Governance,* the group decided, meant how to govern at the highest levels of integrity—deciding the makeup of the board, the structure of committees, setting the agenda, recruiting new members, making sure the staff followed the board's will. *Transparency* meant defining a model of openness, listing what to disclose, making sure no gap remained between how the Conservancy described itself and how it acted. *Accountability* meant defining to whom the Conservancy was accountable, as well as where to step up oversight, what performance benchmarks to set, and the role of members, donors, and partners in evaluating the Conservancy's performance.

The board viewed the charter as critical to making sure the panel took the high road. The board didn't want outsiders conducting a narrow probe—of conflicts of interest on Long Island, or management errors in Texas, or executive loans for homes, or tax treatment of easements. It wanted advice on how the Conservancy could run itself better for years down the line.

To get the right panel, Grassi and McCormick drew up a list of panel candidates. Grassi met or talked with each of them, and by mid-August signed on some of the best and brightest in governance: Derek Bok, former president of Harvard University, Claudine Malone, former chairman of the Federal Reserve Bank of Richmond, Richard Schlosberg, former CEO of the *Los Angeles Times,* Thomas Tierney, former CEO of management consulting firm Bain & Company, and as chairman, Ira Millstein, a preeminent New York attorney.

During this time, McCormick received constant reminders that, however much progress the Conservancy had made figuring out how to respond, the crisis of accountability would rage on until the Conservancy took some more solid public actions. He felt a temporary reprieve after meeting Senator Max Baucus a second time. Baucus sent him a follow-up by e-mail on July 13: "Glad to learn the Conservancy is taking such a high road. In my view it'll pay off in spades."

But three days later, McCormick was stung nonetheless by Grassley and Baucus's promised letter. Seven pages in length, listing eighteen subjects, the letter demanded an extensive set of documents: files on all conservation-buyer deals for the last ten years; all government land deals for the last five years; all loans for the last ten years; all audits for the last five years; all easements for the last five years; data on board members, executive compensation, valuation methods, travel expenses, board-member transactions, litigation, donations, and so on.

"People who donate property and dollars to help protect the environment deserve to know The Nature Conservancy won't betray them," Senator Grassley said in a statement. "Our goal in asking these detailed questions is to shed daylight on what's happened so we can hold the bad actors accountable and prevent wrongdoing in the future."

A formal Senate investigation—this was frightening for McCormick. He didn't have any experience with it. As one adviser told him at the time, "You don't have the muscle tone for this"—and McCormick knew he was right. Over fifty years, the Conservancy had never been tested by any crises to condition itself to wrestle with the challenge coming at it now. Reading the letter, and how exhaustive it was, he wasn't even sure how to think it through. The worst part was that the letter was backward-looking. Unlike the outside panelists, the Senate would be looking at past practices, unearthing every possible questionable detail in former Conservancy transactions.

McCormick took both the long and short view. In the long view, he knew the Conservancy would get through the crisis. It would fall back on its basic values, mission, and strategy. The board had reviewed and reaffirmed all three on June 13. In the short term, the Conservancy would give the Senate everything it asked for, when it asked for it, how it asked for it. The Conservancy would be transparent.

The Senate's wide-ranging request whipped up a new round of panic among the Conservancy's critical constituencies. Members, staff, donors, and the public began wondering: *What other skeletons are in the Conservancy closet?* Conservancy chief financial officer Howell, whose work was entirely free of any malfeasance, began to hear from friends anyway: "Are you going to jail?"

For the job of complying with the Senate's requests, McCormick tapped Karen Berky, head of government relations, who would mastermind the months-long response for information. With the specter of having to testify before the Senate, however, he was more convinced than ever that the outside panel was his best hope to put the crisis behind him.

At 10 A.M. on August 26, almost four months after the *Post* series began, McCormick met for the first time with panel chairman Millstein. The meeting was at Millstein's office in New York, at the Fifth Avenue headquarters of Weil, Gotshal & Manges, a 1,100-lawyer international law firm. Millstein and two partners met with McCormick in Millstein's personal conference room, on the 32nd floor overlooking Central Park. Ironically, the group could look right across the leafy park and its lake to the American Museum of Natural History, where Richard Pough, nearly fifty years earlier, had met often with the Conservancy board to thrash out his own issues of governance with George Fell.

Governance was an old game for the Conservancy, but never had the group played in such big leagues. Millstein was a player without peer. *BusinessWeek* called him the "éminence grise" and "guru" of corporate governance. The General Motors board received his tutelage in 1992, in an era when departing director Ross Perot derided the GM board as a "pet rock" and GM chairman and former Procter & Gamble CEO John Smale forced out CEO Robert Stempel. The move triggered a series of ousters and governance reforms across the United States, in firms from American Express to Eastman Kodak.

Millstein went on to create the model of better corporate governance. In 1996, he chaired a commission issuing a report on model governance for the National Association of Corporate Directors. In 1998, he chaired the commission sponsored by the New York Stock Exchange and National Association of Securities Dealers to reform board audit committees. In 2002, he testified before Congress as it formulated the Sarbanes-Oxley Act, considered a landmark piece of governance legislation. Millstein taught at Yale, Harvard, and Columbia.

At seventy-six, the tall, bespectacled, silver-haired Millstein was the statesman of board reform and the leading advocate of a simple idea: You can often trace bad organizational performance to a poorly run board. Yet despite his age, he was no poke-along grayhair. He was provocative, energetic, and blunt. It was to this man that McCormick described Conservancy culture—the nonconfrontational approach instilled by Pough, the corporate partnerships championed by Patrick Noonan, the radical state-based decentralization engineered by Gregory Low and others. The Conservancy was not like a corporation, McCormick said.

McCormick, pondering Millstein's prescription for change, explained that the people at the Conservancy had struggled for two years to change into a more global organization. He had driven people hard, and he wasn't sure how much more dislocation they could withstand. The fact was, behind the scenes, people griped that his restructuring and layoffs were heartless. Many of the sources so willing to speak to the *Post,* some insiders felt, were probably disgruntled employees jilted by the new boss from California.

Millstein was more concerned with the operation of the board, however. He worried that perhaps Conservancy board members didn't really want a serious examination, and that maybe they were hoping for Millstein to conduct a cursory once-over and blessing. But Millstein had in mind more of a shakedown and awakening. He outlined his view in plain terms: The board members might have thought their role was to give money and lend their reputation. But now they must seriously oversee the organization, too. He told McCormick that the Conservancy might have tapped them for funding and connections, but that McCormick would have to engage them in helping deliver efficiency and performance.

Millstein noted that the public and politicians believed boards were neither monitoring their charges nor delivering expected performance. He basically said to McCormick, "If your board wants to win trust and raise money as a nonprofit, it's going to have to operate more like a for-profit board. Your board members have to be as responsible and accountable to their constituents as a for-profit board's are to their constituents, the shareholders."

After nearly four hours of conversation, McCormick left the meeting galvanized. His team had thrown governance around as a concept while writing the panel charter; now Millstein had given it real meaning. The board was too large at nearly forty people. The board was not engaged in the governance of the organization. When McCormick fretted about some governors not taking the whole affair seriously, Millstein promised to impress on the organization the gravity of his work. He wasn't just going to applaud, he said. He would be an irritant.

The meeting opened McCormick's eyes to the need for the board of a nonprofit to adhere to the highest levels of governance. In other words, board members had to be directors first and ambassadors and fundraisers second. They had to oversee a huge, decentralized organization. In meeting with the guru of governance, McCormick realized he would be charged with participating in a process that would make a major change in the way the board operated. The goal would be to create a real governing board.

RIGHTER THAN RIGHT

When the governance panel met in September with McCormick, Meeks, Grassi, and others in Arlington, Millstein pointed out the problem of a disengaged board. Some of the things that were going on at the Conservancy should have been looked at more closely, he said, adding that good governance wasn't some idle exercise about following a new set of rules. It was about working in a way to preserve an organization's most precious asset, its reputation. Up to this time, neither McCormick nor the board fully understood the governors' roles as so closely connected to the Conservancy's health, image, and performance.

Millstein then noted the Conservancy suffered from another problem: a debilitating attitude of hubris. As Millstein and partner Robert Odle began their work, they heard over and over from governors and staff different versions of essentially the same message: We are a terrific organization, and everything we do is wonderful and exceptional. At the September meeting, Millstein told McCormick and others that the Conservancy might be exceptional, but when an organization's work is tax-exempt, it can't just do great work, it has to do it in a great way. "Your work has to be righter than right," he said.

The panel met five times in the next few months to work out recommendations for the righter-than-right approach. Each panel member talked to different Conservancy constituents. Millstein and Odle, for their part, questioned appraisers, former IRS officials, state attorneys general, charity officials, and Conservancy staff. They got an earful about two issues: Conservancy transactions that gave good deals to insiders, and a property-appraisal process that could shortchange the taxpaying public.

As for appraisals, people said greed, neglect, and lack of enforcement led to suspect valuations of land and easements. Appraisers pleased donors by inflating valuations. The Conservancy facilitated transactions by following the letter of the law and refraining from taking a position on valuations. And the IRS let deals slide through because it didn't have enough money to police the process. Everything was legal. The work often produced great conservation, but Millstein and Odle heard again and again that the processes just didn't strike people as "right."

Millstein and Odle had a simple comment for McCormick and his staff: Whether these deals are legal or not doesn't matter when it comes to preserving the Conservancy's reputation. Instead, they said, "You have to pass the smell test."

The panel examined the Conservancy from the ground up. It even looked at such basic issues as whether the Conservancy was operating in the way Congress intended for a standard 501(c)(3) charitable organization. One controversial proposal floated seriously was to shrink the board to eight members, a number in line with corporate best practice. But Grassi and others talked the panel into considering alternatives; after all, even if governance was job #1, fundraising was job #2, and those governors provided a lot of access to money.

As the panel worked behind the scenes, McCormick continued to manage the crisis playing out on the public stage. In November 2003, he received a second letter from the Senate Finance Committee. On the surface it was damning. The committee suggested subpoenaing documents. It wanted access to papers the Conservancy was legally obligated to withhold owing to confidentiality agreements with donors. It also asked him to craft a whistleblower policy, so Senate investigators could talk to former employees "chilled" by similar agreements.

"We would ask that TNC make a public written statement that it will take no action against any former or current TNC employees or contractors who cooperate with the Finance Committee's investigation," wrote Grassley.

No subpoena was ever necessary, and McCormick issued a whistle-blower statement. But the letter kicked off a tough holiday season with fresh, unflattering developments. In November, the *Post* disclosed questionable expense handling and tax reporting at the Virginia Coast Reserve. In December, it reported another sweetheart deal from years earlier with the donor of an easement in New York. The Conservancy also received a letter from the IRS. Auditors would move onto the premises to examine 2002 tax returns.

The panel took advice from a handful of governors named as liaisons on how to guide the Conservancy away from the approach that led to the crisis in the first place. Chief among the liaisons, besides Grassi, was Goldman Sachs's Paulson. Paulson was invaluable because he had just weathered a storm over conflicts of interest and business practices on Wall Street. Paulson had been outspoken in taking the high road on Wall Street. In 2002, at the same time the *Post* was investigating the Conservancy, he was giving a speech at the National Press Club in Washington, D.C., calling on corporate America to make reforms in corporate governance, accounting policy, and managing conflicts of interest. He told the assembled reporters and editors, "We have not done as good a job as we might have." He pledged changes to clean up the problems.

Paulson, facing an analogous set of issues at the Conservancy, became the main liaison with the committee because he worked near Millstein in New York City. He also became a major player because he knew well how to handle conflicts of interest and other risks. Goldman Sachs had a sophisticated system to manage its own financial and reputational risks. A nature lover, Paulson was nonetheless a strong-willed, take-charge corporate manager known to work at all hours. As he learned more about the Conservancy's problems, he told Millstein that he could change all he wanted at the board level, but the Conservancy also had to change processes and procedures. "The governance at the top is only as good as the systems supporting them from below," he said.

Paulson saw strong parallels between the operations of Goldman Sachs and the Conservancy. Both Goldman and the Conservancy were highly decentralized global institutions, where people in the field had a lot of leeway to invent new ways to conduct business. As he dug deeply into Conservancy affairs, he recognized conservation deals were much more complex and created many more risks than he previously thought. What's more, wherever he dug into the details of Conservancy transactions, he found that 95 percent of them looked fine, but 5 percent had inadvertent or unintended errors.

To prevent Goldman Sachs partners from making such errors, the firm had strict policies on many practices, and an internal review board to vet all deals with unusual risks. Paulson decided he should expose the Conservancy staff to a vetting by people who managed risk for a global financial institution. So on January 9, 2004, he summoned a number of Conservancy staff to New York for a day-long session attended by some of his top risk-control managers. Together, they went over one after another of the Conservancy's most trouble-prone practices: compensation, conservation-buyer deals, conflicts of interest, easements, lobbying, government transactions, and so on. Paulson then urged the staff to draft recommendations to tighten up procedures in every risk-prone business practice.

TWO ANSWERS

With Paulson on the scene, the panel continued to pursue essentially two avenues of reform, similar to those originally proposed by McCormick's team in June. The first was board-governance reform. The second was reform of risk-management procedures—the systems and processes to make sure the details of every deal were righter than right. McCormick saw that both were necessary to turn the tide of the crisis into an opportunity for improved performance.

In late January 2004, Millstein flew to Washington to present the board-governance findings personally. On the eve of the January 29 board meeting, speaking without notes, preaching a sermon he had given many times, Millstein said it was time for board members to roll up their sleeves and get to work governing. If they were on the board as a sort of ceremonial post, they should think about doing something else. The new board member's job would require more work, more face-to-face meetings, and more active oversight.

Paulson, elected chairman of the board just a week before, laid out the case for board change. In today's world, board members have to be more responsible, involved, knowledgeable, and accountable, he explained. They have to face up to the fact that times have changed. If a board is running a for-profit organization, its shareholders vote by bidding up or down the company's stock price; if the board is running a nonprofit, its donors vote by moving up or down their level of giving. The stronger the Conservancy's reputation, the more money the Conservancy is going to be able to raise, and the more work it can do.

Paulson urged the board to adopt the panel's first set of governance reforms. He argued that the status quo was not really an option. A forty-person board couldn't possibly act as a decision-making body. The Conservancy needed a quicker, nimbler body for making decisions. It needed more regular and ad hoc meetings. It needed people to work hard on every committee to do real work and conduct serious deliberations.

The next day, the board members agreed to the changes. By the end of the day, Paulson engineered the initial restructuring the panel called for: Assigning everyone to just one of six committees—and not more than one; designating an eleven-member executive committee, composed of the six committee chairs, the CEO, board chair, secretary, and two vice chairs; delegating oversight to the executive committee, to meet in person at least four times a year, with phone meetings in between.

With these major governance changes in place, the panel turned to the two remaining issues in its charter: accountability and transparency. The staff, spurred by Paulson, had been working on reforms for several months, under the leadership of Coda. On February 18, Coda took a thirty-six-page memo outlining new procedures to a meeting in Atlanta of state directors and state board-of-trustee chairs. The procedures covered reforms in handling eight areas of concern, from compensation and compatible human use to conservation easements and conflicts of interest.

Paulson again gave a pitch about how times had changed. He and McCormick recognized that, remarkably, some directors and trustees still didn't think the crisis was serious. The doubters maintained that the crisis was not a national story. It was a Beltway affair. Trustees said they didn't like talking to donors about the allegations, and didn't like talking to members. After all, they hadn't seen any drop-off in donations or any damage to relationships. Their common refrain amounted to a simple recommendation: Let the story die inside the Beltway!

But neither Paulson nor McCormick could accept this advice. Paulson, speaking for twenty-five minutes and then taking questions for an hour, was adamant. He insisted that everyone was in the crisis together. He stressed, like Millstein, that the Conservancy's reputation was its most important asset, and it was at stake during every Conservancy transaction. Noting that innocent mistakes were all too widespread, he said the Conservancy had to pinpoint its vulnerabilities and manage its risk.

Paulson had one particularly pointed message for his audience: He noted that although everyone had the opportunity to advance the cause of the Conservancy every day, they had an even greater potential to harm the organization should they make a big mistake. The risk on the downside—impairing the organization's national reputation through one wayward deal or misguided act—was much greater than the upside.

Paulson's persuasion carried the day. Coda's memo, the work of multiple working groups, detailed the new procedures. In the past, managers had been given the clear message that they shouldn't let appearances stop them from doing the right thing. If it was legal, and it furthered conservation, they should do it. Now a different threshold would prevail—and a new compliance director, a further recommendation of the governance panel, would help make sure people minded the threshold.

When it came to valuation, for example, new procedures barred the staff from standing by if donors, eager to fatten tax deductions, nudged appraisers to embroider numbers. The Conservancy would refuse to sign the required IRS Form 8283 for tax deductions until the donor submitted an appraisal by a state-certified appraiser experienced in conservation deals using accepted standards. The Conservancy still wouldn't take a position on the valuation, but it would walk away from any deal where the *appearance* was suspect.

With the end of the February 18 meeting, McCormick could breathe easier. The board had bought into governance reform. The staff and state trustees had bought into risk-management reform. The work of the panel was on track to turn the crisis into an opportunity for substantial improvement.

The buy-in by insiders came none too soon. On March 3, Senators Grassley and Baucus sent McCormick yet another letter. In eighteen pages, they laid out not only scores of follow-up questions but new questions about altogether new concerns. Particularly worrisome was their interest in a variety of "related organizations." Observers inferred the Senate was wondering whether the Conservancy was playing an Enron-like shell game with its money, hiding losses or gains in obscure accounts.

Among the related organizations the Senate wanted to know about were Conservation Beef, a unit to encourage ranchers to use environmentally friendly husbandry; Nature Serve, the spun-off science-data unit, once the domain of Robert Jenkins; Forest Bank, a unit, since liquidated, to encourage landowners to log without harsh clear-cut practices; and the Virginia Eastern Shore Development Corporation. The Conservancy had already copied more than forty thousand pages of documents for the Senate. Now it had another exhausting round of document copying before it.

Within days, on March 19, the governance panel issued its final report. Along with reiterating governance changes, the report commented favorably on most of the changes proposed by Coda and suggested additional safeguards recommended by the panel. With this final report, in which the panel urged, among other things, that the Form 990 tax return become the detailed document for disclosure, the Conservancy had in place a game plan for managing governance, accountability, and transparency. Paulson and McCormick now had on hand the template for control and oversight.

Of course, much work remained. The age-old problem of dividing authority and responsibility between state boards and the national board was not totally resolved. This conundrum was to be worked out by a team led by Grassi—and it was no simple task. After all, it was at the root of the worst mistake publicized by the *Post*, namely gas drilling in Texas City. Still, Paulson and McCormick had a road map for taking the high road to establishing true nonprofit accountability. With the panel, they had indeed turned the crisis into a chance for far-reaching reform. And when the Senate held hearings on charity reform on June 22, 2004—a session subtitled "Keeping Bad Things from Happening to Good Charities"—the Finance Committee didn't call anyone from the Conservancy to testify.

McCormick, though still braced for criticism as the Senate investigation continued, had reached a new point in his thinking. In 2001, his first year as president, he gave a speech at the Conservancy annual meeting. Cheering the Conservancy's achievements driven by a daring mix of "dreaming and doing," he asserted the Conservancy was beginning to transform the world. "I really believe that NGOs [nongovernmental organizations] will be the most influential institutions on the globe," he said. "I believe the Nature Conservancy can set that pattern. I believe the Nature Conservancy will set that pattern."

Some in the audience thought he was reaching a bit. The new president was aspiring to an awful lot.

In 2004, though still aspiring to global influence, McCormick hit a different note. People around him spoke of the Conservancy becoming the role model of nonprofit governance—or the benchmark, or the gold standard. But McCormick realized such talk fomented hubris and invited another comeuppance. Hubris, in fact, was becoming ever more apparent as the organization's Achilles heel. Better that the Conservancy worry less about restoring its former angelic reputation and more about fostering continuous improvement.

That's what most of the organization had done in the year since the *Post* stories had broken, a year in which the Conservancy had closed a $1.4 billion capital campaign and McCormick had presided over the protection of more than 700,000 acres in twenty-eight countries around the globe. That pattern of doing more and doing better was written into the theme music of many heroic tales of the Conservancy over fifty years. It was what helped people turn trouble and challenge into repeated success—and helped them live lives that counted, and counted big.

EPILOGUE:
Unsung Heroes

V ICTOR SHELFORD HAD A SIMPLE, universal yearning: to have an impact, to make his mark. He wanted to change the world—for everyone's good. If he succeeded, if he unleashed a chain of events and the energies of other people, the University of Chicago ecologist could have an effect for generations.

But fulfilling his yearning would not come easily. At fifty-eight years of age, the pioneer in the field of ecology watched as the organization he had founded back in 1915, the Ecological Society of America, voted to forbid one of his favored programs: taking action to protect natural areas. The society couldn't even write a congressman to urge saving a virgin forest.

As the society voted in 1946 to abolish the subgroup he'd started in 1917, Shelford fostered a schism. He and fourteen others, including three past presidents, signed a proposal to form a new group to take direct action to *protect* ecosystems. On the other side stood partisans of tradition, society members who would stick with scholarship, the *study* of ecosystems.

Shelford lived in an alarming era for an ecologist, especially one who had written the seminal work, *Animal Communities in Temperate America,* in 1913. He witnessed the extinction of the passenger pigeon and Carolina parrot in 1914. He witnessed the extinction of the Great Plains wolf and the California grizzly in 1925. He was witnessing the tenuous grasp on life of dozens of other plant, fish, mammal, and bird species. So he parted with the society, and in the first year drew 158 members to his new splinter group, the Ecologists Union.

Shelford, father of the natural-areas movement, must remain the first of many unsung heroes in this book. His work doesn't figure in a significant way into any of the nine stories contained in earlier chapters. Nor do the stories of thousands of other heroes who came after him, the volunteers who ran local, state, and national programs and the staff who spearheaded global growth.

Perhaps this, the final lesson of this book, goes without saying: Behind every good leader or manager in any organization stand thousands of people who make the organization's story worth recounting. It takes a vast community of passionate and capable people to build a group of "the size and strength to take its rightful place in a country that does things on a gigantic scale," as George Fell said.

The men and women mentioned in the preceding pages are but a sampling of Conservancy leaders. Their stories represent just a few of those about the courage of Conservancy leadership and power of culture, about the value of focused mission and lively innovation, about building a board and empowering it, about managing teams and building institutional muscle, about instilling accountability and learning the ropes of good governance.

Leaders like Richard Goodwin took the hard steps to assure the steady growth of an organization and its capabilities. Visionaries like Robert Jenkins exercised the discipline to focus the mission on issues of global importance. Entrepreneurs like Patrick Noonan established the culture to stimulate fast action and tangible results. Innovators like Gregory Low helped create the powerful business models to deliver maximum effectiveness. Managers like Kent Wommack, John Sawhill, Katherine Skinner, Kelvin Taketa, and Steven McCormick all played a role in making the organization excel.

But there are many more like them. In fact, in interviews in 2003 and 2004, these chosen few expressed their concern that their stories, told in such detail, would overshadow those of other, more worthy heroes. They repeatedly credited predecessors, peers, and mentors with the successes they were involved in. But one of the hazards of writing a book is that not every worthy member of an organization who deserves credit can get it. Such is the nature of storytelling.

The same is true when giving credit to all those who help in the production of a book. I interviewed more than two hundred people and solicited assistance from countless administrative assistants, librarians, archivists, and others who helped me retrieve thousands of documents, find people, and schedule research. Some of these people figure into stories in this book, but most do not. To them I am indebted. I appreciate their time, patience, and thoughtfulness.

For help in orienting me at the start of my work, I am also indebted to two Conservancy veterans, John Humke and David Williamson, two men who both contributed to and revere the history and legacy of the Conservancy.

I would especially like to thank the seven people I interviewed for their personal stories. They put up with repeated requests and intrusive questions about their motives and mistakes. They are Dick Goodwin, Bob Jenkins, Greg Low, Kent Wommack, Katherine Skinner, Steve McCormick, and Kelvin Taketa. I would also like to thank the many peers and colleagues of Patrick Noonan, whose clear recollections from the 1970s did much to flesh out Chapter Four.

If it takes many unsung heroes to build an organization, it takes many more to publish a book. Those heroes include members of my family, and I want to thank Sue, Jake, and Kye for putting up with my many preoccupations over many months. I also want to thank my agent, Helen Rees, who believed in and cheered on my project even before I got the proposal written, and to my editors, Johanna Vondeling and Dorothy Hearst, who championed and brought the book to market.

Finally, as all managers of nonprofits know, the heroes of any such story must include the people who draw from their bank accounts to fund the dreams of people like those in this book. Donors to the Conservancy provide the fuel to assure the organization has a global impact. Victor

Shelford himself set an example of the generosity that has carried the Conservancy from its start. In 1946 he gave the lion's share of the seed money to get the forebear of the Nature Conservancy on its feet. He donated $300—$2,500 in today's dollars—to launch the Ecologists Union. To these donors, the term "unsung hero" applies particularly well. They are the guardians of the diversity of life.

AUTHOR'S NOTE

I STARTED DEVELOPING THE IDEA for *Nature's Keepers* in late 2002, prompted by my interest in both management and conservation. By mid-2003, I began work in earnest, having been given full access to the Nature Conservancy's people and archives by president Steve McCormick. I conducted about 225 interviews with people inside and outside the Conservancy. I also reviewed thousands of documents— letters, meeting minutes, reports, white papers, plans, e-mail messages, old articles, and speech transcripts. The result is a work entirely of nonfiction. No events have been created. No names have been changed.

To assure the integrity and fidelity of the story, I entered all key events into Casesoft's TimeMap time-line software, with which I created a map of the sequence of events over more than fifty years. I also entered more than a thousand pages of notes into EndNote bibliographic software. During writing I was able to access and double-check this information instantly via keyword searches of my database. I was also able to access and double-check unabridged digital audio of interviews indexed in my notes.

I decided early on that none of my interview sources, no matter how good his or her memory, could reliably recall conversations verbatim— even conversations from weeks earlier. So when I reconstructed dialogue, I often omitted quotation marks, used indirect quotations, or qualified quotations with phrases like "he basically said." I used unqualified quotations only where I was 90 to 100 percent sure the characters in the book uttered those very words. When I used quotes to set off what a character was thinking, the wording comes directly from verbatim transcription of interviews in which I asked people to recall what they were thinking at the time of various events.

Characters' memories of events invariably differ. So when possible I confirmed the accuracy of events with a second or third person, or better yet with a document in the written record. In some cases, I omitted events when nobody could agree on what happened or when the reliability of a single source's memory was questionable. I also tried to omit details that, to me, appeared to stem from historical revisionism rather than from a clear memory of what actually happened.

When I was all done, I spent a month in late 2004 fact-checking the book with all critical sources to weed out errors. I appreciate no end the care many people took in setting my facts straight before they appeared in print. Despite this handling of information, mistakes no doubt remain. I would be grateful to readers who point them out.

www.natureskeepers.net   www.billbirchard.com

INDEX

THE AUTHOR

BILL BIRCHARD is a freelance journalist based in Amherst, New Hampshire. He specializes in writing about business, health, and environmental affairs. His work has appeared in *Chief Executive, CFO, Fast Company, Strategy+Business, Tomorrow,* and other magazines. A business writer for nearly twenty years, Birchard was formerly editor for six years of *Enterprise,* a magazine for senior executives published by Digital Equipment Corporation. He wrote on leadership, finance, strategic planning, quality management, corporate culture change, R&D, globalization, environmental management, and other topics.

Nature's Keepers is Birchard's latest book. Its predecessors are *The One-Minute Meditator* (Perseus, 2001), co-authored with David Nichol, M.D., a how-to guide devoted to the use of meditation for better health, and *Counting What Counts* (Perseus, 1999), co-authored with former Harvard Business School professor Marc Epstein. *Counting What Counts* lays out a unique plan for companies to boost their performance by instilling the practices of accountability. See www.billbirchard.com.